This book is the property of

_____

INTO THE PENSIEVE

The Philosophy and Mythology of Harry Potter

PATRICK McCAULEY

4880 Lower Valley Road • Atglen, PA 19310

Designed by Justin Watkinson
Type set in Blackadder ITC/
Bodoni PosterCompressed/Minion Pro
Photo illustrations by Patrick McCauley

ISBN: 978-0-7643-4945-4
Printed in China

Published by Schiffer Publishing, Ltd.
4880 Lower Valley Road
Atglen, PA 19310
Phone: (610) 593-1777; Fax: (610) 593-2002
E-mail: Info@schifferbooks.com

For our complete selection of fine books on this and related subjects, please visit our website at www.schifferbooks.com. You may also write for a free catalog.

This book may be purchased from the publisher.
Please try your bookstore first.

We are always looking for people to write books on new and related subjects. If you have an idea for a book, please contact us at proposals@schifferbooks.com.

Schiffer Publishing's titles are available at special discounts for bulk purchases for sales promotions or premiums. Special editions, including personalized covers, corporate imprints, and excerpts can be created in large quantities for special needs. For more information, contact the publisher.

For my father,
whose fierce Patronus has stood guard
over me every day of my life.

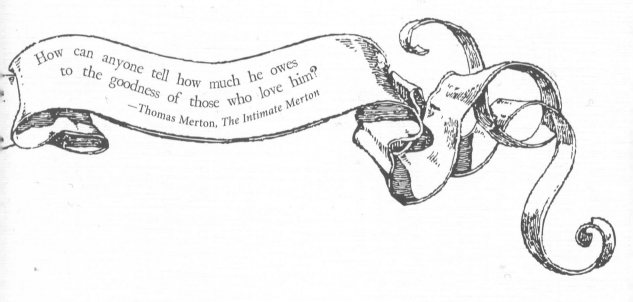

How can anyone tell how much he owes
to the goodness of those who love him?
—Thomas Merton, *The Intimate Merton*

Contents

INTRODUCTION
Of House-Elves and Children's Tales

Why do we find ourselves so intrigued with the story of Harry Potter? So, let's return to the world of J. K. Rowling and Harry Potter as if through the magic of Professor Dumbledore's Pensieve. This book is designed to take you back in time, back into the books you fell in love with but with a new perspective and insight. Many of you will have read these books as a teen or young adult, drawn through the stories by the delightful intrigue and mystery of Rowling's plot. This book invites you back into the magical world of J. K. Rowling through a serious and structured respect for the depth element that lies just below the surface of Harry's story. As we progress again through the seven-year voyage, we will see more than an epic battle with evil. We will see that Harry's story also charts the intricate progression of human character as it develops over a great deal of time and through a tremendous variety of circumstances and experiences.

Wasn't it just a little over a decade ago that many of us had given up on the idea that the new generation of children would be drawn to reading books? Hadn't we all come to the conclusion that video games, the Internet, and Netflix would prove just too tempting to allow for the possibility of a child sitting in her quiet bedroom poring page after page over paper and ink? Could any of us have imagined a line of young people standing in the cold waiting for a book to be released while perfectly good movies were being ignored down the street?

Over the last few years a colleague and I have offered a year-long honors seminar situated at the intersection between religion, literature, and science. The course is intended to raise the question of the nature and ground of individual human meaning and significance. In other words, the course asks how we as human beings determine the truth? How do we come to decide where our priorities lie? The course is designed as an exploration into the unknown to be taken by each of the students individually. In an effort to aid in this process, we frame the course within year-long readings of *The Lord of the Rings* and the Harry Potter series. One of these students was a recognized standout in the English department. There was little within the canon of

great English literature to which the student had not been exposed, and yet it is difficult to express the giddy joy with which she received the information that we would be finishing our class with an intensive reading of all seven of the Harry Potter books.

As we began to open these books, this student, who had written extensively on William Shakespeare and Jane Austen, sat straight up in her chair, with eyes wide and pencil tapping. I've seen a similar look in the eyes of my children as we are about to enter a new amusement park for the first time or descend the stairs on Christmas morning. I asked her, "When did you begin reading the Harry Potter books?" She said "I was roughly the same age that Harry and Hermione were for every one of the books. I have been waiting all year to get back into them for this class." I then asked her, "Given your considerable understanding of literature, what, in your opinion, accounts for the draw of the Harry Potter novels? There are a seemingly endless supply of stories involving magic and children. There are also quite a few works of fiction involving the drama of English boarding schools. What is it about Jo Rowling's work that allows it to stand out so in the minds of the voracious readers of your generation? What about these books draws you

back into them even though you know every turn of plot across the entire series? When you find yourself yearning for these stories, what is it that you are yearning for? What is that characteristic or essence that pulls you so tangibly back into this narrative?" The entire class turned to hear her response. She sat looking straight back at me for an awkwardly long period of time before she said, "I have no idea."

Robert Pirsig, best-selling author of *Zen and the Art of Motorcycle Maintenance*, once wrote,

> There is a Swedish word, *kulturbärer*, which can be translated as "culture-bearer" but still doesn't mean much. It's not a concept that has much American use, although it should have. A culture-bearing book, like a mule, bears the culture on its back. No one should sit down to write one deliberately. Culture-bearing books occur almost accidentally, like a sudden change in the stock market. There are books of high quality that are a part of the culture, but that is not the same. They are a part of it. They aren't carrying it anywhere. […]Uncle Tom's Cabin was no literary masterpiece but it was a culture-bearing book. It came at a time when the entire culture was about to reject slavery. People seized upon it as a portrayal of their own new values and it became an overwhelming success. The success of *Zen and the Art of Motorcycle Maintenance* seems the result of this culture-bearing phenomenon. (ZMM, Afterword)

So, is the Harry Potter series a culture-bearer? If Pirsig is right, then a culture-bearing book gives expression to a society-wide awakening that is just about to happen. A culture-bearing book is about something that is just about to be imagined. It is embraced precisely because it expresses an idea or feeling that was up to that point largely unthinkable.

People who originate new ideas that break the mold of cultural pre-determinism usually receive them in a form that is disjointed, disorganized, and easily mishandled. These ideas often arrive in the form of intuitions, hunches, and semiconscious daydreams. If they remain in this state they are forgotten as easily as a vivid dream that fades by lunchtime. Left on their own they will be abandoned, forgotten so completely that we will not even remember that something has been lost. New ideas and new values need to be housed, sheltered within an amenable structure. Like a leaf preserved within two sheets of wax paper, or a child's handprint in plaster, new ideas and new priorities are too fleeting, too gossamer to last by themselves for longer than the blink of an eye. Something real, something tangible, something material must submit itself as the form through which this new content can be expressed and sustained.

Dr. Martin Luther King Jr.'s "I Have a Dream" speech was a culture-bearer. We can look back now at white reception for the civil rights movement and see that resistance tipped over into support at the majority level at exactly the point that the speech was first broadcast on the nightly news. We may also notice with what fervency we hold on to images and snippets of that speech more than fifty years later. For the reluctant individual in 1963, the mere consideration of supporting the civil rights movement might very well have been daunting and confusing. For many, the inspiration or intuition to consider supporting this new and radical idea required the material presence of King's speech as the house within which their own budding support would reside. This is part of the reason why we cherish images of the speech even now.

So if Rowling's Harry Potter series is a culture-bearer, if it is the house within which a new idea is being sheltered and shared, what is the new idea? This is a serious question. We can begin to answer this by asking what it is that the culture needs. I mentioned earlier the possibility of an intersection between science, literature, and religion. Ever since Galileo ran afoul of the Catholic Church, there has been an antagonistic battle between proponents of truth as determined by science and proponents of truth as determined by religious authority. For many of us, this has turned into an exercise of choosing up sides. Little in Western culture has been left unaffected by the nearly constant mutual mudslinging of the last four hundred years. Both sides share a sense of entitled self-assuredness that they employ as the foundations of their catapults. The battle over truth and relevance between science and religion has resulted in a fundamental and dangerous redefining of the very nature of religion. We will delve into this issue in far greater depth in ensuing chapters. What we need to address at the outset is the idea that religion has undergone such a serious cultural re-understanding that for many of us, it has lost its ability to perform its mythological function. So, let us turn to that. What is religion's mythological function?

Most of what we experience in everyday human life can be easily explained. For example, there is little need for explanation with regard to the role and importance of shelter. The same can be said of things like food, clothing, and medicine. The basic utility of transportation, technical education, and energy are seen by many as so obvious that few of us need these things explained. They all play obvious roles with regard to our desires for survival and comfort. So much of human activity is dedicated to or grounded on the desire for survival that it forces us to wonder if there is much that we do beyond this. If so much of our life is based on our desire for survival and safety, then what is the purpose and point of religion? Where does religion come from? Why does it emerge in nearly every culture on the globe and during almost every period in history? Burial ceremonies or funerals were one of the first things that early humans did that were

not directly connected to survival. In earlier periods we find caves complete with fire pits surrounded by animal bones and hunting tools, but lacking evidence of funerals. We even find brilliant cave paintings concerned primarily with the hunt. Tools help sustain life, but a funeral does not. What happened, what changed that produced the desire to have a burial ceremony?

Regardless of whether or not we believe in the existence of a divinity, regardless of whether or not we see ourselves as believers, agnostics, or atheists, we will still be presented with the archetypal, character-determining decisions that are inherent to human existence. Despite the popular presumptions to the contrary, religion has never been so small as to be limited to a discussion of the existence of some supernatural being. Religion is a human endeavor that emerges out of our unenviable and inevitable search for meaning in a field where none is guaranteed. We inherit our DNA but we are the sovereign creators and authors of our decisions. This process of being thrown into free responsibility both thrills and terrifies us.

In his novel *The Plot Against America*, Philip Roth observes "the unfolding of the unforeseen was everything. Turned wrong way round, the relentless unforeseen was what we schoolchildren studied as 'history,' harmless history, where everything unexpected in its own time is chronicled on the page as inevitable. The terror of the unforeseen is what the science of history hides, turning disaster into an epic"(Roth, 2005, 114). What Roth seems to be pointing to is that idea that once something happens we tend to want to believe that this occurrence had always been inevitable. We tend to want to believe that other choices and options never really existed. For some reason, we tend to want to believe that history was always going to turn out the way it actually did. This is true about history, but is also true of our own individual past. To acknowledge the reality of our own past alternatives is to encounter the reality of our own responsibility. None of us make it to adulthood without a few decisions we would do anything to go back and change. The pain of this acknowledgment is often so intense that it fuels our desire to reinterpret the decisions as having always been fated, inherent to our circumstance or destiny. But this is a lie. Much of the Harry Potter series is dedicated to an expression of the pivotal importance of character-shaping decisions occurring relentlessly in real time and under duress.

For the adult reader, Rowling takes us back to childhood and adolescence and forces us to remember that at that age there exists an incredible contrast between our limited understanding and the immensity of impending choices. Rowling makes the future again the unforeseen, the undetermined, the undecided, and the unknown. She forces us to look again at the majesty of the moment before a choice is made. She invites us to remember what this really felt like. For the adolescent reader, none of this aspect of Harry's story needs to be explained. The daunting grandeur of imminent decisions is not something that they need to recall. This is all too familiar to people of that age. At the gravitational center of everything in Harry Potter's world, Rowling places, as if in a cradle, the transcendent primacy of individual deliberation.

However, on what are young people to base their life-altering decisions? As a culture, we have come to question unfounded claims of moral authority. Few would deny the radical importance of our evolving re-understanding of the concepts of race, class, gender, and romantic orientation that has emerged out of our rebellion against somewhat arbitrary cultural traditions. However, even if there were very good reasons for questioning the biased judgments of traditional arbiters of propriety and privilege, to question all claims of meaning and significance is to leave us with little upon which to base our own interpretations of priority. Even if the scientific revolution has, for so many of us, made the acceptance of the supernatural an insurmountable impediment to any serious religious participation, we are nonetheless destined to make all of our own most serious decisions. For unnumbered generations,

religion served not only as a source of supernatural explanations for unfathomable mysteries, but also as the source of patterns though which a life of significance and integrity could be achieved. What will guide and inspire our own best choices now? What will serve as the foundation and ground of our priorities and meaning? These questions remain even if the easy acceptance of the supernatural and of traditional authority does not. If we throw all religion out along with its supernatural claims and arbitrary authority, where will we turn for our definitions of character, worth, and purpose?

We are, every one of use, meant to embark on a voyage by which we will discover the central principles of our life. Harry reminds us that we are destined for a hero's journey and that it is high time that we, like Neville Longbottom, shall reach into a ragged hat to pull forth the Sword of Gryffindor. One of the main reasons that Harry's story has been so passionately embraced is because Rowling has reminded us that even if claims of moral authority have been questioned, morality itself has not been. Our decisions matter, they matter more than everything else. It is no good pretending that morality is relative when we all know that we are responsible for our conclusions. Even if the culture can defer on the issue of objective moral authority, we as individuals will, nonetheless, have to select the determining principles of our own lives and causes. The idea that there is no objective moral truth is no excuse for denying that there has to be a subjective one. Human decisions are inevitable and decisions require moral principles, principles for which we will hold ourselves accountable even if no one else does. Harry reminds us that what we desire more than all else is a life of integrity, bravery, and excellence in the service of a worthy mission. He also reminds us that we are responsible not only for the bravery but also for the worthiness of the undertaking.

CHAPTER 1

The Symbol of the Father in Harry Potter and the Prisoner of Azkaban

What should I decide to be? Which vision of my own future makes the most sense? It can often be difficult to determine our own most excellent or fulfilling aspiration. Paul Tillich discusses the necessity of orienting symbols within the search for our most appropriate individual purpose. Joseph Campbell focuses in on the specific symbol of the Father as inspiring guide toward authentic identity and personal mission. J. K. Rowling offers a sophisticated glimpse into the nature of this empowering symbol in *Harry Potter and the Prisoner of Azkaban*. Rowling effectively and purposely brings the external and internal image of the Father into productive and powerful tension. The literal existence of a Father figure may perform an indispensable role in a young person's search for his or her most appropriate future.

We meet Harry Potter as an orphan. For many of us one of the most difficult scenes in the entire series occurs in the very first book, *Harry Potter and The Philosopher's Stone*, where we find the young Harry standing before the Mirror of Erised, yearning for the presence of his mother and father. Throughout the series we find Harry looking for shreds, fragments, and clues as to the nature and character of his parents. We also find him holding on to an irrational hope for their possible return. From the Mirror through to the Resurrection Stone, we can see that Harry never strays for long from his quest for his parents.

We also find Harry looking for surrogates of one type or another. Molly Weasley is revealed as a mother figure in her encounter with the Boggart at 12 Grimmauld Place. If we look merely at the father figure, we find a list of potential candidates including Sirius Black, Vernon Dursley, Albus Dumbledore, Arthur Weasley, Severus Snape, Barty Crouch Jr., Remus Lupin, Minerva McGonagall, and Tom Riddle. What is so important about the quest for the father? (I must note here that I am not referring to the father in a gender specific manner. I am discussing the father quest as symbolic or archetypal in nature).

Joseph Campbell, noted author of the *Hero with a Thousand Faces* and renowned religious scholar, makes the following points:

You're born from your mother, and your father may be unknown to you, or the father may have died […] the hero has to go in quest of his father […]. [In *The Odyssey*,] Odysseus' son Telemachus is a tiny babe when Odysseus goes off to the Trojan War. The war lasts for ten years, and then, on his journey home, Odysseus is lost for ten more years […]. Athena comes to Telemachus, who is now twenty years old, and says, "Go find your father." He doesn't know where his father is. He goes to Nestor and asks, "Where do you think my father would be?" And Nestor says, "Well, go ask Proteus." He's on the father quest […]. Now, the finding of the father has to do with finding your own character and destiny. There's a notion that the character is inherited from the father, and the body and very often the mind from the mother. But it's your character that is the mystery, and your character is your destiny. So it is the discovery of your destiny that is symbolized by the father quest […]. You remember the story of Jesus lost in Jerusalem when he's a little boy about twelve years old. His parents hunt for him, and when they find him in the temple, in conversation with the doctors of the law, they ask, "Why did you abandon us this way? Why did you give

us this fear and anxiety?" And he says, "Didn't you know I had to be about my father's business?" He's twelve years old -- that's the age of the adolescent initiations, finding who you are. That father quest is a major hero adventure for young people. That is the adventure of finding what your career is, what your nature is, what your source is. You undertake that intentionally. (Moyers and Campbell, 1988)

Aristotle argues that we must first set a target before we can take aim. I must determine what I want before I can pursue it. Aristotle felt that each of us possesses a unique and excellent potential. He called this eudaimonia.

Eudaimonia can be understood as complete individual human flourishing or fulfillment, my own personally defined excellence (Cates, 1997).

Eudaimonia can be seen as a question that asks me what my own most appropriate life path might be. It is not the question of my potential from the point of view of a guidance counselor or other such person. It is the question of my potential from my own perspective, from deep within my own point of view, experience, and judgment. Aristotle suggests that we each have a deep and unrelenting desire to seek out the best possible expression of our own infinitely unique existence and potential. He seems to say that while physical pleasure and the approval of others can both bring significant happiness, they can never satisfy our desire for the intimate intuition of our own most excellent aspiration. Pleasure and approval can never bring happiness that is as fulfilling as that of eudaimonia.

Unlike Sinclair Lewis's *Babbit*, we must not arrive at the end of life having to admit "I've never done a single thing I've wanted to in my whole life!" (B, 379). I personally met a man who told me on his deathbed, "I spent my life doing things that I did not care about and now it is over. Nothing to be done." Our society tends to direct young people toward conformity, financial reliability, and obedience. It is a rare voice that asks such a person about thoughts regarding their possible unique contribution to the wide world. It is the rare person who can offer trusted guidance in regard to a question that can only be answered within the subjectivity of the individual.

So what of Harry's parents? One of the fundamental characteristics of Rowling's Harry Potter series is the question of whether or not Harry more fervently desires the physical presence of his parents or their guidance. We meet Harry at the age of eleven and under the regrettable control of the Dursleys. It cannot be said that the Dursleys physically torture or seriously starve Harry, but there can be no question that Harry is ignored, bullied, and derided for much of his early life. We find Harry understandably wishing for care and comfort, for protection and nurture. This is made evident in chapter twenty of *Harry Potter and the Prisoner of Azkaban*:

> "Yes …," said Black. "But I'm also—I don't know if anyone ever told you—I'm your godfather."
>
> "Yeah, I knew that," said Harry.
>
> "Well … your parents appointed me your guardian," said Black stiffly. "If ever anything happened to them …"
>
> Harry waited. Did Black mean what he thought he meant?
>
> "I'll understand, of course, if you want to stay with your aunt and uncle," said Black. "But … well … think about it. Once my name's cleared … if you want a … a different home …"

Some sort of explosion took place in the pit of Harry's stomach.

"What—live with you?" He said, accidentally cracking his head on a bit of rock protruding from the ceiling. "Leave the Dursleys?"

"Of course, I thought you wouldn't want to," Said Black quickly. "I understand, I just thought I'd –"

"Are you insane?" said Harry, his voice easily as croaky as Black's. "Of course I want to leave the Dursleys! Have you got a house? When can I move in?" (PA, 379)

This is an expression of the desire for a parent from the point of view of the child who doesn't have one. The child, painfully aware of his or her own inability to protect, provide, or care for him or herself, desires the care and protection of a powerful and compassionate adult. The powerless child stands in conscious need of the protective power of a merciful adult. We see a much more vivid presentation of this at the very end of chapter twenty:

But then, from beyond the range of their vision, they heard a yelping, a whining: a dog in pain.

"Sirius," Harry muttered, staring into the darkness. […] The yelping had stopped abruptly. As they reached the lakeshore, they saw why—Sirius had turned back into a man. He was crouched on all fours, his hands over his head.

"*Nooo*," he moaned. "*Noooo … please …*"

And then Harry saw them. Dementors, at least a hundred of them, gliding in a black mass around the lake toward them. He spun around, the familiar, icy cold penetrating his insides, fog starting to obscure his vision; more were appearing out of the darkness on every side; they were encircling them […]. The dementors were closing in, barely ten feet from them. They formed a solid wall around Harry and Hermione, and were getting closer […]. Harry felt his knees hit the cold grass. Fog was clouding his eyes […]. By the feeble light of his formless Patronus, he saw a dementor halt very close

[…]. A paralyzing terror filled Harry so that he couldn't move or speak. His Patronus flickered and died. (PA, 379)

At this moment we are with Harry as he is losing both his own life and that of the man who was to be his protector and provider. Harry the child tries in vain to conjure a protective Patronus. He does not have the power to protect either himself of his newly acquired father figure. We might note here that the word Patronus comes from the Latin meaning "defender, protector, former master (of a freed slave); advocate," from pater (gen. patris) "father" (www.etymonline.com). More than anything, Harry needs to *have* a protector, not to *be* one.

It is just at this point that the following occurs:

And then, through the fog that was drowning him, he thought he saw a silvery light brighter and brighter…. He felt himself fall forward onto the grass…. Facedown, too weak to move, sick and shaking, Harry opened his eyes. The dementor must have released him. The blinding light was illuminating the grass around him…. Something was driving the dementors back…. It was circling around him and Black and Hermione…. With every ounce of strength he could muster, Harry raised his head a few inches and saw an animal amid the light, galloping away across the lake…. It was as bright as a unicorn…. Fighting to stay conscious, Harry watched it canter to a halt as it reached the opposite shore. For a moment, Harry saw, by its brightness, somebody welcoming it back … someone who looked strangely familiar … but it couldn't be … (PA, 384–5)

Here we have Harry at his most vulnerable receiving the very intervention he needs and desires. At the very moment that his own power is revealed as insufficient, an outside force rides to the rescue. He has been taken under someone's wing.

Later Hermione asks,

"Harry, there is something I don't understand. … Why didn't the dementors get Sirius?"

Harry sat down too. He explained what he had seen; how, as the nearest dementor had lowered its mouth to Harry's, a large silver something had come galloping across the lake and forced the dementors to retreat.

"But what was it?"

"There is only one thing it could have been, to make the dementors go," said Harry. "A real Patronus. A powerful one."

"But who conjured it? […] It must have been a very powerful wizard, to drive all those dementors away …. If the Patronus was shining so brightly, didn't it light him up? Couldn't you see—?"

"Yeah, I saw him […] but … maybe I imagined it…. I wasn't thinking straight."

"*Who do you think it was?*"

"I think—" Harry swallowed, knowing how strange this was going to sound. "I think it was my Dad […]. Maybe I was seeing things […]. But […] from what I could see … it looked like him … I've got photos of him … "

He was thinking about his father and his three oldest friends … Moony, Wormtail, Padfoot, and Prongs … Wormtail has reappeared this evening when everyone thought has was dead…. Was it so impossible his father had done the same?" (PA, 406–7)

Harry knows his father is dead, and Hermione makes sure he does. However, we see here Harry as the desperate child desiring the protective parent he hasn't had since his first birthday. His desire adjusts his interpretation of events. This Harry does not desire advice or guidance. This Harry merely wants to be taken care of and this is exactly what he receives. For the space of about an hour, Harry lives under the belief that his actual father had appeared and rescued him. Belief does not have to be true to be powerful.

Paul Tillich writes " 'Father' is a symbol for God in so far as he preserves man by his sustaining creativity and drives him to his fulfillment by his directing creativity" (ST 1967, 287) .This reflects the ideas from Joseph Campbell we saw earlier. Tillich also writes,

Whatever is essentially mysterious cannot lose its mysteriousness even when it is revealed […]. Revelation of what is essentially and necessarily mysterious means the manifestation of something within the context of ordinary experience which transcends the ordinary context of experience […]. Revelation always is a subjective and an objective event in strict interdependence. Someone is grasped by the manifestation of the mystery; this is the subjective side of the event. Something occurs through which the mystery of revelation grasps someone; this is the objective side. These two sides cannot be separated […]. Ecstasy (standing outside oneself) points to a state of mind which is extraordinary in the sense that the mind transcends its ordinary situation. Ecstasy […] is a state of mind in which reason is beyond itself, that is, beyond its subject-object structure […].There is no reality, thing or event which cannot become a bearer of the mystery of being and enter into a revelatory correlation […]. Religious symbols are double edged. They are directed toward the infinite which they symbolize and toward the finite through which they symbolize it. They force the infinite down to finitude and the finite up to infinity. They open the divine for the human and the human for the divine. (ST, 109, 113, 118, 240)

In other words, Tillich is saying that a physical thing or event can be the finite or real-world occasion or location for a subjective or personal insight or awakening. The transcendent, the divine, so to speak, appears through some object. This object is not itself the transcendent or the holy. The object is the location through which the holy appears to a person. That person will, however, often see the object as holy in that the transcendent appeared there. The physical substance that becomes symbolic is not to be confused with that which is sacred. The symbol points beyond itself to something that cannot exist in reality or finitude. The symbol is the temporary occasion within which the ineffable, the unthinkable, becomes momentarily graspable. Of course, this is a subjective and personal, perhaps even private experience. The symbol is only a transcendent symbol for the person who is grasped by it. This experience is, as the existential philosopher Søren Kierkegaard (Denmark 1813–1855) says, intimate. These objects that become symbols have the capacity to deliver revelatory insight about siagnificance, about meaning.

This brings us to the other side of the lake. By means of the Time-Turner, Harry and Hermione gain the power to exist in two places at once.

> Harry stared out toward the lake, his heart doing a kind of drum roll in his chest… Whoever had sent the Patronus would be appearing at any moment…. he had to know … Harry began to run. He had no thought in his head except his father…. If it was him … if it was really him … he had to know, had to find out… A terrified excitement shot through him—at any moment now—
>
> "Come on!" He muttered, staring about. "Where are you? Dad, come on—"
>
> But no one came. Harry raised his head to look at the circle of dementors across the lake. One of them was lowering its hood. It was time for the rescuer to appear—but no one was coming to help this time—
>
> And then it hit him—he understood. He hadn't seen his father—he had seen *himself*—
>
> Harry flung himself out from behind the bush and pulled out his wand.
>
> "Expecto Patronum!" he yelled.
>
> And out of the end of his wand burst, not a shapeless cloud of mist, but a blinding, dazzling, silver animal […]. He saw it lower its head and charge at the swarming dementors. … the dementors were falling back, scattering, retreating into the darkness…. They were gone.
>
> The Patronus turned. It was cantering back toward Harry across the still surface of the water. It wasn't a horse, It wasn't a unicorn, either. It was a stag […]. It stopped on the bank. Its hooves made no mark on the soft ground as it stared at Harry with its large, silver eyes. Slowly, it bowed its antlered head. And Harry realized …
>
> "*Prongs*," he whispered. (PA, 410–2)

What is happening here? As both Campbell and Tillich suggest, the symbol of the father is not limited to a presentation of protective parental power. The symbol of the father can provide a powerful intuition of my own mysterious calling or eudaimonia. A child waits for rescue. The hero, however, is delivered onto his or her quest through his or her own deliberate and courageous action. Rowling will later reveal that the Patronus of each witch and wizard has a specific animal form. It is suggested in this that your Patronus reveals something of your authentic identity. However, while every witch and wizard will glimpse a clue as to her or his own authentic nature in the shape of her or his Patronus, there is more than this going on from Harry's perspective.

In this scene by the lake Harry is both rescuer and rescued, protector and protected, both parent and child. It is crucial too that we remember that a symbol is a subjective event and can only be understood from the perspective of the particular individual who receives it. From the moment we are introduced to Harry Potter we find him yearning for his parents. But as we have seen, parents play a dual role. They are both my protector and the symbol of my own true nature and destiny. As an orphan Harry has been denied both. We all go through the transition whereby we release our desire to be taken care of and assume the mantle of responsibility. In this transition we release the image of our parents as protectors and look to them in a new way, as symbolic intimations of our own true epic voyage into the future. We look to them in the hope that we might catch a glimpse of our own future self, something "blinding, dazzling … [something that can] lower its head and charge." In *Harry Potter and the Prisoner of Azkaban*, we are permitted a front row seat as Harry crosses this threshold.

However, Harry has no father to perform this role. If it is true that Harry's father has not been permitted the chance to protect his son, how can we assume that he could perform the role of eudaimoniac symbol? Tillich helps us here. The physical symbol is only a stand-in for the transcendent truth that is revealed in the experience of that symbol. When I stare at an object that is holy for me, it is not the object per se that receives my esteem and reverence. It is that to which the symbol points or alludes (not the symbol itself) that grabs me and throws me into ecstasy. For the first Harry, the Harry that passes out by the lake, the protector father arrives just in time. For an hour or two Harry is granted leave to recline into the belief his father is alive and has come to rescue him. Harry was, after all, really rescued. For the boy who spent days in front of both the Mirror of Erised and Dudley Dursley, how wonderful must this have felt? For at least one hour, he knows what it feels like to have had his missing father return.

Despite the explanation Harry gives to Hermione, it is this very real feeling that fuels the later Patronus. It is this real feeling that makes that Patronus possible at all. We must remember that the Patronus Charm is one driven by only the deepest feelings. Harry had not been able to cast a strong one for lack of the very feeling we are discussing here. For one hour Harry Potter lived under the belief that his father had come to protect him. For one hour Harry Potter knew what it felt like to finally receive the embracing protection of his real father. It is this feeling, this real feeling, that fueled his stag Patronus. His belief in the existence of his father made him literally capable of something he had not been capable of before. Even when he comes to discover that his father had not actually come, he will retain the glorious memory of having believed. It was his belief that he had been protected by his father that made him capable of not needing that protection any longer.

One last question. As we have seen, the Patronus stag canters back across the water and is said to stare at Harry. Harry stares back and names it Prongs. It is not hard to notice that Harry's Patronus, his image of his authentic identity and future potential, just happens to be his father's animigus shape. So who is it that is looking at Harry when the silver stag stares at him? Whose gaze is that? Rowling leaves this in delicate and poetic indefiniteness. It is, of course, Harry and James, mysterious and paradoxical as that may be. We will leave the discussion about how the paradoxical unity of father and son walks across water to a later chapter.

According to Aristotle, we are all destined for a unique and important epic voyage. We all feel ourselves called to this personal mystery. And yet, epic voyages always require confidence and courage from those who so often are scared and self-doubting. They also require the development of confidence in their own subjective judgment over and against the tendency to conform to habit or cultural authority. A symbolic presentation of one's own unseen capabilities may be required to initiate such a challenge. According to Paul Tillich and Joseph Campbell, it is the symbol of the Father that can provide this presentation. In the end it is always of moment of deliberate and defining existential decision that allows me to step out of the role of the protected and into the realm of authentic and courageous self-determination.

CHAPTER 2

Aesthetic Distance

owling's seven novels about Harry Potter center around the question of the real and the imaginary. Late in the last novel of the series, *Harry Potter and The Deathly Hallows*, there appears a chapter titled "King's Cross." In what is perhaps the series's most pivotal scene, Harry encounters his guiding mentor Albus Dumbledore, former headmaster of Hogwarts School of Witchcraft and Wizardry, in a realm within which both characters are presumably dead. Following a long conversation, the following interchange occurs:

> "Tell me one last thing," said Harry. "Is this real? Or has this been happening inside my head?" Dumbledore beamed at him, and his voice sounded loud and strong in Harry's ears even though the bright mist was descending again, obscuring his figure. "Of course it is happening inside your head, Harry, but why on earth should that mean that it is not real?" (DH 2007, 723)

In this chapter I will address what I will call aesthetic distance, a literary device closely related to the willing suspension of disbelief. As we encounter written material, we are drawn to ask what ontological or reality status the world within that material attains? Is this a true story or not? As a teacher of religion courses, I am often asked by students whether the Bible and the Koran are to be read literally or figuratively. Any serious reader of sacred writing is forced to ask the same question. Is this story real or imaginary? Should I apply what I find here to my real life, and if so, to what degree? Where some would shy away from this question, Rowling instead courts and emphasizes the border between the real and imaginary.

We may notice that in many of the books and movies aimed at a juvenile audience, there is an element of magical power. In Disney's *Escape from Witch Mountain*, the two young protagonists can either see the future or move objects telepathically. In C. S. Lewis's *Chronicles of Narnia* series, the main characters find that they have the power to enter another world through a wardrobe. L. Frank Baum's Dorothy has the power to travel somewhere over the rainbow. In Lynne Reid Banks's *The Indian in the Cupboard*, we find a boy who can bring toys to life with his magical cupboard, and J. M. Barrie's Peter Pan can teach us to fly. There is a very long list of such works. It is not hard to understand why. Children often possess very little power or control over the circumstances of their existence. From food to bedtime to schoolwork, most of their day is determined by authoritative outside forces. Santa is beloved precisely because he offers the wish fulfillment and power agency that children find they are so commonly denied. It is often for a similar reason that we see so many orphan protagonists in this genre. If I don't have a parent to tell me what to do, I am free to have adventures.

However, few of those children who love orphan stories desire to actually find themselves orphans. I may desire the vicarious pleasure of imagining myself escaping the control of my parents, but that does not mean that I also desire the loss of their protective power. Such stories are fun only so long as I read them while safely tucked into my bed. If roller coasters or horror movies posed any actual risk, very few of us would choose to try them. The thrill of a double looping coaster is undeniable so long as my safety is assured. Adventure stories are like roller coasters. They both allow me to flirt with the idea of danger even while I am actually safe. I am calling attention

to the crucial importance of the distance between the human being reading the book and the characters and events within that book. Without the safety provided by this aesthetic distance, the books could not be popular. The safety bar is an essential element to any roller coaster experience.

Yet for the characters within the story, it is precisely that very border that is crossed. Wendy is invited to leave her familiar and safe nursery in order to fly past the "second star to the right and straight on till morning." Dorothy is drawn up in a tornado that deposits her in Oz. Even Shakespeare's Hamlet is invited to speak to a ghost. The very border that must be maintained in order to sustain the perception of safety for the reader is the same border that must be crossed to bring about the adventure for the characters. As a reader of adventure literature, I am always assured that my own safety will never be gambled even while I am also assured that the safety of the characters within the adventure always will.

Turning to Harry, it is helpful to notice that nearly all of the novels begin at 4 Privet Drive, Little Whinging, Surrey. Rowling takes significant pains to offer the reader a starting point that is mundane, boring, and normal. Many readers will not fail to notice that the house at 4 Privet Drive bears at least some resemblance to the very house in which the book is often being read. What with school, brutal siblings, and dictatorial parents, young readers will often believe that they share many of Harry's experiences. At the outset, many young readers will connect and identify with Harry on the grounds of the perceived similarity of their circumstance. However, just as this connection is accomplished, Rowling sends Hogwarts' letters down the Dursleys' chimney. At that moment, the real paths of the reader and the character part ways.

Why do we so enjoy characters in literature that we would never want to meet in real life? Would anyone be comfortable with the prospect of Walter White or Hannibal Lecter getting your address? Would you ever willingly spend five minutes with either Beavis or Butt-head? I suspect that part of the reason is that the distance between the real-world reader and fictional action within the imagined world dulls the intensity of the perceived action. In real life, dealing with a traffic ticket is a serious plot point. Nothing is more relevant than when I myself get sick. A C+ on a chemistry test can seem like the end of the world. However, these significant dramas usually come across as dull and boring when presented within the bounds of a written narrative. If network television is any indication, we cannot get enough of cop shows and crime dramas. Why? It is because there is always something exciting happening at the police station. But it is only exciting from the point of view of the spectator. For those directly impacted by the events, it is a completely different story. Just consider the traffic jams that occur as a result of our desire to peep at a traffic accident as we pass by safely within our own cars.

But why do we desire the excitement of the police station? It is at least in part the result of aesthetic distance. The very border that guarantees my safety also blunts the emotional impact of a story. When I know something is made up, it is harder to get excited about it. Aesthetic distance exacts a tax. The excitement of the story is muted by the fact that it is received as not real. We often say with Coleridge that we willingly suspend disbelief in order to engage in the story. We suspend the belief that the story is fictional. We are willing to pretend that it is real. And yet, not completely. If we could, we would allow any story about a traffic ticket to engage us as if it were happening to us.

But we do not. In order to reach us out there beyond the border between the imaginary and the real, a story must be bigger than life. How many of us would have read seven novels about Harry's unmagical life with the Dursleys? For the reader aesthetic distance guarantees safety, but simultaneously and for the same reason dulls the emotional force of the narrative.

However, this reduction in emotional impact can be overcome merely by magnifying the scale or ratios of the drama. All I have to do is deliver a story with such dramatic and emotional intensity that some of that force survives the transition across the border. In fact, the willingness to suspend disbelief relies on the degree to which I am engaged by the emotional intensity of the narrative. So long as a story is engaging, I have no problem pretending that it is real. In fact, I usually do so primarily because of my own desire for the pleasure I hope to derive from the narrative. I will conditionally believe in your story so long and only so long as you entertain me. Nothing makes this more obvious than the contrast between *Silas Marner* and *Harry Potter and the Sorcerer's Stone* in regard to the attention of young readers. George Eliot just does not deliver to the average young reader what J. K. Rowling does.

This is only half of the formula. While the intensity of the drama must be strong enough to engender and maintain the suspension of disbelief, it must also avoid becoming too intense. Just as boredom can cause me to discard a book, so, too, can an overabundance of violence or terror within the narrative. Few would offer *The Godfather* movies to a group of seven-year-old children. Even for adults there are movies and television shows that simply go too far. With the intension to offer a narrative emotionally charged enough to survive the border between the real and imaginary, some creators produce something that is simply too heavy to maintain its ability to entertain. While slasher movies do enjoy a predictable and reliable audience, these films almost never attract as large an audience as genres that are more restrained regarding violence. Gibson's *The Passion of the Christ* is often cited as too violent in this way. So, while the aesthetic border does blunt the emotional strength of a story, its power to mute is not so great as to completely tame the force of fiction. Stories, no matter how distant from my actual existence, will maintain their ability to shock, disturb, or even harm me.

A balance must therefore be crafted. As Aristotle might say, a mean between the extremes must be achieved. We might say that for the reader, adventure is the mean between boredom and terror. Deference to either extreme taunts the perfectly free reader to drop the book. One of the great mysteries of the Harry Potter phenomenon is the question as to why an entire generation of young readers put down every form of electronic pablum to read a book despite the assurances of the older generation that these kids were just far too lazy to ever do such a thing. It is therefore important for us to note that Rowling is among the very few who intended a series to impact an audience of changing age. In the Harry Potter series, we see the assumed maturity of the audience advance along the same line the characters do in the books. In order to reach this young audience, Rowling needed to craft a story just scary enough for an eleven year old. She then had to create something just one year scarier, exactly one year scarier and just scary enough. Her ability to do this across seven novels indicates a sophistication and sensitivity for the dynamics of aesthetic distance that has yet to be seen in another recent author. We can see Rowling's direct discussion of this in some of the Dumbledore commentary in *The Tales of Beedle the Bard*:

> The final objection to *The Wizard and the Hopping Pot* remains alive in certain quarters today. It was summed up best, perhaps, by Beatrix Bloxam (1794–1910).... Mrs. Bloxam believed that *The Tales of Beedle the Bard* were damaging to children, because of what she called "their unhealthy preoccupation with the most horrid subjects, such as death, disease, bloodshed, wicked magic, unwholesome characters, and bodily effusions and eruptions of the most disgusting kinds." Mrs. Bloxam took a variety of old stories and rewrote them according to her ideals, which she expressed as "filling the pure minds of our little angels

with healthy, happy thoughts keeping their sweet slumber free of wicked dreams, and protecting the precious flower of their innocence […]. Mrs. Bloxam's tales have met with the same response from generations of Wizarding children: uncontrollable retching, followed by an immediate demand to have the book taken from them and mashed into pulp." (TBB, 17–19)

Rowling is reminding us that children will simply not read books that fail to meet them at their level.

Another point on this issue is emotional or metaphoric ratios. If an author understands the muting effect of the real/imaginary border, that author can learn to directly address it. *Buffy the Vampire Slayer* is one of the most highly regarded and critically acclaimed series in the history of television. Many have noted that *Buffy*'s vampires are extended metaphors for the Machiavellian social powerbrokers in every high school. As a teen engrossed in this series, I do not have to consciously know about this intended metaphor to be drawn in by it. I simply do not have to know why I like a show in order to find myself watching it. I do not have to draw the connection between my own fears in high school and the battles within *Buffy* in order to draw serious pleasure from a drama about the protection of the weak from the malevolent and strong. However, the similarity of ratio must be maintained if the unconscious connection is to be effectively and spontaneously drawn by the reader or viewer.

In other words, in order to survive the emotional drop of the aesthetic border, a narrative has to be appropriately larger than life, and yet the power ratios between the main characters have to mirror those power ratios the reader experiences in his or her real life. The scale has to be different but the ratios have to be the same. It is this similarity in power conflict ratio that ultimately grabs the reader. Harry's story parts ways with his reader as soon as letters from Hogwarts start coming down his uncle's chimney, but this same Harry finds himself encountering struggles that immediately mirror in relative ratio the struggles of his readers. Young readers are drawn to the idea of Harry's newfound

magical ability for the same reason they love Santa Claus; children desire the power that they do not have. However, they keep reading because his challenges reflect the power ratios of their own. In other words, readers are initially attracted to Harry because of his magical difference, but they stay with Harry because of the similarity between his struggles and theirs. A trust fund bully is the same with or without a wand. As G. K. Chesterton noted:

Fairy tales, then, are not responsible for producing in children fear, or any of the shapes of fear; fairy tales do not give the child the idea of the evil or the ugly; that is in the child already, because it is in the world already. Fairy tales do not give the child his first idea of bogey. What fairy tales give the child is his first clear idea of the possible defeat of bogey. The baby has known the dragon intimately ever since he had an imagination. What the fairy tale provides for him is a St. George to kill the dragon. (Chesterton, G. K. (Gilbert Keith), 2012)

Or, in another form, "Fairy tales do not tell children that dragons exist. Children already know that dragons exist. Fairy tales tell children that dragons can be killed." (*Criminal Minds*, 2007). It does no good to tell a child that there are no vampires in his high school or under his bed for it is a lie. To tell him so only serves to assure him that you will not help when they descend.

So why highlight the border between the real and the imaginary? Tolkien, for example, draws almost no attention to the real world of the reader in his crafting of Middle Earth. It would seem to enhance the ability to suspend disbelief to do so, and yet Rowling goes so far as to have her Minister of Magic confound the British Prime Minister of the real world. Why call attention to the fictionality of her imaginary world? It is my contention that Rowling is taking advantage of the border between the real and fictional worlds in order to highlight two real borders encountered by her readers. Rowling uses the aesthetic border between the real and the imaginary as an extended metaphor for the real borders between both childhood and adulthood and between life and death.

The border between childhood and adulthood is nearly opaque when viewed from the child's side. We, most of us, completely and utterly forget this. This forgetting is part of the corruption of power. To children, parents and other adults have so much power that it is as if they have magic wands. Note the power ratio between wizards and muggles on the one hand and between parents and children on the other. Rowling places this power in the hands of children who then fumble with it. To a child in the real world the acquisition and wielding of adult power or agency is a mystery. As a child I don't know how to earn money. I can't fathom the intricacies of housing or shopping. The majestic size of the whole process of acquiring food, clothing, and shelter is so overwhelming that the mere consideration of it often inspires dread or terror. It is, in part, because of this that children fear the potential loss of their parents.

Despite presumptions to the contrary, children are usually worried about the responsibilities of power. Rowling's series centers around the idea that the transition from childhood to adulthood requires the emergence of a hero from within a child. In every one of the seven novels we are presented with children who learn to develop a reliance on their own reason, strength, and courage despite the presence of adult authorities. We are also presented with the fact that children never learn self-reliance without making many mistakes along the way. Each of the books presents the main characters with seemingly insurmountable challenges and we watch as they rise, sometimes limpingly, to ever greater levels of determination, self-reliance, and fortitude.

The young reader of the Harry Potter books is exposed to the wizarding world at the same time Harry is. This reader comes to recognize that the wand that a character buys at Ollivander's does not come ready to use. In every one of the novels, young characters are seen practicing and developing hard-won magical skill and power. What we must see here is that the young real-world reader is going through the same process as the students of Hogwarts. While the young person may not receive a letter from Hogwarts, that person nonetheless, receives ever more power every year beginning seriously in about fourth grade. From the point of view of the recently powerless child, this introduction to previously only imaginable power is always both thrilling and daunting. Babysitting for the first time, taking the outboard out to fish, riding into the center of town alone on a bike—only the forgetful recall memories like these as anything short of an adventure. I once snuck out at 3 a.m. with my best friends Doug and Gordon during a third-grade sleepover. We spent two hours skulking around Wakefield, Massachusetts, in the middle of the night. We ended up being the lone and important witnesses of a car crash amid extensive police activity. Despite a grounding so severe that I am still in it today, no trip to Hogwarts could ever have exceeded the impact of the epic voyage I embarked upon that night with my trusted and stalwart companions.

Courage is not magic, it is not a gift. Leaping into the unknown is something that some people decide to do and others do not. Nor can courage be confused with brash recklessness or uncalculated risk taking. Courage must include the honest intention to accomplish worthy yet intimidating goals. Therefore, courage requires rational hope, imaginable feasibility. Courage requires that I can imagine, in some dim form, my own possible success. No, courage is not a gift. It is a subjective determination, an act of rational will. Rowling does not hide the border between the magical and the real precisely because for the child reading the Harry Potter books there is almost no border at all. After all, Harry has to face all of those trials endemic to his age regardless of his magical ability. He must face them in just the same way that his reader must. One of the main draws of the series for the young reader is that she has already intuited her own wand, her own trip to the sorting hat, her own encounter with Voldemort, and the inevitable necessity of manifesting her own real courage. This is a magic that is going to come true, for better or worse. She will have to face all of this in reality, Harry cannot do it for her. Just as the aesthetic border protects me from Voldemort, it also prevents Harry from reaching across to help as well.

So in the end, Harry's is not a vicarious salvation. Despite the fact that Harry walks deliberately and willingly into the woods to meet

Tom Riddle—the self-styled Lord Voldemort and central antagonist of the entire series, despite the fact that he relinquishes defense and allows for Riddle's curse, Harry's sacrifice will not provide for my salvation. There is no magical alleviation of my own fear or despair in Harry's Gethsemane. There is only the discovery, much to his surprise, that he actually can do what he thought he might not. And for the young reader, this, precisely, is my rational hope. If hopeless Neville of the first book can become the magnificent leader in the seventh, then maybe I can, too.

Character, some say, is forged where principles encounter power. Anyone can have principles and every living person has some power. The question is, will I apply my power to my principles or will the desire for power tempt me to subordinate those principles? Will I amass power to serve my principles, or will I develop principles that serve my desire for power? This leads us to a discussion of the desire for safety and survival and the fear of death. Rowling courts the border between life and death with a resiliency and daring not found in many other works with a young adult audience. The border between life and death, like the border between childhood and adulthood, is intentionally symbolized by means of the attention Rowling draws to the border between the real and imaginary that exists for the engaged reader.

We are never far from a reminder of the death of Harry's parents or of the mortal threat imposed by Tom Riddle. Dumbledore's withered hand is flaunted before us as a continuing intimation and reminder of his impending and inevitable death. Rowling is not merely trying to offer her readers a cheap and thrilling scare. She is trying to render a serious and crucial message: Your life will be sacrificed to something, it is only a question of what. If gravestones were magical, they could be bewitched to reveal a life's true priorities and dedications. There is no life that is not willingly sacrificed to these priorities. The question that I am presented with at the border between childhood and adulthood is the question I will ask of myself at the border with death: To what will I or have I been willing to dedicate my life? In what do I live and move and have my being (Acts 17:28)? The guard and keeper of the threshold will say,

you have a life and you will empty it into whatever you will. Will you pick a purpose that is worthy of an entire human life? Rowling's novels remind us constantly that mere survival is a hopeless and foolish enterprise. The trick is not survival, as Tom Riddle believes, it is meaning, it is purpose. There is no greater threat to the subjective authentic determination of personal meaning and purpose than the many faces of the fear of death. To conquer the fear of death one must decide to prioritize purpose. To prioritize one's own individual eudaimoniac purpose, one must confront one's desire for safety and thus the fear of death.

So, J. K. Rowling highlights the aesthetic border between the real and the imaginary in an effort to address the borders of both adolescence and death. Rowling reaches beyond the bounds of the physical book to the reader through the resonance of intuitively recognizable power ratios. As the young reader, I feel the relevance of these ratios rather than think them. For this reader, the assumption of physical safety draws him or her into ever more precarious emotional yet aesthetic risks. The aesthetic border is broken or crossed once the reader grasps, at some level, that the power ratios that undergird the fictional story are, in fact, a real description of his or her progressing life. While Rowling's novels are a delightful escapist fantasy, they are also meant to serve as an effective wake-up call to the young reader who is just about to encounter the threshold of his or her own epic voyage. A life dedicated to principled eudaimoniac causes is one that requires real and practiced individual courage. I must come to individually accept the unnerving demands of my own potential excellence or else risk the internal condemnations of a personal mediocrity or irrelevance born of cowardice. Rowling's series shares this with nearly every great coming-of-age ritual from religions throughout the world. While it is commonly believed that I must face death in these ceremonies to be accepted as an adult, I do not think this is the key point: What I must do is come to grips with the bald inevitability of death, and thus with the dire and latent risk of a life poorly applied and thus tragically wasted.

CHAPTER 3
Agency

One of the reasons the Harry Potter series has attracted such a large and devoted audience is because, like many lengthy works of fantasy fiction, there is much going on below the surface. Jo Rowling spent at least five years establishing the historical, social, magical, and political setting for a story that would float on top of it. The story of Harry Potter, the actual words that we read are only the uppermost surface of a three-dimensional saga whose Silmarillion details have been carefully and meticulously worked out. We do not need to know the entire history of the Black family in order to feel and experience its gravitational pull within the dynamics of the drama. J. K. Rowling possesses notebooks filled with lists of Hogwarts students organized according to year, house, and magical ability. The audience never comes to know most of them. We as readers do not need to know about these particular students to feel the invisible detail that exists just below the surface of the story we read.

One of the key components just below the surface of the Harry Potter series is the concept of human free will. As we've said, human agency, the ability to make decisions in the real world, is at the center of the Harry Potter series. Free will is so inherent to everyday human experience that it is quite easy to step right over it without even noticing. There is nothing so common as looking down at a glass of water, deciding to reach for it, and then doing so with my actual hand in real space and time. One of the key components of human free will is physical power. Most of us have the ability to move a glass of water whenever we so desire. We can see how significant this is when we reference a paralyzed person by contrast. Both a physically able person and a paralyzed person can mentally wish to move the glass. I do not need physical power to formulate the desire to move or change something for that is a strictly mental enterprise. However, a person suffering from advanced Lou Gehrig's disease, for example, progressively loses the ability to translate the mental wish into physical action. At the center of free will is the common human ability to transform a human wish into physical action in the real world. Humans have the ability to make changes in the physical world that are grounded on purely mental desires and whims. This ability is fundamental to the definition of being human. This ability to reach out and change my world as a result of a thought within my head is miraculous, it is magical. It is only due to its everydayness that we fail to regard it with amazement.

Rowling calls attention to this in many locations within the seven novels. Transfiguring a thought into action is difficult for those who are new to the skill required. In *Harry Potter and the Philosopher's Stone*, we find the students in Professor Flitwick's class trying to levitate a feather. Professor Flitwick says,

> "Now, don't forget that nice wrist movement we've been practicing […]. Swish and flick, remember, swish and flick. And saying the magic words properly is very important, too—never forget Wizard Baruffio, who said 's' instead of 'f' and found himself on the floor with a Buffalo on his chest." It was very difficult. Harry and Seamus swished and flicked, but the feather they were supposed to be sending skyward just lay on the desktop. Shamus got so impatient that he prodded with his wand and set fire to it. (SS, 171)

Picking up a glass of water is so automatic for most people that we forget it was a skill hard-

won during early childhood. Any parent of a toddler can provide evidence for this. All action in the real world requires practice.

Rowling also calls attention to the transition from wish to action in her early emphasis of the house ghosts of Hogwarts. The ghosts of Hogwarts are first mentioned during the opening feast and sorting ceremony in the first novel. "About twenty ghosts had just streamed through the back wall. Pearly-white and slightly transparent, they glided across the room talking to one another and hardly glancing at the first years" (SS, 115). Initially Rowling's ghosts are simply a fascinating magical detail in the description of the Great Hall and of Hogwarts in general. Rowling has said in interviews that these ghosts were part of her original intuition of the Harry Potter series on a train ride from Manchester to London. Ghosts will play a very large role in our understanding of the main themes and ideas below the surface of Harry's story. What we must see about Rowling's ghosts for our current discussion is that they can't move anything. They have lost the ability to translate wish into action. This is made plain in *Harry Potter and the Chamber of Secrets* while Harry is caught in Mr. Filch's office. Mr. Filch releases Harry after hearing a loud bang. While leaving the office Harry sees Nearly Headless Nick.

"Harry! Harry! Did it work?"

Nearly Headless Nick came gliding out of a classroom. Behind him, Harry could see the wreckage of a large black-and-gold cabinet that appeared to have been dropped from a great height.

"I persuaded Peeves to crash it right over Filch's office," said Nick eagerly. "Thought it might distract him —"

"Was that you?" said Harry gratefully.

"Yeah, it worked, I didn't even get detention. Thanks, Nick!" (CS, 129)

We can see in this that Nick needs the poltergeist Peeves to drop the vanishing cabinet on Filch's office. Nick cannot do it himself. Sir Nicholas de Mimsy-Porpington, resident ghost of Gryffindor Tower, cannot move objects in the reality of space and time.

This seems to be an echo of a famous passage of one of Rowling's favorite authors, Charles Dickens. In *A Christmas Carol*, Dickens writes,

The air was filled with phantoms, wandering hither and thither in restless haste, and moaning as they went. Every one of them wore chains like Marley's Ghost; some few (they might be guilty governments) were linked together; none were free. Many had been personally known to Scrooge in their lives. He had been quite familiar with one old ghost, in a white waistcoat, with a monstrous iron safe attached to its ankle, who cried piteously at being unable to assist a wretched woman with an infant, whom it saw below, upon a door-step. *The misery with them all was, clearly, that they sought to interfere, for good, in human matters, and had lost the power for ever.* (Dickens, 24)

We can see here the same crucial characteristic of ghost agency. For both Rowling and Dickens, ghosts can speak but they cannot interfere in human matters for they have lost the power to do so. This inability to change a wish into action is a fundamental ingredient to their misery. Rowling makes this poignantly clear in a short scene from *Harry Potter and the Chamber of Secrets*, where she writes,

Harry watched, amazed, as a portly ghost approached the table, crouched low, and walked through it, his mouth held wide so that it passed through one of the stinking salmon.

"Can you taste it if you walk though it?" Harry asked him.

"Almost," said the ghost sadly, and he drifted away. (CS, 133)

The reflecting reader can detect in this the sense of loss that is embedded in the word "almost." The key point is that the portly ghost cannot taste the food. The ghost's use of the word emphasizes the contrast between what he wants and what he cannot have. Nick himself says, "I haven't eaten for nearly five hundred years [...]. I don't need to, of course, but one does miss it. (SS,125)." Nearly Headless Nick raises the issue again at the end of *Harry Potter and the Order of the Phoenix.* In response to Harry's questions about the death of Sirius Black, Nick says,

"I was afraid of death [...]. I chose to remain behind. I sometimes wonder whether I oughtn't to have ... well, that is neither here nor there ... in fact, I am neither here nor there...."

He gave a small sad chuckle. "I know nothing of the secrets of death, Harry, for I chose my feeble imitation of life instead." (OP, 861)

Rowling is clearly taking advantage of the genre of fantasy in order to make a point about the border between life and death. As we have seen, the border between life and death is one of the cardinal themes in the entire Harry Potter series. Beyond the mere discussion of ghosts, Rowling makes many references to consciousness without power throughout the novels. Take, for example, the portraits of the former headmasters of Hogwarts that hang in Dumbledore's office. The portraits can talk. Characters within the story can carry on in-depth conversations with these long-departed figures. Figures in portraits, like the house ghosts, have the ability to communicate, to advise, and even to persuade. However, they do not have the ability to move or affect objects

in the real world (Moaning Myrtle is the exception in that she does seem to have the power to splash water, however).

We might also notice that Rowling bookends the series with a heavy emphasis on the Resurrection Stone. The reader of the Harry Potter series is introduced to Nicholas Flamel, owner of the Stone, as early as the train ride to Hogwarts in the first novel. The Stone itself is introduced in a Gringotts vault within Diagon Alley in that same book. We return to the Stone in the final novel as the third of the Deathly Hollows that Harry uses to allow his parents to accompany him as he enters the Forbidden Forest to face his own impending death at the hands of Tom Riddle. We can see here that both the first and last novels are named at least in part for this stone.

But what power does the Resurrection Stone actually possess? Let us return to the *Tale of the Three Brothers* where we first come to an understanding of the powerful magical artifact called the Resurrection, Sorcerer's, or Philosopher's stone.

Meanwhile, the second brother journeyed to his own home, where he lived alone. Here he took out the stone that had the power to recall the dead, and he turned it thrice in his hand. To his amazement and his delight, the figure of the girl he had once hoped to marry, before her untimely death, appeared at once before him.

Yet she was sad and cold, separated from him as by a veil. Though she had returned to the mortal world, she did not truly belong there and suffered. Finally the second brother, driven mad with hopeless longing, killed himself so as truly to join her. (DH, 408–9)

Rowling is clearly making a point here about how far the Resurrection Stone can bring a person back from death. Not only does she mention that the resurrected woman was separated "as by a veil," but also that her fiancé was "driven mad with hopeless longing." What was the second brother longing for? What was it that he could not have? Whatever the resurrected woman is, she is not enough to provide the second brother with what he wants. Isn't it true that hopeless longing is precisely what mourners feel in regards to their lost loved ones? We are forced to imagine the manner in which this woman has "returned to the mortal world." She is "sad and cold," she does not truly belong, and she suffers. In comparing her to the Hogwarts ghosts, we must ask what she can do. It does not appear that she can move objects in the real world.

This brings us to discussion of Harry's parents. Harry's status as an orphan is one of the foundational elements of Rowling's extended story. This story begins at Privet Drive mere hours after Harry's parents have been killed by Tom Riddle. The story starts at the point at which Harry's parents end. Harry's parents haunt the entire series as a vacancy and a vacuum. There is nothing that happens in Harry's story that isn't directly or indirectly related to the absence of Harry's parents. Nonetheless, this is a magical tale, and Harry's parents appear three times. We first see Harry's parents in the Mirror of Erised. We see Harry's parents again at the end of *Harry Potter and the Goblet of Fire*, when they emerge from the end of Tom Riddle's wand during the duel with Harry through the rare version of the spell Priori Incantatem. Lastly, we see Harry's parents, as we've said, by means of the Resurrection Stone in the final novel.

However, Rowling is relentless in her intention to assert that "no spell can reawaken the dead" (GOF, 697). This quote from Dumbledore is echoed by Hermione in *Harry Potter and the Deathly Hallows* where she says "no magic can raise the dead, and that's that!" (DH, 427) Dumbledore calls these raised figures "a kind of reverse echo" (GOF, 697). In response to Harry's assertion that his parents had appeared when his wand connected with Tom Riddle's, Hermione says "but they weren't really back from the dead, were they? […] Those kinds of—pale imitations aren't the same as truly bringing someone back to life." (DH, 427)

We discussed the chapter "King's Cross" in the last chapter. King's Cross is, of course, the train station where Platform 9¾ is. So, just as with the Resurrection Stone, Harry's story begins and ends here. In the final novel, Harry finds himself in a version of King's Cross train station

in the bewildering moments following his willing self-sacrifice at the hands of Lord Voldemort/Tom Riddle. There, Harry encounters Professor Dumbledore, who had died at the end of the previous novel:

> "But you're dead," said Harry.
> "Oh yes," said Dumbledore matter-of-factly.
> "Then … I'm dead too?"
> "Ah," said Dumbledore, smiling still more broadly. "That is the question, isn't it? On the whole, dear boy, I think not." (DH, 707)

As we've seen, Rowling is not shy about using magical means to bring about interaction between the living and the dead. However, in this particular instance, Harry himself is among those who are not capable of moving objects in the real world. In the real world Harry is face down in the Forbidden Forest and presumed to be dead. Nonetheless, Harry finds himself in a position to have an extended conversation with Professor Dumbledore. So where are they? Harry asks this himself:

> "Where are we, exactly?"
> "Well, I was going to ask you that," said Dumbledore, looking around. "Where would you say that we are?"
> Until Dumbledore had asked, Harry had not known. Now, however, he found that he had an answer ready to give.
> "It looks," he said slowly, "like King's Cross station. Except a lot cleaner and empty, and there are no trains as far as I can see."
> "King's Cross station!" Dumbledore was chuckling immoderately. "Good gracious, really?"
> "Well, where do you think we are?" asked Harry, a little defensively.
> "My dear boy, I have no idea. This is, as they say, *your* party."
> Harry had no idea what this meant. (DH, 712)

There is a key clue here in Professor Dumbledore's reaction. Even though we see Dumbledore interacting with Harry as if they were both embodied, Professor Dumbledore cannot see where they are. He is surprised when Harry tells him that it looks like a train station. When Harry asks what he thinks, Professor Dumbledore unexpectedly says that he has no idea where they are and then cryptically calls the whole experience "*your* party." Even Harry doesn't know what this means. The reader is no better off. Is Professor Dumbledore really there with Harry, and if so, in what manner?

We find another clue in a chapter that occurs just prior to this one. In the chapter "The Forest Again," Harry succeeds in opening the snitch and retrieving the Resurrection Stone.

> He closed his eyes and turned the stone over in his hand three times. He knew it had happened, because he heard slight movements around him that suggested frail bodies shifting their footing on the earthly, twig-strewn ground that marked the outer edge of the forest. He opened his eyes and looked around. They were neither ghost nor truly flesh, he could see that. They resembled most closely the Riddle that had escaped from the diary so long ago, and he had been memory made nearly solid. Less substantial than living bodies, but much more than ghosts [...].
>
> "—right after you'd had your son … Remus I'm sorry—"
>
> "I am sorry too," said Lupin. "Sorry I will never know him" [...]
>
> "We are part of you," said Sirius. "Invisible to anyone else."
>
> And he set off. The dementors' chill did not overcome him; he passed through it with his companions, and they acted like Patronuses to him. (DH, 698–701)

There is much to see here. Rowling gives us a very articulated description of the figures that appear after the turning of the Resurrection Stone. She describes them "memory made nearly solid. Less substantial than living bodies, but much more than ghosts." Rowling emphasizes again what these figures cannot do. These figures will not rise to Harry's rescue. It is not clear if they offer any physical assistance at all. Some might say they physically protect him from the Dementors

by acting as Patronuses. This is unlikely to be true since it was Harry's not James's Patronus that deflected the Dementors in the third novel. If James is capable of offering protection from Dementors, then why wouldn't he have done so in the earlier opportunity?

Further, there is a clue here in the use of the word Patronus. Why is Rowling calling our attention to such a significant magical tool? The plot does not demand the reference. We will recall that a Patronus is cast by means of recalling a very powerful memory from within our own authentic individual experience. We will also recall that the animal-shaped shield that emerges from the wand gives a clue as to the witch or wizard's authentic individuality. Unlike the protective charms inherited by Harry through the love and sacrifice of his mother, a Patronus is a product of a witch or wizard's own true self. The power of a Patronus is not inherited. So what is the connection between Rowling's mention of the Patronus Charm and the emergence of these figures?

Sirius gives the answer: "They won't be able to see you?" asked Harry. "We are part of you," said Sirius. "Invisible to anyone else." Just as Professor Dumbledore had explained that the experience in King's Cross station was Harry's "party," here Sirius explains that the very existence of Harry's parents and the other companions are products of Harry. We might remember that Harry's Patronus was already an image of his father. Might the Resurrection Stone perform a similar form of magic? If this is the case, then we may imagine that Professor Dumbledore of King's Cross station and Harry's companions in the Forbidden Forest were in actuality projections from within Harry himself.

It is particularly poignant to acknowledge that Remus Lupin is aware that he will never know his son. Here Rowling is taking her stand on her understanding of death. In Rowling's understanding and in the world that Rowling created, Remus Lupin does not watch over his own son. Remus Lupin, unlike Nearly Headless Nick, has "gone on." (OP, 861) Unlike the ghost of Hogwarts Castle who are privileged every year to see the new students get sorted, Remus Lupin will not be there at platform 9 ¾ when his orphaned son is helped onto the Hogwarts Express by Andromeda Tonks and Harry Potter. Rowling does not offer her reader a panacea for the pain of mourning.

On this point let us return to the Mirror of Erised from the first novel. There Professor Dumbledore explains to Harry that the mirror

> shows us nothing more or less than the deepest, most desperate desire of our hearts. You, who have never known your family, see them standing around you [...]. However, this mirror will give us neither knowledge or truth. Men have wasted away before it, entranced by what they have seen, or been driven mad, not knowing if what it shows is real [...]. It does not do to dwell on dreams and forget to live, remember that. (SS, 213-4)

With the help of the scene from the Forbidden Forest, we can see that Professor Dumbledore is warning eleven-year-old Harry about the risks of dwelling too long in bereavement. The Mirror of Erised does not show Harry his parents, or even an image of his parents. It only shows his desire (Erised spelled backwards) for them. Many of us dwell in afterlife images that function to reduce the pain of mourning. How many of these merely reflect our own desires at the cost of knowledge or truth? And how many of us while in the throes of bereavement recline in reflections of our desires at the cost of our own progress in the real world? We must act, for the dead cannot.

This brings us to Merope Riddle. The reader is introduced to Merope Riddle, the mother of Tom Riddle, in *Harry Potter and the Half-Blood Prince*. Professor Dumbledore invites Harry to private lessons. There, both Professor Dumbledore and Harry Potter enter the Pensieve, a magical portal for retrieving and reliving memories. In particular, Professor Dumbledore wants to introduce Harry to Tom Riddle's family and the conditions of his upbringing. Merope Riddle gives birth to Tom in an orphanage and dies shortly thereafter. This disturbs Harry, who says,

"But she can do magic!" said Harry impatiently. "She could of got food and everything for herself by magic, couldn't she?"

"Ah," said Dumbledore, "perhaps she could. But it is my belief—I am guessing again, but I am sure I am right — that when her husband abandoned her, Merope stopped using magic. I do not think that she wanted to be a witch any longer. Of course, it is also possible that her unrequited love and the attendant despair sapped her of her powers; that can happen. In any case, as you are about to see, Merope refused to raise her wand even to save her own life."

"She wouldn't even stay alive for her son?"

Dumbledore raised his eyebrows. "Could you possibly be feeling sorry for Lord Voldemort?"

"No," said Harry quickly, "but she had a choice, didn't she, not like my mother —"

"Your mother had a choice too," said Dumbledore gently. "Yes, Merope Riddle chose death in spite of a son who needed her, but do not judge her too harshly, Harry. She was greatly weakened by long suffering and she never had your mother's courage." (HBP, 262)

What we see here is the very border between life and death. For Rowling, everything hinges on the ability to affect change in the real world. The living can do it and the dead cannot. Here, we see Merope straddling this line. Professor Dumbledore reflects upon Merope with a modicum of mercy and understanding in his suggestion that despair might indeed have robbed her of her magical powers.

Rowling has not been unclear about the role that depression played both in her own life and in the formation of the Harry Potter series. However, Harry counters by emphasizing the stakes at hand when he says, "She wouldn't even stay alive for her son?" Harry seems to assume that Merope could have decided not to die. Professor Dumbledore seems to agree when he says "Merope refused to raise her wand even to save her own life [...]. Yes, Merope Riddle chose death in spite of a son who needed her." If both Professor Dumbledore and Harry are right in their assumption that Merope had a say in her impending death, then what we must see in this is that Merope was making the decision to give up making decisions. (In ancient Greek, the word Merope means to "turn away.") This makes Merope the border figure in between those who can perform actions in the world and those who cannot.

We have considered death in this chapter as a means for addressing the issue of human power and agency. In particular, we have emphasized the idea that agency is a characteristic of the living, not of the dead. Agency refers to the ability to make changes in the real world at will. Rowling emphasizes this by indicating that even in a magical story, the dead do not have this kind of agency. Nonetheless, this subject has raised serious questions that we have not yet addressed sufficiently. We leave a more extended discussion of the implications of death to the final chapters.

CHAPTER 4

Responsibility

We saw in the last chapter that free will is a matter of a person's ability to translate individual desire into real-world action. This chapter will consider the implications of this individual free will. As any child can tell you, freedom for children is remarkably restricted. Rowling's series charts the development of human free will across a very specific and important threshold. In particular, Rowling is interested in the development of moral independence. No one, however, begins as a person who can think and act for themselves. We all begin to a greater or lesser degree as Harry does in the opening chapters of the first novel.

"Up! Get up! Now!"

Harry woke with a start. His aunt rapped on the door again.

"Up!" she screeched […]. His aunt was back outside the door […].

"Are you up yet?" she demanded.

"Nearly," said Harry.

"Well, get a move on, I want you to look after the bacon. And don't you dare let it burn, I want everything perfect on Duddy's birthday."

Harry groaned.

"What did you say?" his aunt snapped through the door.

"Nothing, nothing…" (SS, 19)

It is often noted how cruel and neglecting the Dursleys are in regards to Harry. However, the preceding scene is one that is all too familiar to almost any child reading the novel. In fact, the first five lines of the above quotation were repeated in my house this very morning. Unless you are one of the lost boys who lives with Peter Pan in Neverland, it is very unlikely that, as a child, you will be left to yourself to determine your own bedtime. Children are subject to nearly perpetual authoritative commands. As we've noted earlier, they are told what to eat, where to go, what to do, what words they may or may not use, what to wear, and many, many other things. Those of us who impose these demands on children tell ourselves it is all for their own good, and it almost

always is. Children simply do not have the practical wisdom to understand what is in their own best interest most of the time. A child will run into traffic without looking both ways, and it is the responsibility of the attending adult to monitor the safety of such a child.

However, it is probably impossible for children to understand these commands this way. As adults, our care and concern for children is a kindness that we show them. We are looking out for their safety, their nutrition, their intellectual and social development. We find it sad and disturbing when we hear about children who are at a loss for this type of adult supervision. However, for the child who cannot imagine the danger of a speeding car, the command to look both ways is almost always understood as an arbitrary and frustrating dictatorial imposition. One Halloween, after they'd emptied their trick-or-treat bags into huge salad bowls, I warned my boys not to eat too much candy because it would make them sick. Their reaction made it clear that they thought I just had to be crazy or stupid. No matter how well-meaning and well-grounded the parent, our children will almost always see us as Petunia and Vernon Dursley.

It is also important to notice that when we are very young, we have no choice but to concede to parental authority. As infants sitting in high chairs, children must open their mouths to whatever's on the spoon. We acquire language in

part by means of not questioning the words our parents use. Also, both parent and child often become used to the idea that parents give orders and children take them.

> *Don't ask questions*—that was the first rule for a quiet life with the Dursleys.
>
> Uncle Vernon entered the kitchen as Harry was turning over the bacon.
>
> "Comb your hair!" He barked, by way of the morning greeting. (SS, 20)

Almost all adults interact with children in this way to a greater or lesser extent.

> Harry was left behind with Mrs. Figg, a mad old lady who lived two streets away. Harry hated it there. The whole house smelled of cabbage and Mrs. Figg made him look at photographs of all the cats she'd ever owned. (SS, 22)

Second-time readers of the series will notice that Mrs. Figg is not a Muggle. These readers know that Dumbledore placed Mrs. Figg in proximity to the Dursley household to watch over Harry. She is another of Harry's caretakers, and another of the adults who impose rules upon him. This is just part of life while living at the Dursleys'.

> "I'm warning you," [Vernon] had said, putting his large purple face right up close to Harry's, "I'm warning you now, boy—any funny business, anything at all—and you will be in that cupboard from now until Christmas." (SS, 24)

Adult readers of the novels will commonly see the Dursleys as humorous exaggerations, but it is important to remember that children won't.

One of the most disturbing things about human power relations is that we can afford to ignore or disregard those who have little or no power over us. This is so common that we often fail to notice that we do it. When we ignore the fact that we ignore people, the entire event disappears from our reflection. Usually we won't even remember the interaction, and we don't second-guess what we don't remember.

> "We could phone Marge," Uncle Vernon suggested.
>
> "Don't be silly, Vernon, she hates the boy."
>
> The Dursleys often spoke about Harry like this, as though he wasn't there—or rather, as though he was something very nasty that couldn't understand them, like a slug. (SS, 22)

The tendency to ignore or disregard those with less power is one of the cardinal themes that runs throughout the entire Harry Potter series (Sirius Black addresses the issue directly when he says, "If you want to know what a man's like, take a good look at how he treats his inferiors, not his equals." (GOF, 525)

While those with power can afford to ignore those without, the powerless have no such discretion. The customer can afford to ignore the waitress, but the waitress cannot afford to ignore the customer. Further, while parents may disregard an instance of ignoring their own child, the child never will. In the Dursleys, Rowling provides her reader with an obvious example of the inappropriate application of power. Young people seem to have heightened concern for fairness and thus will pay special attention to how different Harry's life is from Dudley's. Few of us rest easy when we feel ourselves the victims of injustice. When forced to suffer unfairness, we often chafe with the desire for explanation and justification. This desire for justification commonly breeds questioning, or even rebellion. As a result, children often begin to insistently ask why decisions are made the way they are. The word "why" can often ring repeatedly throughout a household for years.

This demand for justification is a very important step in a child's development to moral maturity. It is a demand for motive and then for a justification of the motive. While I am a child, you may have power over me, but the ideal of justice, an idea from within my own head, permits me the right to question the legitimacy of your decisions. As almost any parent can tell you, this type of questioning and interrogation happens very early in the child's life. It is not enough for most children to know *that* it is bedtime, they want to know *why* as well. Like most people, children have a tendency to rebel against unexplained dictatorial power. However, like most people, they must do so with the understanding of the potential costs that will almost certainly result. Rebellion in the face of power is almost always punished. However, swallowing and repressing perceived injustice is also very difficult for us to do. Our indignance usually comes out in one way or another.

> About once a week, Uncle Vernon looked over the top of his newspaper and shouted that Harry needed a haircut. Harry must have had more haircuts than the rest of the boys in his class put together, but it made no difference, his hair simply grew that way—all over the place [...]. Once, Aunt Petunia, tired of Harry coming back from the barber's looking as though he hadn't been at all, had taken a pair of kitchen scissors and cut his hair so short, he was almost bald [...]. Next morning, however, he had gotten up to find his hair exactly as it had been before Aunt Petunia had sheared it off. He had been given a week in his cupboard for this ... (SS, 20–21, 24)

Every child knows that those in power bring no guarantee of justice or beneficence. Any bully can show you that. Being in charge does not make a person right. A person's ability to punish does

not make the punishment legitimate. A child's understanding of this will be fundamental to his or her later moral development. In the short term, however, perceived injustice inspires the temptation to revolt. It is important to notice in the above passage that Harry's hair is rebelling even if Harry himself is not. Harry will later find himself on top of his school after attempting to escape Dudley's gang. In neither case did Harry intentionally try to frustrate those who held power over him. Rowling seems to be tipping her hat to the possibility that rebellion against injustice can begin even before we are conscious of it. In Mark Twain's classic tale, Huckleberry Finn decides to help the slave, Jim, escape even before he recognizes why.

> It would get all around that Huck Finn helped a nigger to get his freedom [...]. I was stealing a poor old woman's nigger that hadn't ever done me no harm [...]. I about made up my mind to pray, and see if I couldn't try to quit being the kind of a boy I was and be better. So I kneeled down. But the words wouldn't come. Why wouldn't they? It warn't no use to try and hide it from Him. Nor from me, neither. I knowed very well why they wouldn't come [...]. I was playing double. I was letting on to give up sin, but away inside of me I was holding on to the biggest one of all. I was trying to make my mouth say I would do the right thing and the clean thing [...] but deep down in me I knowed it was a lie, and He knowed it. You can't pray a lie—I found that out [...]. So I was full of trouble, full as I could be; and didn't know what to do. At last I had an idea; and I says, I'll go and write the letter [...]. I felt good and all washed clean of sin [...]. But I didn't do it straight off, but [... I] got to thinking over our trip down the river; and I see Jim before me all the time: in the day and in the night-time, sometimes moonlight, some-times storms, and we a-floating along, talking and singing and laughing. But somehow I couldn't seem to strike no places to harden me against him ...and then I happened to look around and see that paper [...]. I was a-trembling,

because I'd got to decide, forever, betwixt two things, and I knowed it. I studied a minute, sort of holding my breath, and then says to myself: "All right, then, I'll go to hell"—and tore it up […]. I would go to work and steal Jim out of slavery again. (Twain, 2001, 342-3)

The resentment of injustice is that fundamental to human individuality. During his first meeting with Harry, Hagrid asks,

"Not a wizard, eh? Never made things happen when you was scared or angry?"

Harry looked into the fire. Now he came to think about it … every odd thing that had ever made his aunt and uncle furious with him had happened when he, Harry, had been upset or angry … Chased by Dudley's gang, he had somehow found himself out of their reach … dreading going to school with that ridiculous haircut, he managed to make it grow back … In the very last time Dudley had hit him, hadn't he got his revenge, without even realizing he was doing it? Hadn't he set a boa constrictor on him? (SS, 58)

There is something fundamental to being human that resents injustice and unfairness even though we also like to avoid the wrath of the powerful. Just as the Patronus Charm and the Cruciatus Curse are grounded on deep human feeling, these acts of underage wandless magic are driven by specific emotional reactions to unjustified domination. This is not just anger, this is righteous anger.

Rowling seems to be implying that our negative reaction to injustice is powerful and thus not easily subdued or denied. She also seems to be saying that our perhaps inborn human ability to recognize and resent injustice is strong enough to inspire us to stand up against our own fear of reprisal. Plato suggested that the ability to understand and recognize justice is a divine and miraculous human inheritance. It is magic that we are born with. It should be no surprise then, that Harry's magic arises out of it. However, the natural world is an arena of relative power and applied strategy. In a context in which only the strongest survive, there is and can be no room for the concept of fairness. The philosopher Thomas Hobbes called this the state of nature in his *Leviathan*. In the animal world of eat or be eaten there is no place for mercy. The philosopher Immanuel Kant observed that justice is an idea so ideal that it could never have arisen by means of observing the power competitions of the natural world. The idea of justice must be brought into a violent world through the inspired rational imagination of the human mind and by no other means. The world does not bring the idea of justice to humans, humans bring this idea to the world, a world that could never have predicted or imagined it.

Even when Harry seeks to do what he's told so as to avoid punishment, his own desire to take a stand against arbitrary power squirts out of him, despite himself. We may also recognize that while a magical resistance to injustice seems to sort of leak out of Harry in response to the Dursleys, it veritably explodes out of Ariana Dumbledore, Albus's sister, in response to a far more severe violation. Rowling seems to be saying that the ability to recognize and understand justice is so basic to the very definition of being human that it cannot be controlled even by those who wield this understanding. We are not so free as to be able to disregard our awareness of and care for justice. Our spontaneous resistance to injustice can be redirected, even postponed, but never subdued or tamed. The suppression of it can be only temporary and perhaps dangerous and damaging.

This brings us back to the issue of motive within human decision making. As we've seen, young people find themselves in a situation in which they must submit to the demands of their caretakers. Therefore, children will often develop their initial understanding of the difference between right and wrong by means of the external rules given them by teachers or parents. This begins as a result of the fact that children are so often at a loss to know what to do.

"Yes," said Harry. "The thing is—the thing is, I don't know how to –"

"How to get onto the platform?" she said kindly, and Harry nodded.

"Not to worry," she said. "All you have to do is walk straight at the barrier between platforms, nine and ten. Don't stop and don't be scared you'll crash into it, that's very important. Best do it at a bit of a run if you're nervous. Go on, go now before Ron." (SS, 93)

Few would fail to see this as a kindness shown to Harry by Molly Weasley. Even the most basic things can be mysteries to the young. However, we must also note that in the above passage, there are four distinct commands. As children, our lack of practical knowledge and wisdom teaches us to rely on the advice of adults. At that age, it is in our best interest to trust the superior understanding of guiding adults.

The question then becomes, to what extent should we trust the guiding advice of adults? Trust always comes with risk. What is at stake when children find the need to trust mentoring adults? The nature of adult guidance falls into two categories. The first category is made up of advice intended to help children make it through the day with practical tips, suggestions, and explanations. Molly Weasley's advice about the barrier to platform 9 ¾ is of this type. The second category is made up of advice intended to help children understand the difference between right and wrong. It is very important to recognize the difference between these two forms of advice.

Because children are in the habit of trusting adults regarding practical advice, many of them will then turn and trust the same adults in regards to the criteria of good and bad behavior. Harry Potter is eleven when he boards the train to Hogwarts for the first time, and children of that age either do not know how to determine right and wrong for themselves or they do not usually have the self-confidence to do so. Therefore, children of this age have a tendency to rely on external parental/authoritative rules for the determination of right and wrong. For most children, most of the time, when the teacher says that a child is bad, then the child *is* bad. Usually this is not dangerous. It is well recognized that children need clear and consistent boundaries

within which to begin the process of determining their own identity. Rules of behavior within a classroom will be imposed upon children without their input. Few would deny the practical necessity of in-class rules of behavior for first graders. Dudley Dursley stands as a testament to the problems that can occur when parents fail to provide consistent limitation.

External rules come in many forms. For example, governmental laws are external rules. They are imposed upon us from without. Religious rules are almost always external in a similar way. External rules are rules that do not originate from within my own subjectivity and imagination. They are rules that are imposed or provided to me by someone else. One of the benefits of external rules is clarity. When rules are written down, we can all be clear on what the rules are. Raise your hand before talking. Form a line in the cafeteria. The speed limit is 65 mph. Wear your robes for the sorting ceremony. Eleven-year-old Hermione Granger loves external rules.

"I've learned all our course books by heart, of course, I just hope it will be enough [...]. You'd better hurry up and put your robes on, I've just been up to the front to ask the conductor, and he says we're nearly there. You haven't been fighting, have you? You'll be in trouble before we even get there [...]. I only came in here because people outside are behaving very childishly, racing up and down the corridors [...] you've got dirt on your nose, by the way, did you know [...]. Madam Hooch told us not to move — you'll get us all into trouble [...]. I almost told your brother [...] Percy — he's a prefect, he'd put a stop to this [...]." Hermione was the last person to do anything against the rules [...]. (SS, 105–6, 110, 144, 148, 155, 178)

It is not by mistake that Rowling gives Hermione two parents who both happen to be dentists, for dentists are famous for dishing out rules to children. First-year Hermione has been convinced of the benefits of following the rules. Hermione is one of the most capable first-year students. Her ability to grasp and follow external instruction distinguishes her as an excellent young witch. This first-year Hermione trusts adults to know what's best.

However, this young Hermione does not distinguish between practical and moral advice. The followers of external rules often put themselves at risk of having their identity determined by these rules. If I deeply trust or respect the teacher or relative who then tells me I'm stupid, then I will likely believe I am stupid. We can see this in Neville Longbottom when he remarks, "the family thought I was all-Muggle for ages [. . .] they thought I might not be magic enough [. . .] and everyone knows I'm almost a squib" (SS, 125; CS, 185). Marvolo Gaunt's treatment of his daughter Merope is a far harsher example. The Sorting Hat is also an external determining authority.

> "What house are your brothers in?" asked Harry.
> "Gryffindor," said Ron. Gloom seemed to be settling on him again. "Mom and Dad were in it, too. I don't know what they'll say if I'm not. I don't suppose Ravenclaw *would* be too bad, but imagine if they put me in Slytherin." (SS, 106)

We should note the anxiety that the students demonstrate in regards to the Sorting Hat. The anxiety is born of the belief that they have no control over or input in the Sorting Hat's decisions. Like many judgments that happen during childhood, these decisions happen to children, not with them. The children on the Hogwarts Express believe they have no say in the matter of the house into which they will be placed. They are, however, aware of how significant the decision will be for them. The clarity and confidence that can arise from our reliance on external authority often comes at the cost of letting others determine our fate.

Ron Weasley by contrast has been taught to question and even flaunt authority through the example of his older brothers. He is therefore less likely to be as seriously affected by external judgments. So why would someone like Hermione submit herself so willingly to outside judgment? The first reason, as we have said, is the clear benefit of developing practical expertise and skill. By trusting the authority of the textbook, you improve

the chances of acquiring the skills held within it. The second reason for trusting authority has to do with a desire for moral superiority.

We must recognize that the follower of external rules may also be inadvertently shirking or deferring the responsibility for the writing of those rules. When the know-it-all Hermione derides Harry and Ron regarding robes or being out of bed after hours, she is not insinuating that she herself is in charge. By appealing to external and established rules, she is appropriating the authority of those rules. By expressing allegiance to the rules, she assumes the power of those rules, even if only as a mere conduit.

This is one of the most enticing and tempting elements of external rules. Since I did not write the rules, I do not have to be responsible for them. It is not my fault that the rules are what they are. Further, the clarity of written laws provides me with a certainty that then grants me the option of self-righteousness on the grounds of those clear laws. The follower of unquestioned external laws can feel certain in her goodness. In other words, if a good person is a person who follows the rules, then all I have to do is follow the rules to be a good person. It is not difficult to see this in first-year Hermione.

This pattern of justice that is based on external rules works fine so long as the legitimacy of those rules never comes under scrutiny. The follower of external rules is always at risk of adopting a sense of superiority over those who do not follow the rules as well. The holier-than-thou person will often feel entitled in their negative and diminishing judgment of others. Dolores Umbridge, tyrannical temporary headmistress of Hogwarts and senior undersecretary to the Minster of Magic, represents this attitude. This is the second reason for adopting an allegiance to external rules. It is not hard to see this in first-year Hermione as well.

A third reason for following external rules is a threat of punishment. As Tom Riddle himself understands, the alliegiance of Peter Pettigrew, deadly traitor of Lily and James Potter, is grounded solely on this fear. This brings us back to the role of motive with regard to morality and justice. As we saw earlier, even very young children will interrogate their parents about reasons for decisions they dislike. Motive matters. Further, the source of the motive matters. As already noted, relying on external rules means adopting the rules of someone else. Do we have the right as individual human beings to leave the question of what is right and what is wrong in the hands of another? Have justice and morality ever been as easy as following a rule book? More importantly, we can never trust that the wielders of power will dedicate themselves to universal principles of justice and human dignity. Hermione shows how easily we can be tempted into unquestioning allegiance. In fact, almost every child will have been doing so most of their lives. However, one of the key reasons for the existence of the Harry Potter series is to initiate a serious reflection on the point at which it becomes appropriate to leave the easy adherence to external principles behind.

Heteronomy, rule from another, must be abandoned in favor of autonomy, rule from within oneself. Rowling has carefully chosen the age at which the children first go to Hogwarts. Harry and the other students who attend Hogwarts get their letters at the age of eleven. It is at this age that many young people begin to acquire the ability to question the rules of authorities to the degree that they may actually rebel or resist. It is also at this age that young people begin to recognize a private and individual morality. It is not by mistake that most of the adult initiation rites found around the world occur at just about this age. These rights are not about entry into the status of adulthood in the sense that these children will be granted the right to vote or to drive. They are about entering through a threshold into the ability to think independently about morality and justice. It is at this point that the consistent parental boundaries that were once necessary to help me in determining my identity become much more problematic. We must see that the identity a child forges within the secure boundaries of established external rules then becomes the vehicle through which he or she begins to question those very rules. It is a shame to find a child who has been deprived of consistent guiding and parental boundaries. It is also a shame to find the older child who has never learned to question these boundaries.

Anyone who makes the case that we should resign ourselves to an external authority has the dilemma of explaining the negative examples from history. The call to trust religious authority must always be confronted by the questions of the Spanish Inquisition and the nearly uncountable additional examples. The call to trust political or patriotic authorities must always be confronted by the many, many examples of dictatorial authoritarianism such as the Khmer Rouge or the Nazis. Rowling names one of her wizarding prisons Nurmengard, which clearly makes reference to the city of Nuremberg where Nazi war criminals were condemned despite their claims to have been merely following orders. Following the rules of another simply does not release us from the responsibility of our actions. While reliance on external authorities can give us clarity and self-certainty, unquestioned allegiance always brings with it the threat that the leaders may become or may already be corrupt. If I rely on an authority to tell me the difference between right and wrong, how will I know when that authority has become the source of injustice? Cornelius Fudge, Dolores Umbridge, the Carrows, Vernon Dursley, Gellert Grindelwald, Tom Riddle and even Albus Dumbledore all provide the young reader with potent examples of adults whose authority should not be trusted or condoned. In fact, it might be said that Rowling's series is at least in part dedicated to expressing just how badly wrong trusting external authorities of justice can go.

This leaves the young person in the precarious position of having to determine how to transition from trust in external authorities to reliance on individual principles. Just as Hermione represented the young person who relies too heavily on the trusted wisdom and authority of adults, she will also give expression to one of the most important transitional moments of the entire series.

Then a small voice came out of the shadows.

"Please, Professor McGonagall—they were looking for me [...]. I went looking for the troll because I—I thought I could deal with it on my own—you know, because I've read all about them [...]. If they hadn't found me, I'd be dead now. " (SS, 177–8)

In this instance Hermione does two things for the first time since we have met her. She breaks the rules, and she lies to a Hogwarts professor. She does this on the spot with very little time to think about it. Why does she do it? How does she do it? Hermione Granger is in the habit of getting her ideas of justice from those in authority around her. And yet, in this circumstance, she seems to derive the rule of her decision from within her own reflection. Upon learning of the mountain troll, Ron and Harry go looking for Hermione because they know she will not have heard about the danger. By showing up at just the right time, they prove that they were thinking about her safety when they need not have been. Both Ron and Harry then put themselves at significant risk in order to respond to her need. Throughout the event, Hermione is seen cowering and near to fainting. However, when professors Snape and McGonagall arrive, Hermione snaps to attention and takes the blame for the event.

In a matter of minutes Hermione has gone from a person whose most serious fear is disappointing a teacher to a person who will disappoint that very teacher in order to demonstrate loyalty and gratitude to trusted comrades. In a matter of minutes, Hermione Granger has discovered within herself a principle of justice based on the idea of reciprocated loyalty. This principle from within bears upon her with such force that it is able to topple the former priority of her loyalty to authority. As readers, we have been hoping that Hermione would become less of a know-it-all, so it is easy for us to ignore or disregard what this must have felt like for the individual experiencing it. We must remember how hard it is for most of us to let go of something that had so recently grounded the direction of most of our decisions. What must it have felt like for Hermione to hear the respected Professor McGonagall say "Miss Granger, five points will be taken from Gryffindor for this [...]. I'm very disappointed in you" (SS, 178).

However, most readers will recognize that this decision cemented the relationship between the three main characters of the seven-novel series. "But from that moment on, Hermione Granger became their friend. There are some things you can't share without ending up liking each other" (SS, 179). She herself will say "Books! And cleverness! There are more important things—friendship and bravery" (SS, 287). But how does one do that? How does one demonstrate loyalty to authority all one's life only to overthrow it in a single moment? And how is it that figures like Dolores Umbridge never seem to come to this conclusion? How is it that Hermione Granger can come to understand the significance of demonstrating loyalty to friends so quickly while figures like Peter Pettigrew never do? From this point on, Hermione becomes almost as much of a rule breaker as Ron and Harry are when serious issues are on the line. While she remains one of the most ardent and diligent students, she will never easily trust adult authorities in the same way again. In this moment, Hermione Granger adopts the responsibility of independent moral judgment. She learns to think for herself. Hermione's ability for moral and rational self-reliance will prove an absolutely essential ingredient to the heroic adventures on the horizon.

We see a similar move to decisive independence in Harry upon his first encounter with the entitled pure-blood Draco Malfoy.

> "You'll soon find out some wizarding families are much better than others, Potter. You don't want to go making friends with the wrong sort. I can help you there."
>
> He held out his hand to shake Harry's, but Harry didn't take it.
>
> "I think I can tell who the wrong sort are for myself, thanks," he said coolly. (SS, 108–9)

First-time readers of the series may find this encounter a bit surprising given Harry's willingness to accept advice and insight from those who have so much more understanding of the wizarding world. After all, Draco is offering Harry some form of help. However, after eleven years under the influence of Dudley Dursley, Harry knows a bully when he sees one. Harry knows that bullies never offer help free of charge. Yes, Harry is aware that standing up to Malfoy in this first encounter could cost him, but he is also aware that conceding to him could cost him more. What we must see here is that Harry, like Hermione, is demonstrating ability to arrive at a deliberative conclusion on his own and in the heat of the moment. How many eleven-year-old readers of *Harry Potter and the Sorcerer's Stone* have dreamed of producing such a snappy comeback in the face of their own real-world bullies?

Nonetheless, decisions always come with consequences. Just as Hermione's decision to demonstrate loyalty at great cost cements the relationship between the series' three main characters, Harry's retort to Draco grounds an enmity between the two that will never be reconciled. Therefore, it is very important that decisions like these not be made lightly or foolishly. Those who are new to making judgments on their own will commonly make mistakes. Independent judgment, like any other difficult skill, requires practice. His experience with Dudley grants Harry the ability to make a snap judgment about Draco, a judgment that turns out to be spot-on. Many readers will admire Harry in this moment for his insight and quick courage.

However, Harry is guessing about Draco. Appearances do not always translate to reality. The human tendency to jump too quickly to conclusions is also one of the main guiding themes of the entire Harry Potter series. Upon seeing Draco Malfoy flanked by intimidating attendants Crabbe and Goyle, Harry recognizes a similarity with patterns he encountered first under Dudley, as we have seen. He then allows the similarity to inspire his confidence in the assumption that Draco is just like Dudley. His certainty in his own judgment of Draco grounds and drives his antagonistic retort. If he hadn't been so sure he was right, his comeback could not have been so quick and biting. Harry's certainty in his read of Draco allows Harry to respond with confident action. The more certain I am that things are as they seem, the more confidently I can respond. Action requires faith in my own guesses. This is where a serious problem arises. How can I be sure that my assumptions are accurate enough to act upon? The more I question my assumptions, the less I am able to act upon them with confidence. However, the less I question my assumptions, the more quickly I can act on them as if they were true.

This is one of the key elements of *Harry Potter and the Philosopher's Stone*. Harry, Ron, and Hermione become so convinced that Professor Snape is the villain of the story that they begin to merely take the idea for granted. Just as Harry was all too ready to act on his assumption about Draco Malfoy, Harry comes to a snap decision about Professor Snape and demonstrates very little ability to question this interpretation. Those of us who make snap judgments are right some of the time. However, when we do happen to be right we are largely getting lucky. Assumptions are bets ("I'd bet my broomstick *he* let that troll in, to make a diversion!" (SS, 183). Bets are susceptible to the odds. Sometimes your guess will be accurate, and sometimes it will not. Harry, Ron, and Hermione make a guess about Professor Snape that is not accurate.

> "But I thought—Snape—"
>
> "Severus?" Quirrell laughed, and it wasn't his usual quivering treble, either, but cold and sharp. "Yes, Severus does seem the type, doesn't he? So useful to have him swooping around like an overgrown bat. Next to him, who would suspect p-p-poor, st-stuttering P-Professor Quirrell?"
>
> Harry couldn't take it in. This couldn't be true, it couldn't.
>
> "But Snape tried to kill me!"
>
> "No, no, no. *I* tried to kill you. Your friend Miss Granger accidentally knocked me over as she rushed to set fire to Snape at that Quidditch match. She broke my eye contact with you.
>
> "Another few seconds and I'd have got you off that broom. I'd have managed it before then if Snape hadn't been muttering a countercurse, trying to save you."
>
> "Snape was trying to *save* me?" (SS, 288–9)

Professor Quirrell makes a very important point here. The assumptions that students made about Professor Snape significantly benefited Professor Quirrell, the real villain of the story. People have an amazing tendency to jump unquestioningly to conclusions and Professor

Quirrell used that fact as part of his overall strategy. In other words, the very tendency that allowed Harry to act so admirably in his first meeting with Draco Malfoy also put the entire wizarding world at great risk by aiding Tom Riddle. Every time Harry, Ron, and Hermione focused their attention on Professor Snape, they were turning their attention away from the actual threat. In this first book of the series, Rowling fittingly allows for eleven-year-old protagonists to stumble in an effective direction despite their prejudicial mistakes. However, if her plot had required the young wizards to make accurate judgments, their quest would have failed.

Children must mature beyond their dependence on external authority, and this requires that they learn to develop confidence in their own ability to perform independent judgment. However, independent judgment is a skill hard-won over a long period of time. Novices must be expected to make mistakes as they practice the overall skill. However, practicing judgments in the real world, while necessary for improvement, will always also come with consequences. Everyone has to practice making decisions, but even as they do, they will have to pay for their mistakes. This is one of the most difficult and dangerous aspects of childhood and adolescence. It is messy and probably unfair. Adults rarely acknowledge it and as a result rarely find themselves offering young people credible advice or support on the issue. Rowling offers young readers an honest and detailed presentation of this reality. This is unquestionably one of the reasons for the great popularity of the series among this audience. Rowling acknowledges how messy and serious the transition to adulthood commonly is, and she expresses it in a manner distinctly recognizable to those currently going through it.

CHAPTER 5
Moral Practice Is Messy

I once had a student who designed and made all her own clothing. In the midst of students who all bought their clothing premade in stores, this student stood out. It is not hard to recognize how bold and rare a decision this must've been for a nineteen-year-old undergraduate. Her designs were unique and creative. Many of her creations were quite beautiful. She clearly had talent and potential in the area of fashion design. However, not all of her experiments were successful. Even she was quick to admit that some of her designs were not as she had envisioned them. No one would expect a novice clothing designer to make masterpieces with every go. We expect those who are practicing a new skill to litter the floor with mistakes and embarrassments. Excellence at any skill can only be grounded on the willingness to make mistakes over a long period of time as one progresses.

However, I can avoid mistakes by letting other people make decisions for me. I do not have to understand fashion to wear fashionable clothes. I do not need to know what styles are cool to be able to buy cool styles. Clothing store clerks in shopping malls are all too willing to help me with this. Any person with a credit card can walk into one of these stores and have the employees there outfit them according to the current trends and styles. That person can then go to a high-school setting on the following day wearing clothes that will almost certainly be accepted as fashion appropriate. In distinct contrast to the young woman who designed and created all her own clothes, purchasing clothes on the fashion authority of clothing store employees requires absolutely no input or insight on my part. Copying the clothing choices of fashion models or celebrities in magazines can never be more than mere repetition. If I choose to wear clothing that reflects the current fashion trends, I must recognize that this is yet another example of adhering to external or outside rules.

As we noticed in the last chapter, following external rules can give me both certainty and clarity. Letting store employees choose all my clothing takes all of the guesswork out of my wardrobe for me. Further, conforming to accepted fashion trends will make my acceptance among my social peers far more predictable and reliable. When I let other people make these decisions for me I simply avoid the need to do any deliberation on my own. If I don't make any decisions, I never have to wonder if I made the right decisions. By letting fashion authorities choose all my clothes, I avoid almost any chance of making mistakes.

However, in letting other people make my decisions for me, I miss the opportunity to practice making decisions for myself. For Rowling, independent decision-making is one of the essential ingredients to legitimate maturity. Dolores Umbridge, Percy Weasley, and Draco Malfoy all exude an air of the juvenile in their unquestioning allegiance to external authority. If I am to avoid this, I must learn to resist the temptation of the easy certainty and social acceptance born of external rules. I must risk looking like a fool. I must open to the possibility that I will look like Neville Longbottom trying to mount a broom for the first time. I must be ready to make mistakes for a very long time before anything like skill or wisdom might emerge.

Let us consider a musician's practice room. As almost any serious musician can tell you, practice rooms usually come neither with audiences nor microphones. In a practice room there is no one but me listening and there is usually no recording. This is a mercy and a blessing. A

brilliant performance on the stage before a live audience almost always rests on a great pile of broken and mangled performances that are safely stored in the perfect amnesia of the practice room. For a musician, a practice room is a Room of Requirement that provides nearly unlimited chances to perform a particular piece of music. A private practice room grants me as many tries as I like to address mistakes and inaccuracies as I drive toward an ever more polished mastery of a particular piece. No record is ever kept of how long it took me to arrive at this mastery.

Regrettably, the same cannot be said of most independent moral decision making. In order to practice making decisions about what I should and shouldn't do, I have to make actual decisions in real life. There is no moral practice room. As a developing clothing designer, I can always choose to throw out projects that didn't turn out well. As a musician I can always disregard my last run through a piece and try again. No one expects the development of skill or excellence to occur through any other means. And yet I am always responsible for my moral decisions even as I am practicing making these decisions. In the 1980 Academy Award-winning film *Ordinary People*, two high-school students are bowling. Jeannine asks, "Can you ever break the ball?" Conrad responds, "You can't break the ball. Can't break the floor. Can't break anything in a bowling alley. And that's what I like about bowling alleys." This gives expression to just how often young people feel like they're just about to break something.

Take the issue of friendship, for example. Defining and developing friendships is one of the most complex things that human beings do. Rowling takes seven novels to give full expression to the establishment and development of the friendships between the series' three main characters. We have already noted how important it was for Hermione to abandon her previous loyalties in the name of prioritizing her relationship with Ron and Harry. However, Hermione does not seem to possess a textbook for maintaining this relationship. When Harry is presented with a mysterious world-class Quidditch broom in *Harry Potter and the Prisoner of Azkaban*, Hermione has to decide whether the safety of her friends is more important than her perceived loyalty to them. Should she do what they want her to do (let Harry keep the broom), or should she do what is safe (tell a teacher about the potentially dangerous broom)? By informing Professor McGonagall about the mysterious broom, Hermione protects Harry from potential harm but at the cost of his trust in her. Both Harry and Ron refused to speak with her for quite some time because of this.

Should Hermione have told Professor McGonagall about the Firebolt? Should Ron and Harry have shut Hermione out for this perceived betrayal? What is important to see here is that these decisions are being made by young people new to the very process of maintaining friendships. In order to get good at having friendships, people have to practice at it. However, the mistakes that we make while we practice leave an immediate impact on the people with whom we are practicing. Every decision I make within a friendship remains a detail and aspect of that friendship. If I make a mistake, I can't take it back. Each decision becomes part of the history of the relationship. There is no practice room for friendships.

Rubeus Hagrid, Hogwarts' gamekeeper and longtime guardian and guide for the stories' three main characters, has been listening to Hermione cry about the damage she did to her relationship with Ron and Harry. Hagrid invites Harry and Ron down for a discussion of the issue.

"I got somethin' ter discuss with you two […]. Firs' yeh weren' talking to [Hermione] because o' the Firebolt, now yer not talkin' to her because her cat […]. She's cried a fair few times, yeh know. Goin' through a rough time at the moment […] but I gotta tell yeh, I thought you two'd value yer friend more'n broomsticks or rats. Tha's all" (PA, 273–4).

Hagrid is letting Harry and Ron know that they have made a judgment error. In particular, they have overprioritized the Firebolt, Harry's Quidditch broom, and Scabbers, Ron's pet rat, and underprioritized their relationship with Hermione. It is important to recognize here that Hagrid is not telling Harry and Ron to change their behavior. He is expressing his disappointment about the decision they made. He is not acting as an external authority about right and wrong. He is appealing to their ability to make these decisions on their own. Hagrid's input is in the form of guidance or advice, not command. The boys almost immediately and spontaneously begin to recognize that they may have made a mistake. Through Hagrid's prompting, the boys quickly begin to reconsider and reinterpret their assumptions on the issue. They are practicing subjective moral deliberation in real time and there is no other way to get better at it.

A similar situation arises the second time Harry decides to enter Hogsmeade with the help of the Marauder's Map. Again, Hermione warns the boys not to put Harry at risk. Despite the belief that Harry is being pursued by a murderer, Ron and Harry decide the risk is one worth taking. Further, the boys decide to increase the risk by taking the opportunity to publicly humiliate Draco Malfoy. Neither Ron nor Harry seems to put much thought into the potentially negative consequences of their decisions. Professor Lupin calls them out on this.

> Don't expect me to cover up for you again, Harry. I cannot make you take Sirius Black seriously. But I would have thought that what you have heard when the Dementors draw near you would have had more of an effect on you. Your parents gave their lives to keep you alive, Harry. A poor way to repay them — gambling their sacrifice for a bag of magic tricks. (PA, 290)

Professor Lupin, like Hagrid, emphasizes the question of priority. Like many children, Harry and Ron are drawn by the fun and excitement of Hogsmeade. It is like being drawn by a circus or fair. As Fred Weasley says "where's the fun without a bit of risk?" (GOF, 190). Even Bertie Bott's Every Flavor Beans are advertised as "A Risk With Every Mouthful" (GOF, 102). Any child or young person can identify with the desire to do fun things even if they are risky. Almost every child can identify with the desire to try to get away with such things. However, there are few things more childish than to take great risks for temporary and shallow entertainments. Professor Lupin, an excellent teacher, demonstrates a keen ability to emphasize this point in the above passage. Professor Lupin takes the opportunity to allow Harry and Ron to recognize that Harry's life has been risked for silly magic tricks. By placing this decision in the context of the sacrifice of Harry's parents, Lupin forces the boys to acknowledge just what was prioritized over what.

Both professor Lupin and Hagrid appeal to what they believed to be Harry's character. Both express that they thought Harry would have displayed better judgment. Both are implying that they believed Harry to be a person with different priorities than his decisions express. Both Hagrid and Professor Lupin are appealing to the strength of this character, Harry's own character, to push Harry into making different decisions on his own. Professor Lupin even acknowledges that he "cannot make" Harry make better decisions. Nonetheless, both the decision to exile Hermione and the decision to go into Hogsmeade reveal Harry and Ron to be rash and juvenile. It may sound strange to say so, but the only reason that Harry and Ron disregard the potential threat represented by the mysterious Firebolt is because it is such a cool broom. This is the same kind of childish disregard that draws children headlong into a street without looking in both directions. Rowling does an excellent job of reminding us just how easily a child's attention can be drawn and at what cost. While we can certainly empathize with Harry's desire for both Hogsmeade and the Firebolt, it is also not hard to recognize how stupid the decisions were. These decisions make Harry look like a child, but it is the input of both Hagrid and Professor Lupin that allow Harry to recognize it as well. "[Professor Lupin] walked away, leaving Harry feeling worse by far than he had at any point in Snape's office" (PA, 290). This spontaneous and subjective emotional reaction to his earlier decision is a clear indicator of the emerging force of Harry's developing character.

We can see a similar emotional outcome in Professor Lupin's reaction to his own decisions. Rowling grants us a glimpse of Remus Lupin, Sirius Black, and James Potter as Hogwarts students the same age as Harry, Ron, and Hermione. In the Shrieking Shack, Professor Lupin reveals the fact that he is and has been a werewolf. He tells the story of how Sirius, James, and Peter Pettigrew learned to become Animagi in an effort to protect Remus with regard to his monthly transformations. Many readers will notice the heavy emphasis on the importance of loyalty to friends that crosses the generations here. However, as she so often does, Hermione spies the crucial risk involved in their decisions. "That was still really dangerous! Running around in the dark with a werewolf! What if you'd given the others the slip, and bitten somebody?"

> "A thought that still haunts me," said Lupin heavily. "And there were near misses, many of them. We laughed about them afterwards. We were young, thoughtless—carried away with our own cleverness [...]. I sometimes felt guilty about betraying Dumbledore's trust, of course ... he had admitted me to Hogwarts when no other headmaster would have done so, and he had no idea I was breaking the rules he had set down for my own and others' safety. He never knew I had led three fellow students into becoming Animagi illegally. But I always managed to forget my guilty feelings every time we sat down to plan our next month's adventure." (PA, 355)

Remus Lupin is an excellent teacher and a good man. In this conversation he connects with these children by admitting his similarities to them. He uses the truth of his own past experiences to prove that he, like they, made foolhardy decisions under the intoxicating influence of promised adventure. He convinces them that he understands and remembers what it was like to be "carried away" and "thoughtless." In other words, he earns the trust of these students by convincing them that he remembers what it was like to be so young.

What Remus is doing here is what Rowling does throughout the entire series. He talks to these young people as people. He does not talk down to them. He looks them in the eye and talks to them seriously and directly. By admitting his authentic understanding of their youthful and reckless draw to adventure, Professor Lupin creates a common frame of reference across the generational difference. Lupin convinces the children that he has thought about things from their point of view and from their mindset. This allows the children to trust him in part because so few adults will act in this way. Without really being aware of it, most adults look at children and adolescents as something of another species. These adults will, like Mr. Filch, often content themselves with the idea that children are inscrutable irritations or ignorant brats in need of molding and refining (consider that the school attended by both Dudley and Vernon Dursley is named Smeltings).

So much of children's literature talks down to children. These books are written by authors who conjure a convenient and simplistic understanding of childhood. This recalls for us the comments of Rowling's fictional Beatrix Bloxam mentioned earlier. According to Dumbledore, Bloxam

> believed that *The Tales of Beedle the Bard* were damaging to children [...]. Mrs. Bloxam took a variety of old stories, including several of Beedle's, and rewrote them according to her ideals, which she expressed as "filling the pure minds of our little angels with healthy, happy thoughts, keeping their sweet slumber free of wicked dreams, and protecting the precious flower of their innocence." (TBB, 17–19)

This erroneous convention about what childhood is like bears little resemblance to children's actual lived experience. This is one of the main reasons why record numbers of young people have flocked to Rowling's books. Children see an authentic and detailed expression of their own real experiences reflected there. How many of us are drawn to literature by the uncanny joy and alleviation of loneliness we experience in finding ourselves reflected in the pages of another's writing?

However, like Rowling, Professor Lupin has an ulterior motive. In order to influence someone, you must first convince them that you understand them, that you have listened to them. So, if in fact, Professor Lupin has convinced Harry, Ron, and Hermione that he was indeed like them and does understand them, what does he intend to influence them to do? He is trying to convince them to abandon the very recklessness that he himself has just admitted to.

> This time tomorrow, the owls will start arriving from parents…. They will not want a werewolf teaching their children, Harry. And after last night, I see their point. I could have bitten any of you…. That must never happen again. (PA, 423)

While the teenage Remus Lupin could forget and disregard his "guilty feelings" in order to plan "next month's adventure," the adult Lupin decides to confess to Professor Dumbledore and leave the school before the worst can happen. Despite the fact that he may very well have been the best Defense Against the Dark Arts teacher that Hogwarts had seen for a generation, this fact takes a backseat to the rare yet real threat he poses as a werewolf. While children and adolescents will easily take risks if the potential payoff is high enough, responsible adults will assess real risks far more gravely. The adult Lupin does not wait until the unthinkable occurs. He has come to realize that certain things are so important that they ought never be risked. While an irresponsible person will recognize his mistake only after the tragic occurs, a responsible person will make changes so as to avoid the potential tragedy before it happens. The teacher Lupin is trying to model this behavior for his students.

Yet it takes Lupin his entire life to this point to finally come to this conclusion. Remus Lupin has admitted that his decisions betray a faulty assessment of priority. Knowing how to properly assess priority, what matters more and what matters less, is one of the hallmarks of mature responsibility. It has, however, taken Lupin this long to arrive at this point:

> All this year, I have been battling with myself, wondering whether I should tell Dumbledore that Sirius was an Animagus. But I didn't do it. Why? Because I was too cowardly. It would have meant admitting that I'd betrayed his trust while I was at school, admitting that I'd led others along with me…. And Dumbledore's trust has meant everything to me. He let me into Hogwarts as a boy, and he gave me a job when I had been shunned all my life, unable to find paid work because of what I am. (PA, 356)

Even the adult Lupin wants to "get away with it" just as Harry, Ron, and Hermione so often do. Practicing responsibility is a messy process.

This signals a very important transition in the moral development of the individual person. Those who are governed by external rules fear external punishment. Those, like Professor Lupin, who are ruled by subjective internal principles, fear internal punishment. If I live in a world in which good and bad is determined by those in authority outside of myself, their judgments and their potential punishments are largely what concern me. This is well expressed in the 1983 film *A Christmas Story* directed by Bob Clark and based on the writings of Jean Shepherd. After one third-grade boy has been abandoned by his friends with his tongue stuck to a freezing poll, the teacher expresses the following:

> Now I know that some of you put Flick up to this, but he has refused to say who. But those who did it know their blame, and I'm sure that the guilt you feel is far worse than any punishment you might receive. Now, don't you feel terrible? Don't you feel remorse for what you have done? Well, that's all I'm going to say about poor Flick.

The boy responsible then responds "adults loved to say things like that but kids know better. We knew darn well it was always better not to get caught."

Those who are governed by external rules will almost always think, to a greater or lesser extent, in this manner. More importantly, people at this stage often do not yet experience subjective guilt in the manner assumed by the teacher in the above passage. The children in this passage find the teacher's suggestions about guilt silly. The idea of being driven by autonomous internal ideas of decency and justice has not yet occurred to them. If, however, I actually have begun to hear the voice of my own conscience, my concern for external punishments will begin to diminish in relation. Outside authorities may begin to take a backseat to my concern for the condemnation of my own subjective principles. For people like this, external punishments are bad, but guilt is worse (just as the teacher in the passage suggests). This transition from fear of external punishments to the fear of internal condemnation, from heteronomy to autonomy, is a cardinal moment in moral development.

This brings us to a discussion of one of the most achingly beautiful and empathetic images from Rowling's series, the Room of Hidden Things. As we've said, all children begin with external rules. At this stage I'm simply trying to follow rules set down for me by others. And yet even this can be challenging. Children will make mistake after mistake as they try to practice responding to external demands and conditions. This process then becomes magnificently exacerbated by the rise of my own individual conscience. Many young people are at a loss as to when to stand up to authority and when to acquiesce to it. Just as they were developing a skill at following rules, their own character begins to inspire them to question these very rules and authorities. It is, indeed, an insult to adolescents to attribute all of their awkward indecision and halting determinacy to so-called raging hormones. What is becoming clear, however, is just how muddled and chaotic this process can be. The very license that is granted to dressmakers and musicians to make mistakes without consequence is denied to the individual determining his or her own character. Responsibility cannot be practiced without transgressing that very responsibility. It is often under the weight and cost of bad decisions that we come to discover how important it is to make good ones. But what do we do with the bad decisions?

The Room of Requirement shows up at key moments throughout the Harry Potter series. From the practice and training room for Dumbledore's Army through to the staging area for the Battle of Hogwarts, the Room of Requirement plays an essential role in the progress of Rowling's plot. However, while the Room of Requirement often provided strategic and practical equipment for those who stood before it, Rowling makes sure to indicate that it provided something else as well.

> Harry [...] saw Professor Trelawney sprawled upon the floor, her head covered in one of her many shawls, several sherry bottles lying beside her, one broken [...].
>
> She hiccuped loudly [...].
>
> "Professor, were you trying to get into the Room of Requirement?"
>
> "... what?" She looked suddenly shifty.
>
> "The Room of Requirement," repeated Harry. "Were you trying to get in there?"
>
> "I—well—I didn't know students knew about—"
>
> "Not all of them do," said Harry [...].
>
> "I—well," said Professor Trelawney, drawing her shawls around her defensively and staring down at him with her vastly magnified eyes. "I wished to—ah— deposit certain—um—personal items in the Room. . . ." And she muttered something about nasty accusations.
>
> "Right," said Harry, glancing down at the sherry bottles.
>
> "I walked into the Room [...]," said Professor Trelawney, "[...] and I heard a voice, which has never happened before in all my years of hiding—of using the Room, I mean." (HBP, 540–2)

We can see in this that the room is also used to hide things that people are ashamed of. We see in this passage that Professor Trelawney has been hiding sherry bottles for years and that she is facing "nasty accusations" about them. Passages like this reveal that the room is used to hide things, particularly things that are shameful or embarrassing. Under this use, the room gets another name, "the Room of Hidden Things" (DH, 629).

In an extended interview, called *Harry Potter and Me,* that Rowling gave to the BBC in December 2001, she said,

> Unless you can really really really really remember what it felt like to be a child, you've really got no business writing for children … I remember so vividly what it felt like to be that age.

As young people practicing the skill of making decisions for themselves, many, many shameful and embarrassing mistakes will be made along the way. For many of us, these adolescent mistakes are some of our most painful memories and it is not surprising that we resist and suppress our memories of them. It almost feels like a blessing to allow some of them to recede in ever-dimmer recollections until they are all but forgotten. If we are the kind of people who do in fact allow these memories to dim and fade, then we are not good candidates for writing for or about the adolescent age group. Rowling's description of the Room of Hidden Things is a searing and insightful description of the stumbling and uncoordinated chaos of young free will. Her description of the Room of Hidden Things offers the reader a painfully accurate and yet also empathetic expression of the all-too-common panic and desperation of this age group. As Harry enters the Room of Hidden Things,

> he could not help but be overawed by what he was looking at. He was standing in a room the size of a large cathedral, whose high windows were sending shafts of light down upon what looked like a city with towering walls, built of what Harry knew must be objects hidden by generations of Hogwarts

inhabitants. There were alleyways and roads bordered by teetering piles of broken and damaged furniture, stowed away, perhaps, to hide the evidence of mishandled magic, or else hidden by castle-proud house-elves. There were thousands and thousands of books, no doubt banned or graffitied or stolen. There were winged catapults and Fanged Frisbees, some still with enough life in them to hover halfheartedly over the mountains of other forbidden items; there were chipped bottles of congealed potions, hats, jewels, cloaks; there were what looked like dragon eggshells, corked bottles whose contents still shimmered evilly, several rusting swords, and a heavy, bloodstained axe. Harry hurried forward into one of the many alleyways between all this hidden treasure. He turned right past an enormous stuffed troll, ran on a short way, took a left at the broken Vanishing Cabinet in which Montague had got lost the previous year, finally pausing beside a large cupboard that seemed to have had acid thrown at its blistered surface. He opened one of the cupboard's creaking doors: It had already been used as a hiding place for something in a cage that had long since died; its skeleton had five legs. He stuffed the Half-Blood Prince's book behind the cage and slammed the door. He paused for a moment, his heart thumping horribly, gazing around at all the clutter [. . .] the guilty outcomes of a thousand banned experiments, the secrets of the countless souls who had sought refuge in the room. (HBP, 526–7, DH, 632)

The first thing that we notice about the Room of Hidden Things is its awesome scale. It is the size of a cathedral with walls and alleyways that resemble a city. Rowling is taking pains to give her reader the impression of something incredibly vast. However, size is not the only thing she is trying to convey. She is also trying to highlight the fact that each and every inch of this place is covered with individual objects of shame, guilt, or embarrassment. In other words, the Room of Hidden Things is at once both incredibly vast and minutely detailed.

The Room of Hidden Things has been available to receive objects for many generations. Each object within the room has been placed there one at a time. Every object in the room is a key piece in the story of one particular Hogwarts resident. Harry is there to leave behind his copy of the Half-Blood Prince's potions book. The story surrounding this book is detailed and significant for both Harry and the reader. Every other object, therefore, indicates different stories of equal importance to the specific individual who left it there. Each small object in the Room is a remnant or artifact from some other detailed and crucially important story. Rowling then juxtaposes the individuality and specificity of each object to the overwhelming size of the space and number of these objects. The immensity of the space and the incalculable number of objects permits us a glimpse of just how many flawed individuals have felt the need to come to the Room of Hidden Things before Harry.

The Room of Hidden Things is a place people go in an attempt to either hide something or to get away with something. It is a place to go without anybody watching. It is a place where people put things they don't want anyone else to know about. In short, it is about secrets being kept secret. The books there are "banned or graffitied or stolen." There are "mountains of forbidden items." There is a "heavy, bloodstained axe." The Room of Hidden Things is not about modest privacy or the right to keep things to oneself. It is about the desire for concealment born primarily of embarrassment, lawlessness, guilt, fear, or shame. We can imagine that students enter this room looking over their shoulder and trying to be as invisible as possible. One of the most intriguing and unsettling images from the above passage is the description of a five-legged skeleton inside a cage. The five legs seem to suggest an ill-advised experiment on a living creature that in itself is disturbing. However, Rowling also gives the impression that the caged creature had been left in the room alive and it died there. This idea is even more disturbing. We must remember that Harry is there in part because of his recent use of the spell Sectumsempra, which tortured and nearly killed Draco Malfoy. The Room of

Requirement echoes Ginny Weasley's use of Riddle's diary in *Harry Potter and the Chamber of Secrets*. Diaries are, after all, locked and hidden so as to keep secrets.

However, there is something curious about the Room of Hidden Things. Its performance differs significantly from the more general description of the Room of Requirement. When professor Dumbledore needed a bathroom, the room became filled with chamber pots, and chamber pots alone. When Mr. Filch needed custodial equipment, it became a custodian's closet filled only with the appropriate tools (this is, by the way, perhaps the only time we see Mr. Filch performing actual magic). When Harry needed the room to become a training ground for Dumbledore's Army, it provides what he needs and leaves out everything from all previous uses. Why is it that when the room becomes the Room of Hidden Things that every hidden thing from the past is there? When a student comes to hide something, he or she sees not just the space to hide his or her object, he or she also sees every other object that has ever been hidden in the room. By revealing all the other hidden things to each new hider, the room is doing something that it doesn't do any other time. It is doing something that is not required. If all I want to do is hide something, there is no need to reveal the entire history of hidden things at Hogwarts to me. Revealing this immense cascade of hidden things to the eyes of each new entrant into the room is not something that entrant requires. So why would the Room of Requirement do something that is unrequired?

Perhaps it is doing something that is required. As we've said, people between the ages of eleven and seventeen are constantly trying to hide their mistakes. Let us return to Harry's use of the spell Sectumsempra. Harry gets the spell from his potions book that once belonged to the mysterious Half-Blood Prince. The Prince's notes had been allowing Harry to excel in potions class for the entire year. Harry had come to trust that the Prince's notes would always produce benefits. In a very tight spot, Harry uses the spell without knowing what it would actually do. While this may seem overly reckless, we must remember that people of this age are constantly trying things for the first time without really knowing what the outcomes will be. In order to gain experiences, I simply must be prepared to give new things a decent shot. This process is necessary but also inherently risky. This aspect of adolescence is one that is often conveniently forgotten or disregarded by adults.

The five-legged skeleton in the Room for Hidden Things is an echo of Harry's use of Sectumsempra. In both cases, it seems that the risks weren't considered seriously enough. As Professor Lupin has demonstrated, we must eventually learn how to seriously consider the worst case scenario before it actually occurs. In particular, we must come to realize that hurting others is a risk that is often too great to be taken. Harry considers the possibility that Sectumsempra may be too much only after it is too late.

> "SECTUMSEMPRA!" bellowed Harry from the floor, waving his wand wildly.
>
> Blood spurted from Malfoy's face and chest as though he had been slashed with an invisible sword. He staggered backward and collapsed onto the waterlogged floor with a great splash, his wand falling from his limp right hand.
>
> "No—" gasped Harry.
>
> Slipping and staggering, Harry got to his feet and plunged toward Malfoy, whose face was now shining scarlet, his white hands scrabbling at his blood-soaked chest.
>
> "No—I didn't—"
>
> […] Harry was still watching, horrified by what he had done, barely aware that he too was soaked in blood and water. (HBP 522–3)

Harry gapes at the wounds inflicted on Malfoy in shock. Why hadn't he considered this possibility beforehand? While taking risks is part of gaining experience, considering the worst possible outcome is an essential element to authentic responsibility. So, when the risk is taken and the worst occurs, most of us will feel the desire to hide it.

This is when things are brought to the Room of Hidden Things. When I have underestimated the risks or simply done something stupid, I often

desire to hide the evidence. As we've noted, I do this alone, looking over my shoulder and trying not to be seen. This is an inherently lonely enterprise. People enter the Room of Hidden Things almost always privately and on the sly. The desire for secrecy, no matter how practical, breeds feelings of isolation. Further, I will often keep these secrets within myself even after I have left the condemning evidence safely tucked away. These inner secrets will also have the tendency to separate and isolate me from others. Even if I have safely hidden the evidence and gotten away with my negative act, I may be left wondering if I am the only one who would do such a thing. Such secrets can begin to lead me to think of myself as an irredeemable person even while I assume that most of those around me are not. I will often have no idea that nearly every other student will also have had good reason to hide things.

So, what does the Room of Hidden Things provide? The Room makes it inescapably clear that I am not alone in my desire to hide indiscretions and bad decisions. The Room does not provide easy mercy or undeserved reassurance. It does not hug the students and tell them that everything is fine. It does however, allow the student who may be at his most lonely and isolated moment to see that he is not, in fact, the only one. Unlike the Room of Requirement (which is different for every entrant), the Room of Hidden Things allows each new entrant to see everyone else's hidden things. An act of shameful secrecy can leave a person feeling exiled, separated, or marked. This can be exacerbated by the dark and unfounded suspicion that he or she is alone regarding decisions that require such shameful and furtive secrecy. This can leave a person feeling like he or she is one of the few really condemnable people. This isolating self-condemnation can become a trap.

However, the Room of Requirement, in its function as the Room of Hidden Things, can allow me to see that these objects have been, in fact, "hidden by generations of Hogwarts inhabitants," not just me. The sheer volume of hidden things in this Room offers the developing individual the assurance that furtive secrecy may actually be a common characteristic of most school-aged people. In her description of the Room for Hidden Things as overwhelming in both intricacy and scale, Rowling is offering her young reader a form of mercy. Even as I enter the Room in the utmost secrecy and isolation, I will not likely leave feeling as such for I will have come to realize that uncountable "generations" have come to this same room before me and for very similar reasons. The Room does not offer easy or vicarious forgiveness for trusting the Half-Blood Prince when I should have been thinking for myself or for leaving a live creature to die in a cage, but it does allow me to realize that I may not be the only one under this condition. If I can realize that I'm not the only one, if I can realize that there are many who have been through this before me, then I may be able to believe that there may also be hope for me.

However, this is a very specific type of hope. When I realize that I am not the only one who has done bad things, this does not make what I personally did any better. The five-legged creature is still dead and Draco Malfoy was really stabbed. However, when I come to realize that my own decisions have led me to the need to hide things, I can also come to realize that I will have to be the one who makes the commitment to change my decisions. The need to hide things is not a good feeling. If I don't like that feeling, then I have to avoid decisions that result in the need to hide things in the first place. The Room of Hidden Things is, therefore, something of a confessional. It allows me to see that, while I may have done something I regret, there are many who have gone before me in the same situation. If others have had to come here and then were able to move on with their lives, then maybe I could, too. The Room allows me to see that if I am to begin to avoid this place, I myself will need to be the source of the change. I will have to begin to take more seriously all the potential outcomes of my decisions.

Young people are often content to distinguish themselves from those who intend wrong or evil. They will say, "I am not the kind of person who would do bad things." They content themselves with the idea that so long as they don't intend to do bad things directly, then they will never be

responsible for bad things. If bad things happen through lack of caution, young people will often attempt to avoid responsibility by saying, "but I didn't mean it." The young initiate to responsibility has to learn to move beyond mere avoidance of bad intention. He or she must learn to consider the cost of a lack of caution. He or she must learn to recognize that all outcomes, even the worst outcome, must be considered and accepted as part of his or her responsibility. The average drunk driver does not intend to hurt his passengers or other drivers on the road, but the inability to consider the negative possible outcomes is almost as dangerous as actually intending to hurt someone. Ludo Bagman takes too lightly his responsibility to look out for the Ministry employee, Bertha Jorkins, who works for him in his department.

> "Any news of Bertha Jorkins yet, Ludo?" Mr. Weasley asked as Bagman settled himself down on the grass beside them all.
>
> "Not a dicky bird," said Bagman comfortably. "But she'll turn up. Poor old Bertha … memory like a leaky cauldron and no sense of direction. Lost, you take my word for it. She'll wander back into the office sometime in October, thinking it's still July."
>
> "You don't think it might be time to send someone to look for her?" Mr. Weasley suggested tentatively as Percy handed Bagman his tea.
>
> "Barty Crouch keeps saying that," said Bagman, his round eyes widening innocently, "but we really can't spare anyone at the moment. Oh—talk of the devil! Barty!" (GOF, 89–90)

Ludo Bagman is here disregarding the unlikely but realistic negative explanations for Bertha's absence. As head of his department, Lugo has the responsibility to look out for his department members. However, like a little boy, he disregards this responsibility with a wave of his hand and an over-interest in the fun of the Quidditch World Cup. It is not by mistake that Rowling describes him as "a very overgrown schoolboy" (GOF, 87).

Unfortunately, it often takes a bad outcome to get people to take the risks seriously. Remus Lupin learns to regard his condition as a serious risk to Hogwarts students only after things go far wrong. Harry learns that his reliance on the Half-Blood Prince was too cavalier only after he had become "horrified by what he had done." Conscience is a tricky thing. For most people, it is a voice from within his or her own thinking. While nine-year-old Ralphie from *A Christmas Story* can neither hear nor imagine this voice, the sixteen-year-old Harry finds he cannot escape it after his use of the Sectumsempra spell.

We have said in this chapter that moral maturity requires that an individual must learn to begin to question the voices of authority outside of him or her on the grounds of an inner and independent voice of judgment and discretion. The outer voice must be questioned on the grounds of an inner voice. Making such decisions is not easy and requires significant practice. Mistakes and lapses in judgment are inevitable. However, many of us first come to hear this inner voice only after a very bad decision and its very bad outcome. Many of us come to first recognize our conscience in the bruising of it. Once awakened to its force, most of us take our conscience and thus our responsibilities much more seriously.

Learning to trust and rely on this internal voice over and against the external arbiters of justice requires years of messy practice. Yet even while we understand that we need to practice independent decision making to reach any kind of moral maturity or wisdom, we must also come to recognize that we will hold ourselves responsible for each act of practiced judgment. Even the best of us will feel the desire to hide elements of our own past in the Room of Hidden Things. Even as we come to recognize the legitimacy of our deserved regret for past decisions, we may also find a ray of hope in the fact that we are not alone in our need to fully accept the grandeur of our individual permanent responsibility.

CHAPTER 6

Trusted Guides

As we saw last chapter, free will and responsibility can get messy in the hands of novices. Despite the fact that so many adolescents adopt the posture of arrogant know-it-alls, these same people in reality are commonly all too aware of how much they don't know and of how many things they can potentially screw up. People at this age have often become aware at a very deep level that they are responsible for everything they do even while they are equally aware that they are new to the process and thus bound to make significant and frequent mistakes and misjudgments. These mistakes can commonly be morally costly and so people at this stage of development cannot afford to make any more than absolutely necessary. As a result, these people could really use reliable guidance. Because of the combination of their new responsibility and their practical inexperience, young people are morally bound to pursue the insight of trustable guides and mentors. We saw both Hagrid and Professor Lupin performing this function in the last chapter.

However, the search for trustable advisors presents a logical problem. We have said that moral maturity requires the transition from external to internal rules of behavior. As I grow up, I must endeavor to think ever more for myself and to rely less and less on the word of those outside of me. If the point is to rely on my own internal access to principles of moral behavior, my own conscience, then the search for a trustable advisor seems at first blush to be a kind of backsliding, a return to moral immaturity. If the point is to become self-reliant, then why attempt to rely on another even if he or she is a trustable guide?

However, the search for a trustable mentor or guide would only be a return to heteronomy, outside moral rules, if we did so without reflection or independent responsibility. As the young person searches for a trustable advisor, she must not do so willy-nilly. The selection itself is performed on the grounds of internal or personal principles of evaluation. People like Harry, Ron, and Hermione do not let just anyone give them advice. Harry and Ron's criticism of Professor Lockhart, for example, is a strong example of this. For the young person developing true moral maturity, it is absolutely essential that he or she select influencing voices with the greatest care.

If I am a young person, the fact that I am new at making my own decisions requires that I seek out a reliable coach. However, the fact that I'm trying to learn to make my own decisions requires that I choose such a coach on my own. More importantly, I must select a coach who will merely guide and resist the temptation to indoctrinate. We must understand that moral maturity requires far more than making a decision that results in a beneficial outcome or the "right" conclusion. Moral maturity requires that my decisions originate from within my own independent judgment. The mythologist, Joseph Campbell, has something to say on this.

> A good teacher is there to watch the young person and recognize what the possibilities are—then to give advice, not command [...]. The big problem with any young person's life is to have models to suggest possibilities [...]. We have to give our students guidance in developing their own pictures of themselves [...]. It has to be something out of his or her own unique potentiality for experience, something that never has been and never could have been experienced by anyone else. (PM, 143, 150–1)

It is far more important that a young person learn to make decisions independently than it is to goad the child into making the decisions we want them to make. As the young person who is searching for a trustable mentor, I must look to avoid the guide who would direct rather than inspire. This coach must be a coach not of final actions, but of originating motives. Blind obedience must never be allowed to be confused with moral independence and autonomy based on inner principles.

In other words, I can try to avoid the tendency to backslide into external rules by choosing a mentor who understands the importance of thinking for oneself. As Jean-Jacques Rousseau asserted, we have the individual moral responsibility to submit all creeds and authorities to a "thorough and impartial examination." I must learn to "grant nothing to the right of birth and the authority of fathers and ministers, but . . .examine, in the light of conscience and reason, everything they have taught [me] from childhood" (Rousseau 1983, 284, 272). As a young person I have little choice but to allow outside voices to influence me. However, I must never allow those voices to go unquestioned. None of this is easy. One of the best examples arises in Shakespeare's *Hamlet*. Early in the play, the rational Horatio convinces Prince Hamlet of the nightly appearance of a ghost in Elsinore. According to Horatio, the ghost has the appearance of Prince Hamlet's recently deceased father, the King of Denmark.

HORATIO
Look, my lord, it comes!

Enter Ghost

HAMLET
Angels and ministers of grace defend us!

Be thou a spirit of health or goblin damn'd,
Bring with thee airs from heaven or blasts from hell,
Be thy intents wicked or charitable,
Thou comest in such a questionable shape
That I will speak to thee: I'll call thee Hamlet,
King, father, royal Dane: O, answer me!
Let me not burst in ignorance
—*Hamlet*, Act I, Scene iv

This is Hamlet's first meeting with the ghost. While the ghost does look like his father, we can see that Prince Hamlet is well aware that it may not be. He is aware that it could be either a healthy "spirit" or damned "goblin." In other words, Prince Hamlet knows that he does not know who this ghost is or what its intentions are. Hamlet thus regards the ghost with an appropriate and cautious skepticism.

However, things change quickly. The ghost then tells Prince Hamlet the supposed story of his murder. According to the ghost, the murder plot involves both Prince Hamlet's mother and uncle. The Prince is emotionally overwhelmed by it, and by the end finds himself swearing allegiance to this ghost.

GHOST
I am thy father's spirit [...]. If thou didst ever thy dear father love [...]. Revenge his foul and most unnatural murder [...].

HAMLET
I'll wipe away all trivial fond records [...].
And thy commandment all alone shall live
Within the book and volume of my brain [...].
I have sworn 't.
—*Hamlet*, Act I, Scene iv

Despite the fact that Prince Hamlet is aware that the ghost may not in fact be that of his father, we find him conveniently disregarding this insight by the end of the scene. He has sworn himself to action, to vengeance, despite the uncertainty of the information's source.

Should Prince Hamlet trust the word of his ghostly father? Should he choose to kill his uncle on the word of a ghost who may not be on the up and up? Prince Hamlet's uncertainty on this issue drives most of the rest of the play. Prince Hamlet never achieves the information that would give him certainty. As many have noted, this leaves him partially paralyzed with indecision. He cannot make up his mind. He cannot decide what he should do. By the end of the play, most everyone is dead. *Hamlet* shows us that the uncertainty that can arise from a dubious advisor can be tragic.

So, I must question my advisors, but that very questioning can leave me paralyzed and incapable of action. Rowling raises the issue without calling much attention to it in *Harry Potter and the Chamber of Secrets*. Toward the end of this book, the students begin to think about the upcoming year.

> The time had come to choose their subjects for the third year, a matter that Hermione, at least, took very seriously.
>
> "It could affect our whole future," she told Harry and Ron as they pored over lists of new subjects […].
>
> Neville Longbottom had been sent letters from all the witches and wizards in his family, all giving him different advice on what to choose. Confused and worried, he sat reading the subject lists with his tongue poking out, asking people whether they thought Arithmancy sounded more difficult than the study of Ancient Runes. Dean Thomas, who, like Harry, had grown up with Muggles, ended up closing his eyes and jabbing his wand at the list, then picking the subjects it landed on. Hermione took nobody's advice but signed up for everything. (CS, 251–2)

The students are simultaneously aware of how important these decisions are and how hopeless they are at making them. Neville's family also reminds us how difficult and dangerous it can be to look for the advice of others. How many decisions do we make by simply jabbing our wands at a list of options?

The issue of mentors and advisors boils down to the question of who I can trust. As a young person aware of my own ignorance, I know that I must seek out an advisor. However, I am also aware that I will have a difficult time knowing who to trust for this role. Harry expresses this need and desire well in the early pages of *Harry Potter and Goblet of Fire*.

> Harry kneaded his forehead with his knuckles. What he really wanted (and it felt almost shameful to admit it to himself) was someone like—someone like a parent: an adult wizard whose advice he could ask without feeling stupid, someone who cared about him. (GOF, 22)

Many readers will recognize that Harry soon remembers that he can call upon his godfather, Sirius Black, in this manner. Both Harry and Ron trust Sirius.

> "I told Sirius about my scar," said Harry, shrugging. "I'm waiting for his answer."
>
> "Good thinking!" said Ron, his expression clearing. "I bet Sirius'll know what to do!" (GOF, 150)

Harry trusts and relies on Sirius throughout *Harry Potter and the Goblet of Fire*. Harry's godfather seems to get his name from the star named Sirius. This star is also called the Dog Star (which may explain something of Sirius's Animagus shape). But why would Rowling name Sirius after a star in the first place? The star Sirius is more than twice as bright as the next brightest star in the night sky. As such, this star would have been key to any who would have navigated by the stars. For ancient mariners the Dog Star, Sirius, was an absolutely crucial guide. Just as these sailors would have looked to this star for direction, so Harry looks to his godfather. For readers following the orphan Harry through rough waters, the appearance of an orienting and guiding beacon is delightful. Many readers are swept up like Harry in happy gratitude for a trustable guardian in the form of Sirius. For a boy so often at risk and in doubt, it is wonderful to finally see Harry with a reliable reference by which to chart his course. Sirius becomes a star by which Harry can safely navigate.

However, this stands in marked contrast to the fact that not too long before this point, about halfway through *Harry Potter and the Prisoner of Azkaban*, Harry seemed bent on murdering Sirius Black in revenge.

> "So what are you saying?" said Ron, looking very tense. "You want to—to kill Black or something?" [...] Harry didn't answer. He didn't know what he wanted to do. All he knew was that the idea of doing nothing, while Black was at liberty, was almost more than he could stand. (PA, 214–5)

In this particular situation Harry is working from information he overheard while in Hogsmeade. He is also being egged on by advice from Draco Malfoy who said, "If it was me, I'd hunt him down myself [. . .]. I'd want revenge." Given Harry's flawed understanding of his own situation and that of Sirius Black, it is not hard to understand why Harry would feel the desire to exact revenge on the man who will turn out to be his trusted godfather. And yet we must also note how quickly Harry goes from wanting to murder this man to wanting to live with him. Loyalty can be fickle.

Hermione takes another approach in the following example. Harry, Ron, and Hermione are discussing the formation of Dumbledore's Army in *Harry Potter and the Order of the Phoenix*.

> "Let's get this straight," said Harry angrily, as they put their bags back on the floor,
> "Sirius agrees with us, so you don't think we should do it anymore?"
> Hermione looked tense and rather miserable. Now staring at her own hands, she said, "Do you honestly trust his judgment?"

"Yes, I do!" said Harry at once. "He's always given us great advice" [...]. It was a few moments before Hermione spoke again and it sounded as though she was choosing her words very carefully.

> "You don't think he has become ... sort of ... reckless ... since he's been cooped up in Grimmauld Place? You don't think he's ... kind of ... living through us?"
> "What d'you mean, 'through us'?" Harry retorted.
> "I mean ... well, I think he'd love to be forming secret defense societies right under the nose of someone from the Ministry.... I think he's really frustrated at how little he can do where he is ... so I think he's keen to kind of ... egg us on." (OP, 377–8)

Even though Hermione had originally come up with the idea of a Defense Against the Dark Arts group, she begins to question the plan precisely because she's beginning to doubt the fitness of Sirius as a mentor. Harry, on the other hand, perhaps out of desperation, seems a little too willing to accept the advice of someone like Sirius. Hermione plays the role of sober questioner and critic while Harry plays the ready believer. Harry has a little too much faith in Sirius, and Hermione has a little too much doubt. We saw Prince Hamlet play both of these roles within just a few lines.

So, should Sirius play the role of Harry's guide? A major discussion on this topic occurs early in *Harry Potter and the Order of the Phoenix*. Molly Weasley and Sirius Black are debating as to what would be best for Harry. At this point Harry is fifteen years old. He can be considered neither an adult nor a child. Some of the adults around Harry see him as more of an adult and some see him as more of a child.

> "It's not down to you to decide what's good for Harry!" said Mrs. Weasley sharply [...].
> "He's not a member of the Order of the Phoenix!" said Mrs. Weasley. "He's only fifteen and"

"—And he's dealt with as much as most in the Order," said Sirius, "and more than some—" […].

"He's not a child!" said Sirius impatiently.

"He's not an adult either!" said Mrs. Weasley, the color rising in her cheeks. "He's not *James*, Sirius!" […].

"What's wrong, Harry, is that you are *not* your father, however much you might look like him!" said Mrs. Weasley, her eyes still boring into Sirius. "You are still at school and adults responsible for you should not forget it!"

"Meaning I'm an irresponsible godfather?" demanded Sirius, his voice rising.

"Meaning you have been known to act rashly, Sirius …"

"He's not your son," said Sirius quietly.

"He's as good as," said Mrs. Weasley fiercely. "Who else has he got?"

"He's got me!" […]

"I think Harry ought to be allowed a say in this," Lupin continued, "he's old enough to decide for himself." (OP, 88–90)

Should those adults who are looking after Harry see Harry as more of an adult or as more of a child? Should he be allowed, even inspired to take on more responsibility, more risk, and more adventure? Or should the risks be taken by mature adults for the purpose of providing protection and safety for the young Harry? Which of these is the advice of an appropriate guardian for Harry?

In his discussion of the path of the archetypal hero, Joseph Campbell writes,

This is a fundamental psychological transformation that everyone has to undergo. We are in childhood in a condition of dependency under someone's protection and supervision […]. You are in no way a self-responsible, free-agent, but an obedient dependent expecting and receiving punishments or awards. To evolve out of this position of psychological immaturity to the courage of self-responsibility and assurance requires a death and resurrection that is the basic motif

of the universal hero's journey—leaving one condition and finding the source of life to bring you forth into a richer or mature condition […]. The trials are designed to see to it that the intending hero should be really a hero. Is he really a match for this task? Can he overcome the dangers? Does he have the courage, the knowledge, the capacity, to enable him to serve? (PM, 124, 126)

When does it become okay to inspire a young person to begin to take real and serious risks? When should parents give up their role as protectors and take on the role of adventure inspirers? The very person who just yesterday advised the young person to avoid risk is today advising that person to now take risks. It is initially irresponsible to allow a young child to take serious risks. However, as the parent or guardian of that same but now older child, it becomes irresponsible not to allow and inspire the child to take serious and perhaps dangerous chances. In other words, Sirius is an appropriate godfather for Harry if we believe that Harry is ready for the adventure, ready for the risk. It's also important to note that while both Sirius and Molly want to decide for Harry, Remus Lupin wants to ask Harry his opinion on the matter. As always, Lupin resists the temptations of indoctrination and paternalism in favor of a presumption of Harry's own intellectual independence. Lupin does not want to decide for Harry, he wants to decide with him.

Young people, as we have said, are fated to undergo a transition from the need for protection to the need for courage. Those who once protected these young people will have to in turn inspire them to take risks for the sake of a legitimate cause. It is not surprising to see that Hogwarts School of Witchcraft and Wizardry follows a similar pattern. Every year students are introduced to ever more serious and potentially dangerous magic. However, all of this happens under the watchful eyes of experienced witches and wizards. At Hogwarts, students are given both a certain amount of free rein and a certain amount of protection. It is wonderful to see Harry performing very dangerous maneuvers on his broom during Quidditch matches, and it is also wonderful to trust that Professor Dumbledore will be there to save Harry from the fifty foot fall (PA, 181).

Sports and music programs for young people are always supposed to perform this dual function of providing both risk and safety. As a high-school student, I can play football or field hockey and I can play a clarinet in the school orchestra. We shouldn't fail to miss the use of the word play in both instances. Both student athletics and school music programs allow the individual to practice the art of rising to the occasion while under the gaze of an actual audience. It is quite common for students to begin to treat their sport as the center of meaning in their life. On a music stage or on the sports field, a student can begin to test the limits of their strength, endurance, courage, and skill. In this arena the student can begin to encounter real pain and fear and to do so on purpose. Also, both sports and music events allow the student an incredible amount of time to practice before the crucial moment arrives. Further, real concerts and real matches require that I make real decisions in the heat of the moment and on the spot with everything on the line.

In these moments a student can come to discover that he or she is capable of far more than he or she imagined. We see this with Harry during the first task of the Triwizard Tournament (dragons). Harry could hear

> his Firebolt hurtling toward him around the edge of the woods, soaring into the enclosure, and stopping dead in midair beside him, waiting for him to mount. The crowd was making even more noise…. Bagman was shouting something … but Harry's ears were not working properly anymore … listening wasn't important….
>
> He swung his leg over the broom and kicked off from the ground. And a second later, something miraculous happened …
>
> As he soared upward, as the wind rushed through his hair, as the crowd's faces became mere flesh-colored pinpricks below, and the Horntail shrank to the size of a dog, he realized that he had left not only the ground behind, but also his fear…. He was back where he belonged….

> This was just another Quidditch match, that was all… just another Quidditch match, and that Horntail was just another ugly opposing team […]. "Okay," Harry told himself, "diversionary tactics … let's go …"
>
> He dived. The Horntail's head followed him; he knew what it was going to do and pulled out of the dive just in time; a jet of fire had been released exactly where he would have been had he not swerved away … but Harry didn't care … that was no more than dodging a Bludger.
>
> "Great Scott, he can fly!" yelled Bagman as the crowd shrieked and gasped. (GOF, 354)

Readers of the series will remember that Harry has been dreading this moment ("his heart was pumping fast, and his fingers tingled with fear […]. His legs seem to be made of marshmallow" (GOF, 353). The "miracle" mentioned in the passage above is that Harry found a way to leave his fear behind as he became immersed in the act itself. What we need to notice here is that Harry's previous experience in Quidditch matches had prepared him to face much more than just Quidditch.

The playing of sports and the playing of music before an audience allows a young person to begin to take serious risks while simultaneously remaining within a context of care and protection. Even though it is quite common for young people to treat their music and their sports with the utmost seriousness, in the end both remain forms of play. There can be no doubt that serious injuries can occur on a variety of different sports fields, however, this almost always occurs with caring and protective adults looking on. The guardian adults nearby are simultaneously offering me protection and the opportunity to take ever greater risks. If a young person blows the solo or misses the game-winning shot, he or she can experience profound disappointment but in the end, nobody dies. Sports and music (among many other high-school extracurricular activities) allow me the opportunity to practice making important decisions without really risking too much damage. Quidditch, the Triwizard Tournament, and even Hogwarts itself all provide something of a combination of adult protective oversight combined with the opportunity for individual daring, resolve, and initiative.

The adult guide most closely associated with Harry during the Triwizard Tournament is Barty Crouch Jr. in the guise of Mad-Eye Moody. The relationship between Barty Crouch Jr. and Harry is framed very carefully. Harry's most trusted advisor, Sirius Black, is all but absent as a result of being on the run from the law. Nonetheless, Sirius gives Harry the impression that "Moody was the best Auror the Ministry ever had." In this case, one trusted guide gives a recommendation for another (GOF, p. 333). Harry also gets an impression of Moody from Ron's older brothers Fred and George.

> "Moody!" he said. "How cool is he?"
>
> "Beyond cool," said George, sitting down opposite Fred.
>
> "Supercool," said the twins' best friend, Lee Jordan, sliding into the seat beside George. "We had him this afternoon," he told Harry and Ron.
>
> "What was it like?" said Harry eagerly.
>
> Fred, George, and Lee exchanged looks full of meaning.
>
> "Never had a lesson like it," said Fred.
>
> "He *knows*, man," said Lee.
>
> "Knows what?" said Ron, leaning forward.
>
> "Knows what it's like to be out there doing it," said George impressively.
>
> "Doing what?" said Harry.
>
> "Fighting the Dark Arts," said Fred.
>
> "He's seen it all," said George.
>
> "'Mazing," said Lee. (GOF, 208)

Both the Weasley brothers and Sirius lay the groundwork for Harry's respect of Mad-Eye Moody. At the most basic level Moody represents a tough and skilled wizard who can offer Harry protection. But the Moody that Harry meets goes far beyond a merely protective guardian. The Moody that Harry meets also confronts the bullying of Draco Malfoy quite directly by turning the boy into a ferret (GOF, 204) This act not only gives Harry the impression of a protective force, but also one interested in justice.

This impression increases when Harry meets Moody directly. After Harry reveals the secret about dragons to Cedric Diggory before the first task of the Triwizard Tournament, Harry is confronted directly by Mad-Eye Moody. Moody says "That was a very decent thing you just did, Potter"(GOF, 342). Harry told Cedric about the dragons on the grounds of fairness or justice. "It's just ... fair, isn't it?" he said to Cedric. "We all know now ... we're on an even footing, aren't we?" (GOF, 341). It's one thing to decide to do something on the grounds of fairness, but it is another thing to receive acknowledgment for this from a respected adult. Not only was Professor Moody not going to punish Harry for breaking the Triwizard Tournament rules, but this distinguished and experienced Auror was also commending him for the morality of his act. If young people are supposed to choose their mentors wisely, the person purporting to be Mad-Eye Moody seems to be earning points in Harry's eyes at every turn.

Following his compliment to Harry for his decency, Mad-Eye Moody starts to discuss the dragons of the first task with Harry. In this context, Moody gives Harry what he calls "some good, general advice [...] *play to your strengths*" (GOF, 344). Moody is blatantly guiding Harry toward the conclusion that he, Harry, should use his Firebolt against the dragons of the first task. With a lot of help from Hermione, the advice works very well and further predisposes Harry toward trusting Professor Moody as a reliable advisor. All of this leads to something very important regarding the development of Harry's character. It is Barty Crouch Jr. in the guise of Mad-Eye Moody who originally gives Harry the idea of becoming an Auror himself.

> They walked in silence to the door of Moody's office, where he stopped and looked up at Harry.
>
> "You ever thought of a career as an Auror, Potter?"
>
> "No," said Harry, taken aback.
>
> "You want to consider it," said Moody, nodding and looking at Harry thoughtfully. "Yes, indeed [...]."
>
> And Moody thought he, Harry, ought to be an Auror! Interesting idea.... But somehow, Harry thought [...] He thought he'd like to check how scarred the rest of them were before he chose it as a career. (GOF, 477–8)

We find that Harry does, indeed, choose Auror as his career path. Fifth-year students of Hogwarts have to begin thinking about their career choices and discuss them with their Head of House. During his appointment with Professor McGonagall, Harry says,

> "Well, I thought of, maybe, being an Auror," […].
>
> "You'd need top grades for that," said Professor McGonagall, extracting a small, dark leaflet from under the mass on her desk and opening it. "They ask for a minimum of five NEWTs, and nothing under 'Exceeds Expectations' grade, I see. Then you would be required to undergo a stringent series of character and aptitude tests at the Auror office. It's a difficult career path, Potter, they only take the best. In fact, I don't think anybody has been taken on in the last three years […].
>
> "Potter," she said in ringing tones, "I will assist you to become an Auror if it is the last thing I do! If I have to coach you nightly, I will make sure you achieve the required results!" (OP, 662, 665)

In *Harry Potter and the Order of the Phoenix*, Harry reveals that "Being a Dark-wizard-catcher [an Auror] was the only career he'd ever considered after Hogwarts" (OP, 52). In *Dumbledore's Army Reunites at Quidditch World Cup Final*, an original addition to the Harry Potter series written by Rowling and published on the website Pottermore in July 2014, Rowling reveals that the adult Harry has indeed become an Auror.

The Auror career path is one of the most difficult and challenging. We can see that longtime guardian and advocate, Minerva McGonagall, will assist Harry toward this end. But we must also see that Harry is "taken aback" by the advice from Crouch Jr. There can be little doubt that the Harry Potter of *Harry Potter and the Goblet of Fire* is unsure as to whether or not he is up to the significant challenge of become a registered Auror. However, by the time Harry received this advice, Harry has come to hold the figure posing as Mad-Eye Moody in very high esteem. Harry believes that this Moody is a great man and that this great man thinks that he, Harry, could be an Auror. People we hold in high regard can convince us of things that no one else can. These same people can inspire us to consider possibilities for ourselves that no one else can. While many others play contributing roles, it cannot be denied that Barty Crouch Jr., posing as Mad-Eye Moody, is primarily responsible for originally inspiring Harry Potter to take on one of the most demanding of possible careers.

However, as almost any reader of the Harry Potter series will know, Barty Crouch Jr. is in no way a trustable guardian or guide. In fact, we can assume that everything Barty Crouch Jr. does while in the guise of Mad-Eye Moody is designed to deliver Harry Potter to Tom Riddle. (Isn't it odd, however, that Barty Crouch Jr. brings up the option of Auror with Harry only *after* he, Barty, has acquired the Marauder's Map? This conversation about Aurors does not further Barty's agenda one bit, which forces us to wonder why he does it. Does Barty accidentally fall into the role of a decent and caring advisor for a minute or two, despite himself?) All of this is revealed to Harry in the late chapters of *Harry Potter and the Goblet of Fire*. And yet the influence holds fast. Just as Harry's belief in the presence of his father helped Harry produce a Patronus Charm in *Harry Potter and the Prizoner of Azkaban*, so too does his trust in Mad-Eye Moody as a reliable guide help Harry reach beyond his mediocre career assumptions to austere and laudable possibilities. In both cases, the initial belief somehow survives the later disillusionment. Sometimes advice remains good even if the people who give it to us do not turn out to be who we think they are.

This leads us to a discussion of Harry's disillusionment regarding his own father, James. Harry had spent most of his life imagining his father as kind and courageous. However, with the aid of a Pensieve, Harry was permitted a glimpse of his father through the memories of Severus Snape.

James whirled about; a second flash of light later, Snape was hanging upside down in the air, his robes falling over his head to reveal skinny, pallid legs and a pair of graying underpants.

Many people in the small crowd watching cheered. Sirius, James, and Wormtail roared with laughter [...]. What was making Harry feel so horrified and unhappy was [...] that he knew how it felt to be humiliated in the middle of the circle of onlookers, knew exactly how Snape had felt as his father had taunted him [...] he felt as though the memory of it was eating him from the inside. He had been so sure that his parents had been wonderful people that he had never had the slightest difficulty in disbelieving Snape's aspersions on his father's character [...]. For nearly five years the thought of his father had been a source of comfort, of inspiration. Whenever someone had told him he was like James he had glowed with pride inside. And now . . . He felt cold and miserable at the thought of him. (OP, 647–8, 650, 653–4)

Harry's father turns out not to have been who Harry thought he was. Disillusionment regarding a trusted guide or advisor can be some of the most painful experiences of youth. Such experiences can tempt a person into giving up on the whole idea of a trustable guardian. However, as we've already seen, our own inexperience and lack of maturity requires that we look for reliable role models. If I trust people too much I put myself at risk of getting taken or disillusioned. If I trust too little, I'm left to figure out everything on my own. For Harry, Sirius has gone from being a homicidal lunatic to a trusted godfather even while Mad-Eye Moody turned out to be the homicidal lunatic Barty Crouch Jr. So, Rowling makes sure to remind us that people we think are bad can turn out to be very good even while people we think are good can turn out to be very bad.

All of this can leave a character like Harry Potter in Prince Hamlet's precarious position. If I can't trust the advice of anyone, if I can't have faith in any doctrine at all, I run the risk of suffering the paralysis of Hamlet's indecision and lack of direction. Our potential faith in trusted guides and role models resembles the trust that many have placed in religion. However, many atheists and intellectual skeptics content themselves with assumptions that the religiously faithful have been too easily persuaded by unsubstantiated superstition. Many of the well-educated look down their nose at people of faith who look to their religion for trusted guidance and direction. It is however, too convenient to assume that people of faith are as such because of some ignorant reliance on thoughtless tradition. Yes, all trusted guides and advisors may eventually be revealed as frauds. Yes, religion has often been responsible for perpetrating illegitimate external indoctrination with the worst possible results. But that may not be enough of a reason to disregard the possibility of trust-worthy guidance altogether.

CHAPTER 7
Principles

In the last few chapters we have discussed how important it is to learn how to make decisions for oneself. As we grow and mature we need to move away from the expectation that other people will protect us toward a personal resolution to begin to look out for ourselves. We need to learn to move beyond allowing other people to tell us how to behave and learn how to decipher this for ourselves. In order to do this we need to learn how to let go of the rules of behavior given to us by others in order to make room for the rules that we find within ourselves that will govern our decisions and behavior. We need to begin to relinquish behaving like Percy Weasley who "was a great believer in rigidly following rules" (GOF, 90) and progress toward the likes of Harry and his father who were known for "a certain disregard for rules" (CS, 333).

However, Tom Riddle was also known for disregarding the rules. Yes, we must all learn to move beyond the need to unthinkingly follow someone else's principles, but that alone will not tell us whether or not we are moving in an appropriate direction. If the point is to let go of outer principles in favor of those I find within me, how do I know if I can trust myself to choose appropriate principles? We saw in the last few chapters that young people make mistakes at an alarming rate. We also saw that trust of my own judgment can only come through practice. However, if I'm supposed to rely on myself for direction and evaluation, how do I know when I'm heading in a good or bad direction? Is there supposed to be a compass or sensor within me to direct me toward good and away from bad decisions? How do I read such a compass if it does indeed exist? In short, what is a conscience and how does it work?

Does a conscience run on feelings? We've already seen that Ron and Harry both spontaneously felt bad when confronted by Hagrid regarding their exclusion of Hermione. We have also seen that Remus Lupin came to feel that his potential as an unchecked werewolf on the Hogwarts grounds presented too great a risk to Hogwarts students. In both cases these individuals came to decide to change their behavior based on a negative feeling we sometimes call guilt. Is conscience an inner voice that uses the feelings of responsibility or guilt to prod people into making decisions that they might not otherwise make? If conscience is a voice, then whose voice is it? What is its source? Is the voice of a conscience that would direct my decisions my own voice or the voice of some other? Sometimes people are confronted by a decision that pulls them in two directions. If one direction is that of the conscience, what do we call the voice of the other direction? If it is my conscience that advises me not to steal candy, then what do we call the voice that advises me to go ahead and steal it? More importantly, which of these two voices is my own voice?

These are fundamental questions about what it means to be a human being. Questions of independent conscience, free will, and individual judgment have been at the center of many of the great and ancient books of human wisdom. Great works of literature, philosophy, and religion have focused on these questions for millennia. It should come as no surprise that the Harry Potter series is grounded on these questions as well.

At first the question of human judgment and conscience can look complicated and tricky. If conscience is related to motive, we must ask which motives are good and which are not. After all there are so many different motivating desires.

Take jealousy, for example, such as Ron's reaction to Harry's selection as a Triwizard champion.

> "Oh Harry, isn't it obvious?" Hermione said despairingly. "He's jealous!"
>
> "Jealous?" Harry said incredulously. "Jealous of what? He wants to make a prat of himself in front of the whole school, does he?"
>
> "Look," said Hermione patiently, "it's always you who gets all the attention, you know it is. I know it's not your fault," she added quickly, seeing Harry open his mouth furiously. "I know you don't ask for it … but —well—you know, Ron's got all those brothers to compete against at home, and you're his best friend, and you're really famous—he's always shunted to one side whenever people see you, and he puts up with it, and he never mentions it, but I suppose this is just one time too many … (GOF, 289–90)

Fear can also be an effective motivator. Not only do we find Harry and Ron understandably afraid of confronting the basilisk, that monstrous and deadly serpent from the Chamber of Secrets, but we also find that they are afraid of asking girls to the Yule Ball. Percy Weasley seems to be motivated by ambition and a desire for public respect. Hermione seems to be motivated by some desire for academic achievement. Draco Malfoy seems to be motivated by some form of family and class loyalty. Luna Lovegood seems to be motivated by a sense of compassion or even deep empathy. Molly Weasley seems be motivated by a desperate desire for the safety of her family. Sirius Black seems to be motivated by a courageous or perhaps reckless drive for justice. Severus Snape seems to be motivated by a faithful commitment to a lost love. How can we make general pronouncements about judgment and conscience if each and every character seems to have a different palette of emotions and motivations?

In an effort to answer this we need to look at how judgment works in the first place. At base, judgment uses principles to perform decisions. A definition, for example, can function as a principle to help us decide whether or not the thing before us is one thing or another. For example, the definition of a dog can work as a principle to help us determine whether or not a real pet at the end of a leash is or is not a dog. We can look up the definition of a dog in any dictionary and it will provide us with certain characteristics common to dogs. We can then apply these characteristics to the animal at hand to see if that animal possesses the necessary characteristics. The definition is a template or a role model to help us determine whether examples in real life are or are not a member of a certain category. In other words, definitions are codes for identification. Identification is a form of judgment.

We see an excellent example of how principles can be used to perform judgments with the Sorting Ceremony. Every year during the start of term feast, the Sorting Hat is called upon to determine in which house of the four a particular eleven-year-old student belongs. The Sorting Hat uses the following four principles or house definitions to perform the sorting.

> Said Slytherin, "We'll teach just those whose
> Ancestry is purest."
> Said Ravenclaw, "We'll teach those whose
> Intelligence is surest."
> Said Gryffindor, "We'll teach all those
> With brave deeds to their name."
> Said Hufflepuff, "I'll teach the lot,
> And treat them just the same." (OP, 205)

The Sorting Hat takes the principle or definition of each house and then applies it to each student. The Sorting Hat uses the principle of each house as a template or basic guide for determining where a particular student should go. It is by means of these principles that the sorting can occur. If each house didn't have a different principle or definition, there could be no sorting at all. Each house represents a category, and each student must fit into one of the four categories. It is the Sorting Hat's job and responsibility to apply the principles to each real-life student, and thus determine his or her house. This is how principles work.

Our brains use this technique almost every minute that we are awake. We constantly use general definitions to determine the identity of things in our experience. Even if I have never seen a particular table before, I can identify a particular piece of furniture as a table by means of the general definition of table I keep in my head. Take Harry's identification of Hermione as a girl.

> "Hermione, Neville's right—you are a girl …"
> "Oh well spotted," she said acidly. (GOF, 400)

Identifying objects in the real world according to the definitions we carry in our heads usually works just fine. Most objects are identified fairly quickly and easily. It is not difficult, for example, to identify a fork or a house. As a result, there is usually little controversy over the identification of forks and houses.

Things start to get complicated when the definitions get a little too loose. What is the definition of justice? Some people think it is just to repay a slight with an equal and opposite slight, an eye for an eye. These people often define justice as revenge. Other people define justice as treating all people equally and fairly and therefore often see revenge as unjust. Because we use definitions as principles for judgment, different definitions result in different judgments. Remember, definitions work as principles that allow us to identify objects or occurrences in the real world. They work as templates or models. I use the definition to tell myself what I am seeing. If your definition of justice is different than mine, then our judgments regarding justice will be different as well. Wherever there is uncertainty or disagreement about a definition we can usually find an associated controversy. The abortion controversy is in part grounded on a question as to whether or not a fetus is included within the definition of being a human. The death penalty controversy is in part grounded on a lack of clarity with regard to the definition of the words "cruel and unusual."

Perhaps the biggest problem in this regard surrounds the definition of the word good. The philosopher Plato called attention to this over two thousand years ago. In his dialogue *Euthyphro*, the characters Socrates and Euthyphro are debating the question of holiness or what we might call goodness. Try putting the word good wherever Socrates puts in the word holy.

> **Socrates:** I asked you for that special feature through which all holy things are holy. For you were in agreement, surely that it was by virtue of a single standard that all unholy things are unholy and all holy things holy. Or don't you remember?
> **Euthyphro:** I do.
> **Socrates:** So explain to me what the standard itself is so that when I observe it and use it as a means of comparison, I may affirm that whatever actions are like it—yours or anybody else's—are holy, while those not of that kind are not. (Plato 1986, 12–3)

How should we answer a question like this? What is our definition of good or holy? Is our definition of goodness solid enough to be used as a standard for identification? Is the definition of the word good a private, personal matter? Are the definitions of words like good and just a matter of social consensus and majority agreement? If I use the definition of fork to identify forks in real life, then what definition of justice do I use to identify instances of justice in real life? How do we, as individuals or as communities, come to decide the principles by which judgments of goodness are determined? Where do our ideas about the definition of the word good come from?

As we've said, the looser a definition is, the more likely we are to find a controversy in association with it. The words good, right, just, and holy are all related to each other to some degree. In a similar way the words bad, wrong, unjust, and evil are also related to each other. How many of the world's wars have been waged on the grounds of disputes over one or all of these words? In Plato's dialogue, Socrates endeavors to help Euthyphro see that he, Euthyphro, has never really stopped to consider what his definitions of holiness, goodness, or justice are. How many of us are in the same boat as Euthyphro? How many have been brave enough to enter a war in the name of justice without actually being able to explain what they mean by that word? What makes a good act good and a bad act bad? There are many who might say that the questions of good and bad are personal matters. Even if that is the case, there is still the question of whether or not I can explain to myself what I mean when I use the word. Can I explain what makes a good thing good and a bad thing bad even within my own head? Even if our general culture has seen fit to disregard the question as inevitably relative, I, as an individual, will eventually have to come to a reckoning on this question within my own character.

As humans we use these concepts and these words at such an early age and with such frequency later on that few of us stop to think about them. However, we must recognize that at some level our definitions or concepts associated with justice or goodness drive our decisions to become, for example, members of one political party or the other. In fact, there are few decisions that we make in our lives unrelated to our assumptions about right and wrong, good and bad. Should I get married? Who should I marry? What career should I choose? How should I raise my children? How should I treat my parents? What principles should I live by and stand up for? How should I treat my closest friends? How important is money? It is hard to overestimate the importance and individual relevance of our definition of the word good.

Perhaps the definitions of right and wrong are so simple and obvious that they require no reflection. Some will say "I may not know much, but I know the difference between right and wrong." The suggestion here is that the definition of good is simple, basic. Is it? If good is so easy to understand, then why do we fight about it so much? Why are political parties so often in disagreement about this very definition? Why do people who believe that good is simple so often find themselves shooting at each other from different sides of a war?

What makes the matter even stickier is that we use the word good in significantly different ways. I can simultaneously say that an ice cream sundae is good and that donating to the poor is also good. Do I mean the same thing in both instances? If I tell you that I have a good job, does that mean that the job pays well or that the work I do is very moral? Consider the short discussion between Hermione and Ginny Weasley regarding Harry's use of the Sectumsempra Curse on Draco Malfoy in *Harry Potter and the Half-Blood Prince*.

> "Give it a rest, Hermione!" said Ginny, and Harry was so amazed, so grateful, he looked up. "By the sound of it, Malfoy was trying to use an Unforgivable Curse, you should be glad Harry had something good up his sleeve!"
>
> "Well, of course I'm glad Harry wasn't cursed!" said Hermione, clearly stung. "But you can't call that Sectumsempra spell good, Ginny." (HBP, 530)

The issue comes up again on the occasion when Rufus Scrimgeour replaced Cornelius Fudge as Minister of Magic. Harry asks Dumbledore,

> "Is he... Do you think he's good?" asked Harry.
>
> "An interesting question," said Dumbledore. "He is able, certainly. A more decisive and forceful personality than Cornelius."
>
> "Yes, but I meant —"
>
> "I know what you meant. Rufus is a man of action and, having fought Dark wizards for most of his working life, does not underestimate Lord Voldemort." (HBP, 61)

Dumbledore knows that Harry is asking whether or not Scrimgeour is a decent man, and it is interesting to note that this teacher does not answer the question. "Harry waited, but

Dumbledore did not say anything ... and he did not have the nerve to pursue the subject" (HBP, 61). Rowling is calling attention to the very uncertainty we are addressing here.

In order to clear this up, we need to look at the problem as generally as possible. As we've said, in order to tell if any particular thing or decision is good or bad, we need a definition of good to use as a model for comparison. At base, the problem is that we have two distinct and even antagonistic definitions of good. This is a secret that few understand. This is also one of the most important points in this book. On the one hand we ground our understanding of good on power, and on the other hand we ground our understanding of good on morality or ethics.

CHAPTER 8
Power

Let us begin with a look at power. Power is not inherently good or bad. In her 2008 commencement speech at Harvard, Rowling said that "power [. . .] is morally neutral." As we said earlier, power is what people have and ghosts don't. At a very basic level power is the ability to move things in the real world at will. The more power I have, the more things I can move. More specifically, the more power I have the better chance I have of getting what I want. As we watch an infant grow into a child, we see this individual acquiring new powers on a daily basis. First the child can nurse, then he or she can focus his or her eyes. Eventually the child will usually learn to walk and talk. At every step and with every new power, the child can get more and more of what he or she wants. Many of us celebrate these small milestones with pictures and videos that we share with relatives. Most would agree that acquiring new abilities is a very good thing.

The Harry Potter series follows young people from the ages of eleven though seventeen. One of the joys of reading the novels is watching as Harry, Ron, and Hermione acquire new abilities and powers every year. Take, for example, when Harry says, "I'll hex you. I know some good ones now" at the end of *Harry Potter and the Goblet of Fire* (GOF, 733). Rowling makes sure that her reader gets the chance to smile along with her characters as they develop new skills and talents. It is delightful to be there as a reader when Hagrid explains to Harry for the first time that he, Harry, is a wizard. It is a pleasure to watch Harry ride a broom for the first time. It is so much fun to watch as Hermione turns cleverness, determination, and rigor into real-world power at the end of her wand.

There are many other examples and instances of power within the Harry Potter series. The very fact that most of the story's characters carry a wand is a constant reminder of their power and capability. Sirius can turn into a dog. Professor Dumbledore can capture streetlights in a small device called a Deluminator. Hermione can attend two classes at the same time with the use of the Time-Turner. There can be little doubt that one of the initial and sustaining draws of the series for children is the exciting and enticing presentation of magical power in the hands of young people.

If power allows me a better chance of getting what I want, then getting power is good, isn't it? One of the most satisfying and entertaining elements of the Harry Potter series is Rowling's luxuriously detailed descriptions of the Hogwarts feasts.

> Harry's mouth fell open. The dishes in front of him were now piled with food. He had never seen so many things he liked to eat on one table: roast beef, roast chicken, pork chops and lamb chops, sausages, bacon and steak, boiled potatoes, roast potatoes, fries, Yorkshire pudding, peas, carrots, gravy, ketchup, and, for some strange reason, peppermint humbugs. (SS, 123)

· · · · ·

> "Well, I think that's everything of importance," said Dumbledore. "Let the feast begin!"
>
> The golden plates and goblets before them filled suddenly with food and drink. Harry, suddenly ravenous, helped himself to everything he could reach and began to eat.
>
> It was a delicious feast; the hall echoed with talk, laughter, and the clatter of knives and forks … At long last, when the last morsels of pumpkin tart had melted from the golden platters, Dumbledore gave the word that it was time for them all to go to bed. (PA, 93–4)

. . . . .

… for food had appeared out of nowhere, so that the five long tables were groaning under joints and pies and dishes of vegetables, bread and sauces and flagons of pumpkin juice.

"Excellent," said Ron, with a kind of groan of longing, and he seized the nearest plate of chops and began piling them on to his plate, watched wistfully by Nearly Headless Nick … Ron … was now eating roast potatoes with almost indecent enthusiasm. (OP, 208–9)

Her descriptions of Honeydukes sweet shop in Hogsmeade can boggle the mind.

There were shelves upon shelves of the most succulent-looking sweets imaginable. Creamy chunks of nougat, shimmering pink squares of coconut ice, fat, honey-colored toffees; hundreds of different kinds of chocolate in neat rows; there was a large barrel of Every Flavor Beans, and another of Fizzing Whizbees, the levitating sherbet balls that Ron had mentioned; along yet another wall were "Special Effects" sweets: Droobles Best Blowing Gum (which filled a room with bluebell-colored bubbles that refused to pop for days), the strange, splintery Toothflossing Stringmints, tiny black Pepper Imps ("Breathe fire for your friends!"), Ice Mice ("Hear your teeth chatter and squeak!"), peppermint creams shaped like toads ("hop realistically in the stomach!"), fragile sugar-spun quills, and exploding bonbons. (PA, 197)

Rowling's descriptions of the Hogwarts feasts and Honeydukes are set off against Harry's experience at the Dursleys'. While he had so little at the Dursleys', here was an overflowing cornucopia. Any reader of this series can relate to the idea of being presented with an overwhelming feast or magnificent candy shop after having been hungry. The feeling of hunger and the joy of a feast are two of the most basic and relatable of human experiences. Even though many of us resist it, as Rowling said in her speech at Harvard, "imagining ourselves into the lives" of hungry people is not at all hard for us to do.

I first started reading *Harry Potter and the Sorcerer's Stone* to my sons at night when they were just beginning to go to school. My oldest son asked me many questions about Harry's life with the Dursleys. He wanted to know exactly what it was like to live in a closet under the stairs and he wanted to know why Harry never got enough to eat. He also wanted to know if Harry was a real or imaginary boy. I asked him why he wanted to know this. His six-year-old eyes were wet and his little lower lip was sticking out. He told me that if Harry were a real boy, he would want him to come live with us. It is hard to describe the look of relief that appeared on his face when we finally got to the feast at Hogwarts after the Sorting Ceremony.

Many of us can relate to my son's point of view here. We can imagine what it feels like to be hungry, and we would like to be able to respond to that need. My son wanted to give Harry what he did not have. However, in order to do this, we must first possess the power or ability to do so. If I do not have the power to feed myself, I also do not have the power to feed anyone else. Few would deny that it is good to acquire the ability to feed myself and perhaps even others. The ability to feed myself is a form of power. The ability to feed myself is good. Therefore, the power to feed myself is also good. Power is good. Right?

One of the ongoing themes of the Harry Potter series is the financial situation of the Weasley family. Even though Arthur Weasley works for the Ministry of Magic, his interest in Muggles has diminished his potential in the eyes of Cornelius Fudge, the Minister of Magic. We hear from Molly Weasley that "It's Arthur's fondness for Muggles that has held him back at the Ministry all these years. Fudge thinks he lacks proper wizarding pride" (GOF, 711). This has left Arthur Weasley in one of the presumably less lucrative career paths at the Ministry of Magic. When you combine this with the size of the Weasley family, we can understand why the Weasleys have to be so frugal with Ron's school things.

Ron made a loud noise of disgust behind him.

"What is that supposed to be?"

He was holding up something that looked to Harry like a long, maroon velvet dress. It had a moldy-looking lace frill at the collar and matching lace cuffs […].

"Mum, you've given me Ginny's new dress," said Ron, handing it out to her.

"Of course I haven't," said Mrs. Weasley. "That's for you. Dress robes."

"What?" said Ron, looking horror-struck.

"Dress robes!" repeated Mrs. Weasley. "It says on your school list that you're supposed to have dress robes this year … robes for formal occasions."[…]

"I'll go starkers before I put that on," said Ron stubbornly.

"Don't be so silly," said Mrs. Weasley. "You've got to have dress robes, they're on your list! I got some for Harry too … show him, Harry …"

In some trepidation, Harry opened the last parcel on his camp bed. It wasn't as bad as he had expected, however; his dress robes didn't have any lace on them at all—in fact, they were more or less the same as his school ones, except that they were bottle green instead of black.

"I thought they'd bring out the color of your eyes, dear," said Mrs. Weasley fondly.

"Well, they're okay!" said Ron angrily, looking at Harry's robes. "Why couldn't I have some like that?"

"Because … well, I had to get yours secondhand, and there wasn't a lot of choice!" said Mrs. Weasley, flushing […].

"Why is everything I own rubbish?" said Ron furiously (GOF, 155–7)

Ron speared a roast potato on the end of his fork, glaring at it. Then he said, "I hate being poor."

Harry and Hermione looked at each other. Neither of them really knew what to say.

"It's rubbish," said Ron, still glaring down at his potato. "I don't blame Fred and George for trying to make some extra money." (GOF, 546)

Percy, Fred, George, and Ron Weasley all seem motivated toward financial success. As readers we can imagine all four of them saying the things Ron has just said. Few would envy Ron in his position.

However, Ron is not really poor. Yes, he has to live in hand-me-downs and bring bag lunches on the Hogwarts express, but both of his parents are well educated as are all of his siblings. Despite the fact that his house, the Borough, seems to have "once been a large stone pigpen," it also seems to be a property the Weasleys own (CS, 32). While Ron thinks "it's not much," Harry says "this is the best house I've ever been in" (CS, 41). The Borough is always overflowing with breakfast food and family life. While Ron will always envy Harry his family fortune, Ron's family life makes him wealthy in a way that Harry never has been.

Nonetheless, most of the Weasley boys desire financial power precisely because they have never gotten as much as they wanted. As readers we find out in Rowling's 2014 article by the fictional Rita Skeeter that Ron is "co-manag[ing]the highly successful joke emporium Weasley's Wizard Wheezes" with his brother George (Pottermore.com). Most readers cannot help but be happy for Ron who had to go with less for so long. It's nice to hear that Ron no longer has to mark every knut. It's nice to hear that Ron's children will not have to wear secondhand robes to the Yule Ball. We love to hear about young people who make it through the challenges of school and young adulthood to finally achieve gainful employment, or what Remus Lupin calls "paid work" (PA, 356). We often refer to young people with gainful employment within their career as "doing well" and that they are getting "good money." We often celebrate their first paychecks and we have housewarming parties after the purchase of a new home. We like to get what we want, and we seem to think that having the power to do so is good.

We can see the same idea in charity and fundraising. Money is a form of power. Donating money to a charity, whether it's for starving children in destitute countries or for the local public radio station, is simply a way of giving some of my power to someone else. Programs such as Habitat for Humanity give me the option of donating either my time or my money. However, in either case, they are asking for a donation of power. The desire to feed the hungry is largely a desire for the power to do so. It is a simple and undeniable fact that we cannot respond to the needs of those in conditions of poverty or tyranny without the power to do so. To care about the poor is to care seriously about the money that would alleviate their poverty. It is disingenuous to be concerned about the poor without also being concerned about finances, politics, and economics. Power that would alleviate the suffering of those in need is usually seen by all involved as a profound blessing. Power is good. Right?

So, has this given us the definitional template for the word good? Power gives us what we want and need. Getting what we want and need is good. Not getting what we want or need is bad. Therefore, power is the principle of good. Might is right. It certainly can be used this way. There are many who ground all of their decisions on the pursuit of power. I have had many students, for example, who base their career decisions exclusively on projected income potential. One time I had student who was studying finance and investment. When I asked him if he enjoyed this field, he looked at me as if I were crazy. "What does enjoyment have to do with it?" he said. "I'm going to enjoy being rich, not going to work." He made an interesting point. If we are prepared to be serious and honest, how much of the average adult's day is given over

to concerns about the kind of power we call financial security? So many of us spend a great deal of our time fretting over the finances we will use to protect and care for those we love.

I'm sure that many of you who are reading this have begun to sense a problem, however. If we define good relative to the power to acquire what we want and need, then it becomes very difficult to understand any difference between ourselves and Tom Riddle. Professor Quirrell quotes Riddle saying "there is no good and evil, there is only power, and those too weak to seek it . . ."(SS, 291). The character Tom Riddle, who calls himself Voldemort, seems to truly believe this idea. He simply defines good by means of power. More power is good, less power is bad, weakness. Tom Riddle is not the first to say such a thing. In Plato's *Republic* there is a character named Thrasymachus who says, "I say that justice or right is simply what is in the interest of the stronger party" (Plato 1974, 19). What Thrasymachus seems to be saying is that those in power simply define and ground what is good on what benefits themselves. For them, might literally makes right what it is. In other words, if you have enough power, you can make up your own rules about what is right and wrong. We hear an echo of this in *Harry Potter and the Deathly Hallows* in regards to the Death Eater statue within the great Atrium of the Ministry of Magic and its inscription "MAGIC IS MIGHT" (DH, 241).

This idea is taken to another level by a Niccolò Machiavelli. In the early sixteenth century, Machiavelli wrote *The Prince*, a short instruction manual on how to gain and maintain political power. His main point seems to have been that achieving political power is not easy and requires unflinching focus on the goal. He seems to be saying that if power is your goal, then this motive must remain unmixed with other motives.

A prince should therefore have no other aim or thought, nor take up any other thing for his study, but war and its organization and discipline, for that is the only art necessary for one who commands. (Machiavelli 1992)

He also felt that

> whoever desires to found a state and give it laws, must start with assuming that all men are bad and ever ready to display their vicious nature, whenever they may find occasion for it. (Machiavelli 1995)

In order to understand Machiavelli's point, we must see that he is describing the nature of politics and the nature of people as dispassionately as he can. In other words, Machiavelli is simply describing things as he sees them and as he thinks they actually are. He is claiming to be honest and realistic.

If we take Machiavelli at his word, he believes that all people are motivated by the desire for power and power alone. He is aware that we should probably act differently, but we don't.

> Many have imagined republics and principalities which have never been seen or known to exist in reality; *for how we live is far removed from how we ought to live*, that he who abandons what is done for what ought to be done, will rather bring about his own ruin than his preservation. (Machiavelli 1992, my emphasis)

Machiavelli is saying here that there is no point pretending that people behave according to any other principle than the principle of power. This is true both for rulers and the ruled. Machiavelli believes that no one actually uses ethical principles in reality. Therefore, he or she who would rule must be prepared to do whatever it takes to acquire and maintain power. Ethics and compassion should play no part. In a battle between two princes, the one who is prepared to be more ruthless and behave according to fewer restricting ethical principles will probably vanquish the other. These ideas are extremely well represented in Mafia movies such as *The Godfather* and *Goodfellas*.

In other words, power is fickle. Machiavelli's book is a little like a recipe book. There are rules for becoming powerful, and you should follow these rules if you want to be powerful. If you don't follow the rules, the recipe will not come out right. The rules for becoming powerful are strict and specific. Power only comes to those who follow these rules. The bloody and violent history of the Elder Wand or Deathstick gives stark expression to this idea (TBB, 106). Since power is acquired by means of these rules, failure to continue following the rules will result in a ruler's downfall. The rules of power do not know or care who it is that wields them. Only the ruler who is unwaveringly loyal to these rules will acquire and maintain power. If I desire to rule, I must come to understand that it is not me, but my ability to follow the rules of power that puts me in command. My dominance is only a measure of my ability to follow these rules. The rules are really in charge, not me.

So, what are these rules? Well, since, according to Machiavelli, people are motivated almost exclusively by greed and fear, the ruler must make everyone else fear him or her. Criticizing Peter Pettigrew, Tom Riddle says "You returned to me, not out of loyalty, but out of fear" (GOF, 649). Riddle claims that he is disappointed by this ("I confess myself disappointed …" (GOF, 648)). This can't be true, because Riddle has always known that Peter Pettigrew and all the rest of the Death Eaters were eventually and primarily motivated by their fear of his power and ruthlessness. Riddle, trusting no one, never relied on free will loyalty. According to Machiavelli, fear bred of the ruler's ability and readiness to hurt and punish is the primary tool of power. This mentality is expressed simply and directly by Morfin Gaunt, brutal pure-blood uncle of Tom Riddle, while speaking to a live snake in Parseltongue.

> *Hissy, hissy, little snakey,*
> *Slither on the floor*
> *You be good to Morfin*
> *Or he'll nail you to the door.* (HBP, 204)

Machiavelli describes power at the highest levels, the levels of kings and princes. As such, his descriptions have a tendency to appear overwhelmingly brazen and cold. However, we must not fail to see that strategies of power and pecking order can be observed fully engaged in every middle school, high school, and workplace. Harry, Ron, and Hermione get a bracing introduction to this in *Harry Potter and the Deathly Hollows* when they enter the Ministry of Magic disguised as adult workers and are treated as such. What may be even scarier about all this is that we can begin to engage in these strategies ourselves without being fully conscious of it. Most of us find ourselves commonly concerned about things like our grades, our social status, our looks, our job prospects, our career stability, our relationship stability, and our financial status. We dwell on these ideas so commonly that we often fail to acknowledge that we are doing it. For most of us, part of our brain has no other job but to constantly assess our position within the pecking order surrounding us. As a high-school student walking down a school hallway, I find myself constantly aware of the other students and teachers around me. I can't help but try to constantly assess which of these people are allies and which are threats.

Harry's return to Hogwarts at the beginning of *Harry Potter and the Order of the Phoenix* is a prime example of this. In the time period following the end of the Triwizard Tournament and the murder of Cedric Diggory, Harry finds that his credibility has been thrown into question by the Ministry of Magic and *The Daily Prophet*. Even within Gryffindor Tower, Harry is left to assess whether the individual students around him believe his story about the rise of Voldemort or not. Are the people around him with him or against him? Harry simply cannot afford to ignore this question, but neither can the average middle-school student or newly hired corporate employee. We are constantly in a power context, a web of people with different amounts of power, and we cannot afford to ignore it. This is one of Machiavelli's most important points. Much of what Karl Marx wrote relates to this as well.

Frederick Nietzsche took this line of thinking a step further. This German philosopher from the late 1800s seems to have thought that we were fundamentally and primarily driven by a desire to maximize our power over and against those around us. He seems to have felt that there is a part of every one of us that desires above all else to be in charge, in command, the boss. This same part of us heartily resents being told what to do. He called this part of us the "Will to Power."

Wherever I found a living thing, there found I Will to Power; and even in the will of the servant found I the will to be master. That to the stronger the weaker shall serve. (Nietzsche 2012, 144–145)

This part of us loves to acknowledge and take note of every increase of power we come by. We tend to regard every increase in our allowance, every advance in grade at school, every expansion of our liberty as unquestioned benefits. The lottery only interests us because it represents the possibility of a radical increase in our financial power.

One of the only overt references to Christianity within the Harry Potter series is the mention of Christmas and "Father Christmas" or Santa Claus (GOF, 234). There are many people whose fondest memories of childhood are those surrounding Christmas. Many of us have cherished memories of counting down the days with Advent calendars. And yet, what are children counting down to? While many six- and seven-year-old children can point to the baby Jesus in a holiday manger scene, few of these children are marking the days because of Him. For children of this age, the star of Christmas is Santa Claus. While there may always be a few children standing around the Nativity scene at the local church, the line to see Santa often stretches halfway through the mall. This is because for many of these children, Santa brings what they want.

Remember, power is about having the ability to get what you want. For the vast majority of the year, children of this age rarely get to choose what they want. As we've said, their bedtimes are determined for them, their food is often determined for them, their day is often determined for them, and their toys are almost always determined for them. While parents so often say no, Santa says yes. Children so often love Santa because Santa represents the idea of getting what you want. Christmas is that one day a year when events proceed in the way that kids would have it. From a child's point of view Santa represents the power to bring my wishes into reality. From a child's point of view, Santa symbolizes power. The lottery plays a similar role for some adults. We do seem to love power at a very basic and profound level.

The Harry Potter series is riddled with similar symbols of power. Most of the characters within the series are performing acts of extraordinary power almost as a secondary concern. As Ron, Harry, and Hermione do their homework, they are frequently making something fly across the room or turn into something else. Rowling turns even homework into an expression of imagined power. At every stage along the way, the main characters of the series are acquiring new abilities, learning new spells, and being introduced to new magical creatures. The plot never progresses long without introducing the reader to some interesting new magic. Magic, like money, is power. Young people are drawn to the series in part because it is delightful to imagine having so much power.

Nietzsche does seem to have a point. There does seem to be part of us that is really enamored with power for its own sake. Dudley, for example, certainly seems to love power for its own sake, never missing a chance to lord his position in the Dursley family over Harry. Certainly Draco Malfoy never misses an opportunity to highlight his family's wealth over and against those with less, specifically the Weasleys. The students of Gryffindor certainly seem to enjoy winning the House Cup, the yearly points competition among the four houses of Hogwarts. The desire for the House cup infuses significance into every instance in which house points are awarded or lost. Almost every character in the series seems to enjoy being in a position of advantage and seems to resent being in a position of submission. Most of us can relate to this. But what should we think about this part of us? Is the part of us that wills power good? Take Harry's confrontation of Dudley at the beginning of *Harry Potter and the Order of the Phoenix*.

"So who've you been beating up tonight?" Harry asked, his grin fading. "Another ten-year-old? I know you did Mark Evans two nights ago—"

"He was asking for it," snarled Dudley.

"Oh yeah?"

"He cheeked me."

"Yeah? Did he say you look like a pig that's been taught to walk on its hind legs? Cause that's not cheek, Dud, that's true …"

A muscle was twitching in Dudley's jaw. It gave Harry enormous satisfaction to know how furious he was making Dudley; he felt as though he was siphoning off his own frustration into his cousin, the only outlet he had…

Dudley backed into the alley wall. Harry was pointing the wand directly at Dudley's heart. Harry could feel fourteen years' hatred of Dudley pounding in his veins—what wouldn't he give to strike now, to jinx Dudley so thoroughly he'd have to crawl home like an insect, struck dumb, sprouting feelers—(OP, 13, 15)

We are aware of how cruel Dudley has been to Harry for years. Yet, it is also important to notice that Harry rounds on Dudley with a feeling of "enormous satisfaction." Rowling gives her readers a really emotional presentation of Harry's desire to dominate Dudley. She uses phrases like "fourteen years of hatred pounding in his veins," "siphoning off his own frustrations into his cousin," and "what wouldn't he give to strike now." Most readers will not doubt that Dudley deserves everything he's getting in this scene. However, we must also note how seriously dark Harry's motives are. In scenes like this it is not difficult to detect the small fraction of Tom Riddle's soul that resides within Harry.

Nonetheless, it may be true that a part of us does desire power and even dominance. Nietzsche takes this a step further. Remember, we've been considering the possibility that the acquisition of power is the principle or definition for the judgment of the word good. Nietzsche seems to think that it is.

where there is life, is there also will: not, however, Will to Life, but—so teach I thee—Will to Power! […] Verily, I say unto you: good and evil […] doth not exist! (Nietzsche 2012, 144–145)

Note how similar this is to a statement we mentioned earlier by Professor Quirrell at the conclusion of *Harry Potter and the Sorcerer's Stone*.

A foolish young man I was then, full of ridiculous ideas about good and evil. Lord Voldemort showed me how wrong I was. There is no good and evil, there is only power, and those too week to seek it …" (SS, 291)

This is echoed by something said by Mr. Ollivander, the wand master from Diagon Alley.

Is very curious indeed that you should be destined for this wand when its brother—why, its brother gave you that scar … Curious indeed how these things happen. A wand chooses the wizard, remember … I think we must expect great things from you, Mr. Potter … After all, He-Who-Must-Not-Be-Named did great things—terrible, yes, but great. (SS, 85)

Mr. Ollivander is a master of wand lore, and a wand is an instrument of power. It should not be too surprising then that Mr. Ollivander is fascinated with demonstrations of wand power. And yet, Mr. Ollivander seems far more taken with the magnitude of Tom Riddle's achievements with his wand than with the immensity of suffering and injustice caused by him. This causes both Harry and the reader to have an odd feeling about Mr. Ollivander.

Harry was suddenly reminded of how unsure, when they first met, of how much he liked Ollivander. Even now, having been tortured and imprisoned by Voldemort, the idea of the Dark Wizard in possession of [the Elder] wand seemed to enthrall him as much as it repulsed him. (DH, 497)

This character's respect for wand power is so great that it overwhelms his sensitivity for issues of justice and suffering.

There can be little doubt that Mr. Ollivander regards Tom Riddle with a certain disquieting admiration. It is almost as if the atrocities perpetrated by Tom Riddle are of somehow reduced concern in relation to the scale of his achievements in magical power. Mr. Ollivander's statement "terrible, yes, but great" reveals a certain spooky amorality in his character that connects him to

Professor Quirrell and to Tom Riddle himself. All three of these men seem to think about power in some sense outside of the boundaries of morality, just as Nietzsche seems to have. We can also be sure that Mr. Ollivander's use of the word great, a word deeply connected to the word good we are exploring, has nothing to do with morality and everything to do with power. For Mr. Ollivander, the word great in this context is an expression of power alone. This idea is further emphasized by the fact that Mr. Ollivander tactlessly equates Harry's potential greatness with the brutal greatness of Tom Riddle. All of this is set off against Professor Dumbledore's use of the word in relation to Tom Riddle in *Harry Potter and the Half-Blood Prince*. In reaction to Tom Riddle's claims of greatness, Dumbledore says, "You call it 'greatness,' what you have been doing, do you?" (HBP, 443). It is not by mistake that the very word used by Mr. Ollivander to applaud is used by Professor Dumbledore to deride.

Even though Dumbledore does not seem to agree with those who would ground the definition of good on the acquisition of power, Nietzsche makes a persuasive point. Poker is a game of power and strategy that leaves no room for compassion or empathy. Those who play agree at the beginning to behave under these conditions. Chess is also a game of power and strategy with no room for deference or sympathy. It is important to remember that chess plays a crucial role in the first book in the Harry Potter series. Football, soccer, baseball, field hockey, basketball, and Quidditch are all games of power, skill and strategy that do not allow for benevolent cooperation between the teams. In the heat of the typical game, no team gives points to the other team out of the spirit of politeness and compassion. We seem to enjoy making up games that allow for a fundamental disregard for ethics while within the boundaries of the match.

The idea of power as the ground of good is also reflected in Darwinian principles of evolution. According to the basics of Darwinism, both individual organisms and whole species must be strong if they are to survive. Natural selection, which is based upon the idea that only the strongest will endure, is ruthless. Survival of the fittest is a concept that also implies death for the weak. All the animals and plants in a certain area are in competition for limited food and resources. Those best suited for competition will have a better shot at the food. These will likely survive and have offspring. Usually, the offspring will also be better suited for competition. Those more poorly suited for the competition will commonly die and thus not bear offspring. The weak are weeded out in favor of ever stronger genetic competitors.

Rowling calls attention to genetics in the opening chapters of *Harry Potter and the Prisoner of Azkaban* where Aunt Marge says,

> "You mustn't blame yourself for the way the boy's turned out, Vernon," she said over lunch on the third day. "If there's something rotten on the *inside*, there's nothing anyone can do about it … It's one of the basic rules of breeding," she said. "You see it all the time with dogs. If there's something wrong with the bitch, there'll be something wrong with the pup—" (PA, 25)

Even though very few readers would count Aunt Marge among their favorite characters, it's hard to deny her point about dog breeding. Genetic weaknesses are, in fact, often passed to offspring. Despite the fact that natural selection is brutal and devoid of mercy, it is a process that generally assures the production of robust species that produce individuals with an ever-increasing ability to survive in a hostile environment. Weeding out the weak ensures that only the strong remain. Few would deny that strength is good in a hostile environment.

The idea of power as the principle of good is reflected in capitalism as well. Within the capitalist economic system, a number of companies all compete with each other over rare customer dollars. There are only so many customers out there and they each have a limited amount of money. There is not enough money out there for all of the businesses that are trying to make a go of it. So, just as the animals competed for a limited amount of food and resources, so businesses compete for a limited amount of customer money. Those businesses that are ill-suited to the competition will not attract the customer dollars they need

and thus will go out of business. Only the fittest businesses will survive. This ensures that the customers will be left with only the strongest companies to serve their needs. This is captured in the 1987 film *Wall Street* directed by Oliver Stone. The film's main character, Gordon Gekko, addresses a shareholders meeting and says,

> The new law of evolution in corporate America seems to be survival of the unfittest. Well, in my book, you either do it right or you get eliminated […]. The point is, ladies and gentlemen, that greed, for lack of a better word, is good. Greed is right, greed works. Greed clarifies, cuts through, and captures the essence of the evolutionary spirit. Greed, in all of its forms: greed for life, for money, for love, knowledge, has marked the upward surge of mankind.

It is not difficult to notice here that Gordon Gekko is defining the word good by means of the desire to get what we want, which he calls greed. Adam Smith was a Scottish philosopher who produced a groundbreaking description of capitalism in his 1776 book *Wealth of Nations*. In this book he asserts that "self-interest" is the driving and beneficial force of capitalist economics. Smith's idea is given literary expression in Fyodor Dostoyevsky's 1886 novel *Crime and Punishment*. In this work the character Peter Petrovich says

> in earlier times it was said to me: "love your neighbor" and I acted on it, what was the result? […] The result was that I divided my cloak with my neighbor and we were both left half-naked […]. Science, however, says: love yourself first of all, for everything in the world is based on personal interest. If you love yourself alone, you will conduct your affairs properly and your cloak will remain whole. Economic truth adds that the more private enterprises are established and the more, so to say, whole cloaks there are in a society, the firmer will be its foundations and the more will be undertaken for the common good. That is to say, that by the very act of devoting my gain solely and exclusively to

myself, I am at the same time benefiting the whole community, and ensuring that my neighbor receives something better than half a cloak [...]. The idea is simple, but, unfortunately, has been too long in finding acceptance, obscured as it is by vaporous ideals and misguided enthusiasms. (Dostoyevsky, 2008, 142–3)

Dostoyevsky will eventually come to criticize this idea, but it's not as clear that Rowling does. After all, we see Fred and George tirelessly researching new products, such as Skiving Snack Boxes and Ton-Tongue Toffee to sell in what will eventually be their joke shop. Rowling makes sure we understand that the entire entrepreneurial enterprise was made possible by Harry's initial capital investment from his Triwizard Tournament winnings. Rowling's mention of the success of the joke shop in her 2014 Rita Skeeter publication on Pottermore.com further suggests that she is not as opposed to the profit motive as Dostoyevsky was.

So what is good? If poverty and hunger are bad, does that mean that wealth and food are good? If getting beat up by a bully is bad, does that mean the power to defend oneself and even fight back is good? Machiavelli, Nietzsche, and Tom Riddle all seem to hold the power is all there is. Power and strength are good, weakness and submission are bad. It is good, therefore, to maximize our power and to avoid submitting to anyone else's. Further, since power is good, Adam Smith felt that we should not be ashamed of our self-interested or greedy desire for it. We should applaud a person's efforts to acquire as much power or money as possible. If there is something wrong with this assessment, it is crucially important that we are able to explain what it is. Remember, if we're going to claim that greed is bad, we, like Euthyphro, first have to define what makes bad bad. If we are going to claim that Tom Riddle is wrong in his relentless pursuit of power, we have then to explain why it is okay for other characters to pursue their own power desires. Why is it okay for Dumbledore's Army to practice so as to improve their power in battle and wrong for Tom Riddle to do so? Lastly, we must also remember that one of the most important character traits of Albus Dumbledore is his immense magical power. If power and its acquisition are bad, then why does Dumbledore have so much of it?

CHAPTER 9

Ethics

The answer is that power is neither bad nor good. A dollar, for example, is a form of power. It represents the ability to do something in the real world. A person with a dollar can affect change at will. This individual dollar can be donated to a charity that provides children's books to the underprivileged, or it could be donated to an extremist group bent on violent revenge. I might even use it to purchase some Bertie Bott's Every Flavor Beans. It is not the dollar that is bad or good but its application. It's not the dollar, it's what I spend it on that matters. More importantly, it is the reasons behind the spending of the dollar that make the biggest difference. According to St. Paul, it is "the love of money that is the root of all evil," not the money itself (1 Timothy 6:11).

How can this be? As we saw in the last chapter, the love of money drives the entire capitalistic system and provides many people with what can be considered the highest standard of living the world has ever seen. Fred and George Weasley seem to be driven by the love of money, and it doesn't seem to hurt anyone. In the last chapter, we entertained the possibility that power and the acquisition of power lie at the base of all definitions of good. We saw Tom Riddle echoing Frederick Nietzsche's claim that there is no principle of good other than power and the commitment to seek it. We also saw that power could indeed be the rule by which people decide what is good and what is bad. It is at the very least, a strong contender for the base principle of the definition of good. That was Adam Smith's point, that St. Paul was wrong. According to Adam Smith, the love of money is good, not evil.

However, many have had the deep and intuitive suspicion that there has to be something wrong with this understanding of the nature of good. After all, both Tom Riddle and Albus Dumbledore pursue magical power with deep determination and commitment, and yet there can be no two more different men. What is it that makes Dumbledore's pursuit of power fundamentally different from that of Tom Riddle? Well, at the very least, if we are to criticize the position that power is the sole basis of all good, we will have

to propose that there is some other and different principle that lies at the base and foundation of the concept of good. If the pursuit of power is not in itself good, then what is? We will need to come up with an alternative and perhaps competing definition of good. We will need to answer Plato's question again. Just as each of Hogwarts houses have distinct principles for determining their members, we will need a principle that determines good and bad that is distinct from the principle of power. Tom Riddle claims that power is all there is. If he is wrong, then we will have to show him the alternative possibility. If power is not the only principle or measure of good, then what is?

If there is an alternative principle for the definition of good and bad, then where shall we look for it? Nature and its idea of survival of the fittest suggests that power and cunning are all that matter. From the point of view of nature, strength is good. If it is nature that produces this principle, we will have to look somewhere other than nature for the alternative principle we seek. The outside natural world seems to express and reflect the idea that power is good. From economics and politics to nature and evolution, the physical world seems to have no problem confirming that power is good and that weakness is bad. In the realm of the wild, might so commonly seems to make right. So, if we are to look for some possible alternative to this idea, we will have to look somewhere other than

the natural world. If the alternative principle cannot come from nature, that is, from outside of us, then it will have to come from inside of us. This was Plato's suggestion and he was by no means alone. Perhaps we could find a definition of good and bad that is not a part of nature, but of our own thinking. This brings us back to the idea of a conscience, a voice from within that provides a principle or definition for good and bad. However, this returns us to the question that we raised before. How does a conscience work?

Rowling has confirmed in interviews (and on her website, jkrowling.com) that C. S. Lewis, the early twentieth-century author of *The Chronicles of Narnia*, has been one of her strongest literary influences. The seven books of the Harry Potter series reflect that same number of books in the *Narnia* series, a fact that many see as a sincere sign of respect for Lewis. C. S. Lewis became famous for being able to bring new intellectual light to well-traveled Christian ideas. In one of his most famous and most influential books, *Mere Christianity*, Lewis makes the claim that most people find themselves

> haunted by the idea of a sort of behaviour they ought to practice, what you might call fair play, or decency, or morality [...] we cannot get rid of the idea [...] this Rule of Right and Wrong, or Law of Human Nature [...]. This law was called the Law of [Human] Nature because people thought that everyone knew it by nature and did not need to be taught it [...] they thought that the human idea of decent behaviour was obvious to everyone [...]. There have been differences between ... moralities, but these have never amounted to anything like a total difference. If anyone will take the trouble to compare

the moral teaching of, say, the ancient Egyptians, Babylonians, Hindus, Chinese, Greeks and Romans, what will really strike him will be how very like they are to each other and to our own [...]. It seems, then, we are forced to believe in a real Right and Wrong [...] whether we like it or not, we believe in the Law [...] we feel the Rule or Law pressing on us so. (MC, 18–20, 27, 30)

Lewis is making two important claims here. First of all, he is suggesting that there is a universal rule or principle of right and wrong. Second, he is suggesting not only that this rule is "obvious to everyone," but also that we find ourselves "forced to believe" in it. He seems to have said that "we feel the Rule or Law pressing on us," and that we are "haunted by the idea."

Lewis is making the point that there is a principle of right and wrong that resides within us and presses itself upon us. According to Lewis, we as humans simply cannot help but be aware of this principle that we discover within ourselves. So, if Lewis is right, this, then, could be our alternative principle of good. The outside world, the world of nature, business, and politics, presents us with the idea that good is grounded on power. The inside world, the world of our thinking and feeling, presents us with a different idea of what is good and what is bad. So, how does C. S. Lewis describe this internal law of good and bad? In *Mere Christianity*, he describes it as a certain "fair play and harmony between individuals" (MC, 71). In his *The Screwtape Letters,* Lewis expresses this principle as a certain "disinterested [or unselfish] love." People who are persuaded by this principle believe that "the good of one self is to be the good of another. This [... they] call love" (Lewis, 2001, 94, 119). He articulates this internal principle more specifically when he directly mentions the biblical pronouncement to "love my neighbour as myself" (MC, 83).

With this we can begin to see how conscience might work. Our minds are confronted by two competing definitions of good. One definition we receive through our observation of and physical participation in the natural world, the other we receive through some kind of internal intuition of thought and feeling. These two principles are significantly different. The first claims that self-centeredness is good while the second suggests that self-centeredness is not good. These two principles do not appear to be reconcilable. No easy compromise seems available. Yet each claims to be the one and only definition of good. One thing seems clear. There cannot be two contradictory definitions of good, can there be?

Immanuel Kant, a German philosopher from the late 1700s, takes the idea of an internal principle of good one step further. He starts with the question of what it means to be a human being. While he agrees with the idea that there are many specific characteristics that contribute to the makeup of a human being, he felt our most crucial and defining element was free will or what he called "radical freedom." Kant's idea about free will is directly connected to what we have been calling the principle or definition of good. We recall that definitions work as templates or rules to help us identify things in real life. For example, definitions help us to judge whether the utensil before us is a knife or a fork. Kant felt that the definition or principle of good works in a very similar way. The principle of good helps us to judge whether a decision that we make is a good or bad one.

As we've said, if nature had the only say, then power would be the principle of good and thus the only rule by which decisions are made. If the Machiavellian pursuit of power and advantage were our only incentive to action, our only concern, then everyone would be driven by it and no one would feel bad about it. It seems that we see something like this among animals and in nature in general. There seems to be very little mercy or remorse in the jungle and few of us are surprised by that. Animals seem to be driven by instincts that, in

turn, seem designed to maximize advantage. In other words, most if not all animals are driven by a desire to procreate and survive. Are we like that? If survival were our only concern, then it would seem that ruthlessness would not bother us. If power alone grounded our understanding of good, the pursuit of dominance, the pursuit of power for the sake of survival would cause no one a moment's hesitation or qualm of guilt. We can see something of this in the character of Tom Riddle.

Tom Riddle's primary motive is not a mystery. During his duel with Dumbledore at the Ministry of Magic, which occurs near the end of *Harry Potter and the Order of the Phoenix*, he says "[t]here is nothing worse than death, Dumbledore!" (OP, 814). Near the end of *Harry Potter and the Goblet of Fire*, Riddle is speaking to his followers in the graveyard of his father. He claims to have "gone further than anybody along the path that leads to immortality. You know my goal—to conquer death" (GOF, 653). Professor Dumbledore adds to this saying,

> "There is nothing to be feared from a body, Harry, any more than there is anything to be feared from the darkness. Lord Voldemort, who of course secretly fears both, disagrees. But once again he reveals his own lack of wisdom. It is the unknown we fear when we look upon death and darkness, nothing more." (HBP, 566)

Like a simple animal, Tom Riddle's survival instinct drives his desire for power. Further, we see in this character no hesitation in his boundless pursuit of dominance. We see in Tom Riddle none of what C. S. Lewis would call an internal universal law of morality that "presses" on us. No such law seems to press on Tom Riddle. After Riddle kills Severus Snape for the sake of the Elder Wand, he watches his victim fall to the floor.

> "I regret it," said Voldemort coldly.
> He turned away; there was no sadness in him, no remorse [...]. Voldemort swept from the room without a backward glance. (DH, 656–7)

As cold and emotionless as this murder is, it shouldn't surprise us. If power alone grounds our understanding of good, then the Machiavellian pursuit of power will not be hindered by any other serious concern. Why? Because a person like Tom Riddle seems to carry no other idea or principle of good to compete with it. Remorse has to be based on something, some principle of good. If I don't have that principle, I won't feel remorse. I won't *be able* to feel remorse. Without some other principle, a principle that Lewis claims would "press" on us from within, there can be only an instinctual drive for survival with its accompanying prioritization of power.

We see something similar with the figure of the snake, Nagini. In this case we have an actual animal and yet, Harry gives us access to its thoughts and motivations. In *Harry Potter and the Order of the Phoenix*, Harry gains access to Nagini's attack on Arthur Weasley in the Ministry of Magic through a vision he has of the event. However, his vision of the event happens from the point of view of the snake itself. Harry witnesses the event by becoming the snake.

> Harry put out his tongue … he tasted the man's scent on the air … he was alive but drowsy … sitting in front of a door at the end of the corridor …Harry longed to bite the man … but he must master the impulse … he had more important work to do …
>
> But the man was stirring … a silver Cloak fell from his legs as he jumped to his feet; and Harry saw his vibrant, blurred outline towering above him, saw a wand withdrawn from a belt … he had no choice … he reared high from the floor and struck once, twice, three times, plunging his fangs deeply into the man's flesh, feeling his ribs splinter beneath his jaws, feeling the warm gush of blood …(OP, 462–3)

The scene gives us a very vivid description of how strong animal impulses can be. We are given the impression that Tom Riddle is possessing the snake. We also get the sense that Riddle has given the snake a command that it is obeying. However, once Arthur Weasley is perceived by the snake as a mortal threat, the snake disregards her "important work," the command given her by Voldemort, in favor of defending herself. The snake believes that she "has no choice."

This is a key point if we are to understand Kant's idea about moral principles and "radical" free will. When most people think about freedom, they think about it in terms of discretion and selection. Most of us think about freedom in terms of being able to get or do what we want. Walking into an ice cream parlor, we often feel free to choose the flavor we most desire. In a very similar way we think about people in jail as not being free because they cannot choose to go where they want. This is a perfectly good way to speak about freedom. However this is not how Kant talks about freedom. Kant is talking about freedom at the level of principle. It is one thing to be free to choose what I want. It is quite another thing to be able to choose *why* I want it. This is a very important point. If there are two principles or definitions of good, then I am free to choose between them. If I am free to choose between them, I am not stuck with either one.

Let's say that an animal like Nagini has no internal access to Lewis's idea of universal morality. Such an animal will never treat her neighbor as an equal because the thought can never occur to her. She is driven solely by instinct. Because she has no other rule to choose from, she is stuck with the one rule she has. Without at least two definitions of good to choose from, there can be no choice at all. We see a similar animal mentality in regards to the basilisk in *Harry Potter and the Chamber of Secrets*.

> "Come … come to me…. Let me rip you…. Let me tear you…. Let me kill you […] rip … tear …kill …"
>
> It was the same voice, the same cold, murderous voice … so hungry … for so long … (CS, 120, 137)

Notice the same emphasis on instinctual drive and the "cold" lack of remorse. It seems as if creatures like the basilisk and Nagini are not cold because they disregard an internal sense of decency. They are cold, it seems, because they are completely unaware of the possibility of an internal sense of decency. They don't think of their motives as in any way wrong because they can't. It would seem that they have no sense of good other than that based on power and survival.

However, this does not seem to be the case for humans. While most humans find that they are driven by very strong instinctual desires and priorities, these same humans also find that an internal sense of decency presses on them whether they like it or not. As we have said, this grants them the prerogative to choose between these two principles of good. Let's consider a scene from *Harry Potter and the Prisoner of Azkaban*, in which Peter Pettigrew is unmasked.

> Pettigrew burst into tears. It was horrible to watch, like an oversized, balding baby, cowering on the floor.
>
> "Sirius, Sirius, what could I have done? The Dark Lord … you have no idea… he has weapons you can't imagine … I was scared, Sirius, I was never brave like you and Remus and James. I never meant it to happen … He-Who-Must-Not-Be-Named forced me —"
>
> "DON'T LIE!" bellowed Black [...].
>
> "He—he was taking over everywhere!" gasped Pettigrew. "Wh-what was there to be gained by refusing him?"
>
> "What was there to be gained by fighting the most evil wizard who has ever existed?" said Black, with a terrible fury in his face. "Only innocent lives, Peter!"
>
> "You don't understand!" whined Pettigrew. "He would have killed me, Sirius!"
>
> "THEN YOU SHOULD HAVE DIED!" roared Black. "DIED RATHER THAN BETRAY YOUR FRIENDS, AS WE WOULD HAVE DONE FOR YOU!" (PA, 374–5)

This scene provides us with a very clear articulation of what it means to be free regarding the definition of good. On the one hand we have Peter Pettigrew who is claiming that the instinct for survival functions as a legitimate excuse and explanation for his decisions. The most important element of this is Pettigrew's use of the phrase "He-Who-Must-Not-Be-Named forced me —."

If I believe that I must obey my instincts, then threats to my survival can appear to "force" me to do things.

In contrast to this we have Sirius Black who says, "THEN YOU SHOULD HAVE DIED!" His point is very simple. Instinctual demands, no matter how strong, can be defied and refused. That, at base, is what it means to be free over definitions or principles of good. According to Immanuel Kant, as humans we have no choice but to hear and even suffer the demands of our instincts, but we never have to obey them. Just because my instincts push me to do something, that doesn't mean I have to do it. I can simply decide that internal rules of decency are more important than these instinctual concerns. Because of this ability, this freedom, the threat of death or torture can never force me to act. If I come to recognize my internal sense for universal morality as my top priority, I can simply choose to disregard the threat of death as a primary and motivating concern. As humans with two distinct definitions of good, the choice is simply at our discretion. Any claims of having "no choice" cannot be substantiated. Pettigrew could have simply and obviously chosen not to betray Harry's parents even if his, Peter's, life was on the line. We may also note that Peter Pettigrew undergoes a name change at this point in the story. From here on in, he is primarily referred to as Wormtail.

Another example of this is provided in the form of Dolores Umbridge. In *Harry Potter and the Order of the Phoenix*, Headmistress and High Inquisitor Umbridge considers the use of torture for the sake of extracting information from resistant students.

> "Very well," she said, and she pulled out her wand. "Very well … I am left with no alternative … this is more than a matter of school discipline … this is an issue of Ministry security … yes … yes …"
>
> She seemed to be talking herself into something. She was shifting her weight nervously from foot to foot, staring at Harry, beating her wand against her empty palm and breathing heavily. As he watched her, Harry felt horribly powerless without his own wand as he watched her.

"You are forcing me, Potter … I do not want to," said Umbridge, still moving restlessly on the spot, "but sometimes circumstances justify the use … I am sure the Minister will understand that I had no choice." (OP, 746)

Here again we see Rowling repeating phrases such as "I had no choice" and "you are forcing me." Where Peter Pettigrew says, "I never meant it to happen," Dolores Umbridge says, "I don't want to … but." Of particular interest is the idea that Umbridge "seemed to be talking herself into something." The very thing she is trying to talk herself into is the idea that she has no choice when it is most obvious that she does.

What Pettigrew and Umbridge demonstrate clearly is that there is little point in denying we have a choice when we do. Kant's point about radical freedom is that no one can force us to do anything. We may have to suffer sometimes even dire consequences, but this does not mean that we can be forced to act outside of our independent will. Take Draco Malfoy on the Astronomy Tower at the end of *Harry Potter and the Half-Blood Prince*. Tom Riddle has commanded Draco to kill Albus Dumbledore. Draco says, "Nobody can [help me]. He told me to do it or he'll kill me. I've got no choice" (HBP, 591). Dumbledore makes it quite clear that he, Draco, does not, in fact, have to become a killer. "My dear boy […]. If you were going to kill me, you would have done it when you first disarmed me"(HBP, 591). No one can force us to act. If no one can force us to act, then our decisions are our own. In other words, radical freedom implies radical responsibility. We can see a wonderful expression of this in Harry's confrontation with Tom Riddle in the graveyard at the end of *Harry Potter and the Goblet of Fire*. Riddle has just subjected Harry to the Cruciatus Curse.

He wasn't going to obey Voldemort … he wasn't going to beg …
"I asked you whether you want me to do that again," said Voldemort softly.
"Answer me! *Imperio!*"
And Harry felt, for the third time in his life, the sensation that his mind had been

wiped of all thought … Ah, it was bliss, not to think, it was as though he were floating, dreaming … *just answer no … say no … just answer no…*
I will not, said a stronger voice, in the back of his head, I won't answer …
Just answer no …
I won't do it, I won't say it …
Just answer no …
"I WON'T!" (GOF, 661–2)

Where Umbridge and Pettigrew try to claim that they had "no choice," Harry shows that we do. We should notice in the above passage, both an internal and external voice vying for supremacy, vying for control. Other people in dire circumstances can attempt to coerce my next choice, but they can never make my decision for me. If you threaten me with either the Cruciatus or Imperius Curse, you can intimidate and bully me toward making the choice you want me to make. However, if I do make the decision that you are pressuring me to make, the responsibility for the decision rests solely with me, because I am and must always be sovereign ruler over my own next choice.

Kant claims that the voice from within is nothing that complicated. The internal voice is simply the voice of basic garden-variety reason. Every person has reason even if they don't use it most of the time. Yes, there are some people who are more emotional and some people who are more "rational," but Kant is not talking about reason in this way. He is not setting reason and emotion on opposite sides of a scale. He is saying that even the most emotional people have the power to access reason in their heads. The ability to reason is simply a power that all or almost all people have. Even if I ignore my rational power for my entire life, it is still nonetheless at my disposal.

Reason is so common in our everyday experience that most of us don't even notice it. Mathematics is a form of rational thinking. Take change for example. If you sell me a pretzel that costs $1.50 and I give you $2.00 for it, there will be little debate about what the change will be. Reason tells us that the change will be fifty cents. Some people call this a "no-brainer." What they mean is that the answer is so obvious that no one has to waste any time thinking about it. More importantly, the answer is so obvious that there is no controversy over it. There is no difference in opinion over the answer. When reason functions at this level, everyone agrees.

Kant is not saying anything that is much more complicated than this. Human beings, being rational, simply accept obvious rational pronouncements. Cashiers make change for customers millions of times every day and there is almost never an argument over it. When there does happen to be a controversy over change, it is almost always as a result of a mathematical error and not as result of a difference in opinion about how math works. Our ability to make change without controversy commonly crosses cultural barriers. The rational mathematics of making change doesn't even require that we share the same language. This is because, according to Kant, rational mathematics is not a matter of cultural conditioning or authoritative education. It is a product of our own spontaneous and independent brains.

Let us consider the simple math expression $1 + 1 = 2$. When a first grade student learns that one added to one equals two, she does so in a very specific way. When a student learns $1 + 1 = 2$, the truth of it is a product of her own reasoning ability. When her teacher tells her that George Washington was the first president of the United States, the first grade student has to take the teacher's word for it. This is not the case with simple mathematics. $1 + 1 = 2$ is true regardless of whether or not the teacher confirms it. It is the student's own reasoning ability, the student's own individual brain that confirms the truth of this statement, not the authority of the teacher.

More importantly, reason doesn't take suggestions. If my first-grade teacher were to try to convince me that one jellybean added to a second jellybean adds up to three jellybeans, I would not have the capacity to agree. I can choose to say that $1 + 1 = 3$, but I can't actually believe it. One jellybean added to another jellybean can only ever be two jellybeans. Even I don't have the power to make myself believe anything else. Simple mathematics is not a matter of opinion or discretion. It is the same for everybody, and that is why it works so well when money changes hands.

So how does this apply to an internal call to decency that I find within me? Simple mathematics will help us one more time. Let us consider the simple mathematical expression $1 = 1$. This is perhaps the simplest mathematical expression. The truth of it is so obvious that it all but goes without saying. Similarly the expressions $1 > 1$ and $1 < 1$ are so obviously wrong that this also goes without saying. Reason is so powerful within my thinking that I have no ability but to confirm that $1 = 1$ is true and that both $1 > 1$ and $1 < 1$ are obviously false. When I agree that $1 = 1$, I agree because it's obvious, and I agree because I have no other choice. Reason is not a matter of choice.

It is important to make one thing very clear here. This is a discussion of reason at its most basic level. Even the world's most "emotional" people still agree on rational grounds that one does equal one. Even impractical, intuitive, artistic, and flighty people all usually have the ability to make change. Basic rational ideas like simple mathematics are so obviously valid that they receive near universal agreement. While it is quite common to leave many, many things up to individual opinion, mathematics is not one of those things. If mathematics was an element of personal and private opinion or cultural bias, we would never be able to make change without constant argument.

Why are we talking about mathematics? This is because the very same basic and simple reason that runs mathematics also runs our definition of good, according to Kant. As we've said, the most fundamental and important element of our humanity is our radical free will, our ability to stand up against and say no to even our most vivid instinctual desires and needs. Yes, we have different hair colors, different family backgrounds, different innate talents, different genders, different amounts of money, and yet, at the level of radical free will everyone is the same. Every rational human being is a sovereign ruler over his or her next decision. More importantly, each of these rational human beings is in charge of the reason or principle by which he or she will make his or her next choice. In other words, at our most basic and important level, at the level of free will, we are identical. If what is most important about me is my own ability to make my own choices, then the same thing is true of you.

Then, Kant says something very, very simple and yet deeply profound. There can be no superiority among equals. It is my free will that makes me the human that I am and which grounds my importance as a human being. However, it is that same free will in you that makes you equally human and thus identically important. So, one must equal one. This pronouncement, this rule of right and wrong, is a product of my own subjective reason. It comes out of my own individual brain. 1 = 1. No human of free will can ever matter more or less than any other. Your ability to make your next decision can never matter more or less than my ability to make my next decision. My free will is the foundation of my own significance, and free will is the same in all people. Therefore, my significance can never be inferior or superior to any other. I cannot think of my free will and yours without also thinking of their equality. Kant called this universal principle of human equality the categorical imperative and expressed it as follows.

> Act in such a way that you treat humanity, whether in your own person or the person of another, always at the same time as an end and never simply as a means. (Kant, 1993, 36)

He is saying that no one should ever use anyone else for his or her own purposes, because no one instance of humanity can ever matter more than any other. Notice how Kant's concept of "humanity" in the above passage, a concept that is based on the idea of rational free will, is indistinguishable from one person to the next.

What are we to make of this? First of all, when we look at the world around us we rarely see people behaving in this manner. If this rule is so rationally obvious, then why don't more people take it seriously? If the universal rule of human equality is a product of reason itself, then why do we see so many brutal and corrupt governments, ruthless businesses, and middle-school bullies? If the rational rule of universal human equality is as obvious as 1 + 1 = 2, then why are there so many Dudley Dursleys? Well, this is because free will is free. Even if I admit that one does equal one, and that all humans are equal, I can choose to disregard

it. I, like Harry, can yell, "I WON'T" to my own reason just as easily as I can to my own instincts, fears, and desires.

However, we must also recognize that it is my own individual and private reason that "presses" the idea of human equality on me. The voice of reason is an internal and subjective one. I can debate and even disregard any idea that comes from outside of me. I can disagree with a new governmental law, and I can even refuse to obey that law. I can disagree with a teacher or a pastor. If I disagree seriously enough with an outside governmental idea I can even decide to leave or rebel against that jurisdiction. However, if I don't like an idea that comes from within me and is pressed upon me by my own brain, well, where can I go to escape that? How far do I have to run to be away from myself? While I can choose to disobey the voice of my own reason, it seems I am doomed to forever hear that voice, nonetheless. The voice of reason never seems to listen when I tell it to shut up.

Some might say that I can decide to assert that I don't believe in the idea of universal human equality. I can simply decide that one doesn't equal one. The world is filled with people who use a dizzying array of excuses and legitimizations to support their claim that they are somehow more important than others. Peter Pettigrew simply decides that his life matters more than that of Lily and James Potter. Harry feels he is justified as he approaches to attack Draco Malfoy by means of the Sectumsempra Curse. The question is can I convince myself? Can I persuade myself at the deepest levels that I matter more than those I would subject to my will? If I could really convince myself that I mattered more than other people and then behaved accordingly, then it should follow that contradicting voices within me would remain quiet in the aftermath. What does it mean when, for so many of us, these voices do not remain quiet?

This brings us back to our question about the definition or principle of good. On the one hand we have the idea that power and strength is good. It is good to be able to get what we want and need. It is good to be able to fight off those who would attack us. It is good to work hard to build a career with a good salary. It is good to have the ability to offer powerful help to those in need of it. We witness the strategies of power everywhere in the outside world. On the other hand we have a definition of good that according to C. S. Lewis and Immanuel Kant "presses" on us from within. This internal principle of good asserts that all people matter equally and should be treated as such. Most of us can see legitimacy in both points. We can also see that these two principles may come to counteract each other in a very significant way.

CHAPTER 10

Priority

At the end of last chapter we came to see that there are two competing principles or definitions of good that stand in conflict with each other. The location of this conflict, this battleground so to speak, is within our own free will. More specifically we have to decide which of these definitions of good will ground and motivate our decisions in the real world. Will I be primarily motivated by a desire to maximize my power in a dangerous environment, or will I be primarily motivated by the intention to treat those humans around me as equal in importance to myself? Which of these is good predominately? Both definitions reside within me and both seem to make some sense.

Our first move may be to try to perform some form of compromise. Why can't both definitions of good be right to some degree? Can't the desire for power and the desire for decency coexist? Can't I be trying to make something better of myself even as I endeavor to treat my neighbor better? After all, don't most parents want their children to grow up to be adults who handle both money and people responsibly? Those who desire the compromise between power and decency see these two motives as compatible. People who think along these lines often find that mature adults take care of both their financial and moral concerns in turn. These adults find that they can attribute an appropriate amount of time to both of these concerns within the confines of a normal adult life.

Molly Weasley seems to be a person who thinks along these lines. Mrs. Weasley seems to be a caring and attentive mother and wife. It is clear that she sees it as part of her role as parent to assist and guide her children toward decent and moral behavior. Particularly with regard to her sons Fred and George, Molly Weasley can be strict and demanding. Take, for example, the occasion during which Fred and George leave a Ton-Tongue Toffee for Dudley Dursley at the beginning of *Harry Potter and the Goblet of Fire*.

"It isn't funny!" Mr. Weasley shouted. "That sort of behavior seriously undermines wizard-

Muggle relations! I spend half my life campaigning against the mistreatment of Muggles, and my own sons—[…]. *You stay where you are!"* snarled Mrs. Weasley. (GOF, 53–4)

Ron explains to Harry what's been going on between Fred, George, and their mother during the summer. Ron explains that Fred and George had been making things.

"Joke stuff, you know. Fake wands and trick sweets, loads of stuff […] Only, most of the stuff—well, all of it, really—was a bit dangerous," said Ron, "and, you know, they were planning to sell it at Hogwarts to make some money, and Mum went mad at them. Told them they weren't allowed to make any more of it, and burned all the order forms … she's furious at them […]."

Shouts from the kitchen below echoed up to them. It sounded as though Mr. Weasley had told Mrs. Weasley about the toffees. (GOF, 55–6)

Molly Weasley's concern for the character of her children stands in marked contrast to that of the Dursleys. Where the Dursleys are maddeningly permissive, disregarding every cruel and vicious act perpetrated by their son, Molly Weasley establishes rules and boundaries for her children

designed to help them grow into morally responsible and caring adults. There can be little doubt that Molly Weasley takes this element of her parental responsibility seriously.

On the other hand, we can see that Molly Weasley also has a deep concern for the safety of her family. One of the interesting details of The Borough, the Weasleys' house, is Molly's sitting room clock. Instead of telling the time, this clock reveals where all her family members are and how they are doing. Of particular interest is the fact the clock indicates whether or not her husband and children are in "mortal peril." In other words, Molly Weasley always wants to know if her children are safe. This idea is expanded upon in *Harry Potter and the Order of the Phoenix*, during the scene in which Molly confronts the Boggart in 12 Grimmauld Place.

> Someone was cowering against the dark wall, her wand in her hand, her whole body shaking with sobs. Sprawled on the dusty old carpet in a patch of moonlight, clearly dead, was Ron [...].
>
> "Mrs. Weasley?" Harry croaked.
>
> "R - r - riddikulus!" Mrs. Weasley sobbed, pointing her shaking wand at Ron's body.
>
> Crack.
>
> Ron's body turned into Bill's, spread-eagled on his back, his eyes wide open and empty. Mrs. Weasley sobbed harder than ever.
>
> "R -riddikulus!" she sobbed again.
>
> Crack.
>
> Mr. Weasley's body replaced Bill's, his glasses askew, a trickle of blood running down his face.
>
> "No!" Mrs. Weasley moaned. "No ... riddikulus! Riddikulus! RIDDIKULUS"

> Crack. Dead twins. Crack. Dead Percy. Crack. Dead Harry ...
>
> "I see them d-d-dead all the time!" Mrs. Weasley moaned [...]. "All the t-t-time! I d-d-dream about it [...]. I'm just s-s-so worried," she said. (OP, 175–7)

Nothing seems more normal and natural than Molly's concern for her husband and children. It is also wonderful to see Molly Weasley arguing for Harry's safety over and against Sirius who would risk bringing Harry into the Order of the Phoenix at the age of fifteen. However, we must remember that a desire for safety is, at base, a desire for the power to provide that safety. The desire for safety is an instinct. It is a desire for a sufficiently powerful defense against potential threats.

Nonetheless, Molly Weasley seems to be a decent candidate for that responsible adult who can balance a desire for power with a concern for decency. Further, she seems to be able to effectively transmit this balance to her children. Should Molly Weasley be seen as a role model for emulation? Does this character give us a model for understanding how to understand the interaction between power and morality with regard to the definition of good? If this is the case, then why does Rowling seem to name this character after the term "mollycoddling," a word that Rowling reminds us of while mentioning her (OP, 90).

The answer comes from Albus Dumbledore. We find Harry and Professor Dumbledore discussing responsibility at the end of *Harry Potter and the Order of the Phoenix*. Sirius has just died and Harry believes that he, Harry, is to blame.

> It was his fault Sirius had died; it was all his fault. If he, Harry, had not been stupid enough to fall for Voldemort's trick, if he had not been

so convinced that what he had seen in his dream was real, if he had only opened his mind to the possibility that Voldemort was, as Hermione had said, banking on Harry's *love of playing the hero* … (OP, 820-1)

In response to this Professor Dumbledore insists on taking responsibility saying,

"I cared about you too much," said Dumbledore simply. "I cared more for your happiness than your knowing the truth, more for your peace of mind than my plan, more for your life than the lives that might be lost if the plan failed. In other words, I acted exactly as Voldemort expects we fools who love to act.

"Is there a Defense? I defy anyone who has watched you as I have—and I have watched you more closely than you can have imagined— not to want to save you more pain than you had already suffered. What did I care if numbers of nameless and faceless people and creatures were slaughtered in the vague future, if in the here and now you were alive, and well, and happy? I never dreamed that I would have such a person on my hands." (OP, 838-9)

Albus Dumbledore's concern for Harry that is expressed here is echoed by "the corpulent, red-nosed wizard who hung on the wall behind Dumbledore's desk [...] 'Dumbledore thinks very highly of you, as am sure you know,' he said comfortably. 'Oh yes. Holds you in great esteem'" (OP, 821-2). We can see a concern for Harry that echoes that of Molly Weasley, whose Boggart, a creature that reveals our true fears, presented her with the image of a dead Harry along with the rest of her loved ones. Molly's concern for Harry rivals the concern she holds for the rest of the children in her family. Albus Dumbledore cares for Harry's "happiness [...] peace of mind [... and] life" in much the same way that Molly does.

However, Dumbledore calls this care for Harry "the flaw in my brilliant plan." He says,

I should have recognized the danger signs then. I should have asked myself why I did not feel more disturbed that you had already

asked me the question to which I knew, one day, I must give a terrible answer. I should have recognized that I was too happy to think that I did not have to do it on that particular day... (OP, 838)

Why does Dumbledore think it is a flaw to care for Harry's happiness and safety in the way that Molly Weasley does? It is because our concern for an individual person's physical well-being can blind us to things that matter more. One of the most dangerous things that can happen to us, particularly to those of us who play the part of parents, is that we can confuse a person's physical well-being with the person themselves. It is no good to protect *what* a person is only to lose touch with *who* that person is. This is, after all, the mistake that results in the Dursleys spoiling Dudley. It is a flaw. Molly's overemphasis of regular and abundant family meals helps us understand Ron's inability to cope as well as Harry and Hermione do during the tough times in *Harry Potter and the Deathly Hallows*.

Further, and perhaps more importantly, Albus Dumbledore leaves some cryptic lines in the above passage. Somehow, Dumbledore's concern for Harry Potter might result in "numbers of nameless and faceless people and creatures [being] slaughtered in the vague future" and "lives […] might be lost if the plan failed." Remember, Dumbledore is not talking about putting Harry at risk in the current moment. He is merely talking about what he sees as a dishonorable desire to save Harry pain that might come by telling him the truth of the prophecy concerning Harry and "The Dark Lord." Dumbledore's desire to forestall the anxiety Harry would feel upon hearing the prophesy regrettably convinces Dumbledore to risk even more serious and dire outcomes. The desire for safety and the desire to protect others can be too easily granted the status of a blank check. Even if this can seem like a harmless or even commendable motive, we must always ask what this protection costs. We must always ask what must be sacrificed to pay for this safety and protection.

In other words, it is fine to prioritize both safety and decency so long as they don't get in each other's way, but what happens when you can't have them both? Most of us go through our average day trying to be both safe and decent, both prudent and charitable. Most of us raise our children to regard both safety and respect for others as equally important. This ability to prioritize both safety and decency on an average day can lull us into the unreflective and unchallenged assumption that we can always have them both. But what if this is too much to ask? What does one do when one must choose only one of the options? In this choice between the power for safety and the importance of decency, how does one decide which way to go? As Dumbledore implies, the day will come when we have to know which one is to be the master of the other.

Molly Weasley again provides us with the appropriate example. In what is perhaps her most famous scene, Molly Weasley confronts Bellatrix Lestange during the Battle of Hogwarts at the end of *Harry Potter and the Deathly Hallows.*

> Hermione, Ginny, and Luna, [were] all battling their hardest, but Bellatrix was equal to them […].
>
> "NOT MY DAUGHTER, YOU BITCH!"
>
> Mrs. Weasley threw off her cloak as she ran, freeing her arms. Bellatrix spun on the spot, roaring with laughter at the sight of her new challenger.
>
> "OUT OF MY WAY!" shouted Mrs. Weasley to the three girls, and with a swipe of her wand she began to duel […]. Both women were fighting to kill.
>
> "No!" Mrs. Weasley cried as a few students ran forward, trying to come to her aid. "Get back! Get back! She is mine!" […].
>
> "What will happen to your children when I've killed you?" taunted Bellatrix […]. "When Mummy's gone the same way as Freddie?"
>
> "You—will—never—touch—our—children—again!" […]. Molly's curse soared beneath Bellatrix's outstretched arms and hit her squarely in the chest directly over her heart.
>
> Bellatrix's gloating smile froze, her eyes seemed to bulge … and then she toppled. (DH, 735–7)

The Battle of Hogwarts is one of the culminating plot elements of the entire Harry Potter series. It is a serious and violent battle with much hanging in the balance. With the onset of this battle, the time for merely defensive spells had long since passed. There can be no doubt that many of the combatants are fighting to the death. However, there is something odd about Molly's vanquishing of Bellatrix.

Let us look at the details. At first, Molly Weasley is drawing fire away from her own daughter. She is again prioritizing the physical safety of her child. Rowling's use of uncharacteristically strong language alerts the reader to just how high a priority this was for Molly. However, at some point during the duel, Molly turns from defender and protector to killer. Initially Molly jumps in front of the three girls to protect them, but as the duel progresses she says "Get back! She is mine!" Where she had just pushed students aside to protect them, she now pushes them back in order to keep Bellatrix's death for herself. Something remarkably vengeful has crept into Molly Weasley at this point. It was Bellatrix herself who explained with regard to Unforgivable Curses that "you need to *mean* them […]. You need to really want to cause pain—to enjoy it—righteous anger won't hurt me for long" (OP, 810). Molly Weasley was *not* motivated by righteous anger when she slew Bellatrix Lestrange, "Voldemort's […] last, best lieutenant" (DH, 737).

We must also notice that Molly Weasley performs this act in the presence of her children. As parents, everything we do, every act we perform, is received by our children as the act of a role model. Our children will be tempted to emulate almost everything they see us do. What parents may see as simple decisions are often received and interpreted by children as model behavior. Therefore, it is one thing for Molly to kill Bellatrix Lestrange in vengeance, but it is another thing to do this in front of her daughter, Ginny. Is it good, is it okay for Ginny Weasley to watch her mother kill another person out of bitter hatred and revenge? Does it matter what our motives are on the battlefield?

Sirius Black gives one possible response. As he discusses Alistair Moody with Harry, Sirius says, "I'll say this for Moody, though, he never killed if he could help it. Always brought people in alive where possible. He was tough, but he never descended to the level of the Death Eaters" (GOF, 532). Sirius at least contends that even in the heat of battle, unnecessary killing brings a person down to "the level of the Death Eaters." Did Molly Weasley finally descend to the level of Bellatrix Lestrange? Had she found a way to "mean [it and …] enjoy it" when she cast a lethal and perhaps unforgivable curse?

Harry sheds some more light on this question. In *Harry Potter and the Prisoner of Azkaban*, Harry stops Remus Lupin and Sirius Black from killing the traitor Peter Pettigrew. Harry says,

> "NO!" Harry yelled. He ran forward, placing himself in front Pettigrew, facing the wands. "You can't kill him," he said breathlessly. "You can't." […]
>
> "Harry!" gasped Pettigrew, and he flung his arms around Harry's knees. "You—thank you—it's more than I deserve—thank you—"
>
> "Get off me," Harry spat, throwing Pettigrew's hands off him in disgust. "I'm not doing this for you. I'm doing it because—don't reckon my dad would've wanted them to become killers—just for you." (PA, 375–6)

Harry is making two important points here. He is not denying that Peter Pettigrew deserves the death proposed by both Lupin and Black. Harry knows that Peter Pettigrew is, as Sirius asserts, a "cringing bit of filth" who was willing to sacrifice Harry's entire family for his own "stinking skin." However, it is one thing for a person to deserve death, but it is another thing entirely to personally perform the act of a deserved killing. Peter Pettigrew may deserve death, but Harry does not think that Remus Lupin and Sirius Black deserve to become killers. Further, Harry makes the important point that Peter Pettigrew is not worth what it would cost Remus Lupin and Sirius Black to kill him. Even if the person who is killed deserves it, the cost of becoming a killer is significant. With murders of revenge both the killers and the killed pay a price.

Professor Horace E. F. Slughorn may also be able to add something to this discussion. In *Harry Potter and the Half-Blood Prince*, we are granted witness to one of Professor Slughorn's memories by means of Professor Dumbledore's Pensieve. In this memory we see Professor Slughorn and the student Tom Riddle discussing Horcruxes and murder. Riddle asks,

> *"How do you split your soul?"*
>
> "Well," said Slughorn uncomfortably, "you must understand that the soul is supposed to remain intact and whole. Splitting it is an act of violation, it is against nature."
>
> "But how do you do it?"
>
> "By an act of evil—the supreme act of evil. By committing murder. Killing rips the soul apart." (HBP, 497–8)

We must notice here that Professor Slughorn uses the words "murder" and "killing" interchangeably. He seems to be suggesting that if there is a difference between murder and killing then it is not a very great one in regards to the effect they can have on a person's soul. Professor Slughorn seems to be saying that killing under any condition does significant damage to the soul of the person who kills another. Even if the killing is justified, that killing still does remarkable and perhaps permanent harm to the killer. This magnificently underexpressed idea is nonetheless the main theme of the 1992 Academy Award-winning film *The Unforgiven*, directed by Clint Eastwood and written by David Webb Peoples.

This idea also seemed to be supported by J. K. Rowling during her participation on a British television show called *Who Do You Think You Are?* This is a show that traces the genealogy of famous people who agree to appear. While exploring her family tree on her mother's side, Rowling is presented with records pertaining to her great-grandfather Louis Volant (1877–1949). "Louis' service records revealed that, at thirty-seven, he was deemed too old to fight and was enlisted in the territorials. However, with only fifteen days of training, his group became involved in a fierce WWI battle with the Germans at Courcelles-le-Comte. For his courageous actions that day Corporal Volant was awarded the Croix de Guerre" (*Who Do You Think You Are?* October 2011, 26). Rowling, fluent in French, begins translating the service record for Louis's 16th territorial regiment.

> Rowling: "In the October battle he took command of a section and he held his men under violent fire. With the greatest calm, he … (strong intake of breath and hands to her face) Oh my God! He killed …"
> French Archive Assistant: "he killed …"
> Rowling: "… several German soldiers."
> French Archive Assistant : " … for protecting his position and defending his comrades"
> Rowling: "Oh my God."

Rowling is caught off guard and taken aback with the information she discovers in this moment. None of the battle's other details cause her this level of emotional reaction. It is the fact that her great-grandfather became a killer that has clearly disturbed her. Her breath is taken away and the archival assistant with her feels he has to remind her that he killed to protect his position and his comrades. She will later express that she is deeply proud of his courage and resolve. It does not appear that she was in any way ashamed of his service. She seems to be disturbed about the bare fact that he had taken other human lives. After all, this is not a character in one of her books. This is a person who had a profound psychological effect on the people in her own real family.

We must also look at the final duel between Harry Potter and Tom Riddle. In a close reading of the scene we can see that Harry does not kill Tom Riddle. Harry countered Riddle's "Avada Kedavra!" with "Expelliarmus!", a purely defensive spell. In this moment "Voldemort was […] killed by his own rebounding curse" (DH, 743–4). This fact contradicts an earlier conversation between Professor Dumbledore and Harry from *Harry Potter and the Order of the Phoenix.*

> "So," said Harry, dredging up the words from what felt like a deep well of despair inside him, "so does that mean that . . . that one of us has got to kill the other one … in the end?"
> "Yes," said Dumbledore. (OP, 844)

In this particular instance, Dumbledore's prediction turned out to be inaccurate. Though it is true that Tom Riddle ends up dead at Harry's feet, Harry is only responsible for blocking a spell launched by Riddle himself. Molly Weasley's slaying of Bellatrix Lestrange stands in marked contrast to Harry's standoff with Tom Riddle. It is not by coincidence that Harry's duel with Tom Riddle follows immediately upon Molly's duel with Bellatrix. Harry does not become the killer that Molly does. Harry emphasizes the importance of this in a paragraph that appears shortly after the conversation with Professor Dumbledore just mentioned.

> Harry's heart began to race. He had not told Ron, Hermione, or anyone else what the prophecy had contained […]. He was not ready to see their expression when he told them that he must be either murderer or victim, there was no other way … (OP, 849)

It is very important to see here that Harry has no interest in becoming a killer. We must also notice Rowling's rare and careful use of the word "murderer" in this passage. It is easy to forget the fact that Harry is talking about the potential killing of Tom Riddle. If any character in the entire Harry Potter series deserves to be killed, none could deserve it more than Tom Riddle, the self-styled Voldemort. And yet Harry seems to intuitively understand that killing even this man will cost him at least as much as being killed himself. This echoes Harry's earlier resistance to the killing of Peter Pettigrew by Remus Lupin and Sirius Black in *Harry Potter and the Prisoner of Azkaban.* Harry seems to have a deep understanding that violence even in defense of justice has a very serious cost.

This leads us to the very odd debate between Harry and Tom Riddle just before their final duel. Harry says,

> "before you try to kill me, I'd advise you to think about what you've done…. Think, and try for some remorse, Riddle…."
> "What is this?"
> Of all the things that Harry had said to him, beyond any revelation or taunt, nothing

had shocked Voldemort like this. Harry saw his pupils contact to thin slits, saw the skin around his eyes whiten.

"It's your one last chance," said Harry, "it's all you've got left ... I've seen what you'll be otherwise.... Be a man ... try ... Try for some remorse...." (DH, 741)

Many of us reached this plot culmination white knuckled, reading the dialogue as fast as possible. For those in the grip of the tension of this scene, there was little time to reflect and consider how odd it was that Harry suggested that Riddle "try for some remorse."

Why does Harry say this at just this point? Why, right in the middle of a battle for life and death, does Harry raise the issue of personal morality with Tom Riddle of all people? The answer involves the issue of priorities. As we've said, even though most of us would prefer to spend our days being both safe and decent, one of these will eventually have to rise to the level of our primary concern. Desperate circumstances will force each one of us to have to come to a conclusion on this question. Will I harbor my Jewish neighbors even under the threat of the Third Reich? Will it be safety or decency? One will have to take priority over the other "*for neither can live while the other survives*" (OP, 841). Safety and decency, power and moral principle cannot both simultaneously be a person's top priority. Only one of them can "survive" as a person's primary concern. One of them has to be vanquished by the other. In other words, I cannot decide both to help and not help my Jewish neighbors during the Nazi regime. I must pick one or the other, and the choice will reveal my priority, the choice will make me who I am.

In *Harry Potter and the Deathly Hallows*, Xenophilius Lovegood is presented with just such a dilemma. Harry, Ron, and Hermione go to the house of Mr. Lovegood.

"We need some help," said Harry, before Hermione could start again.

"Ah," said Xenophilius. "Help. Hmm."

His good eye moved again to Harry's scar. He seems simultaneously terrified and mesmerized.

"Yes. The thing is ... helping Harry Potter ... rather dangerous ... "

"Aren't you the one who keeps telling everyone it's their first duty to help Harry?" said Ron. "In that magazine of yours?" (DH, 402)

Lovegood's underground magazine, *The Quibbler*, was a staunch and early supporter of Harry Potter and Albus Dumbledore. There can be little question of Xenophilius Lovegood's initial intention to seriously assist Harry and Albus Dumbledore in their battles with both the Ministry of Magic and Tom Riddle. It is clear that Xenophilius Lovegood takes risks in a courageous effort to stand up for what he thinks is right. However, his willingness to take risks only goes so far.

"They took my Luna," he whispered. "Because of what I've been writing. They took my Luna and I don't know where she is, what they've done to her. But they might give her back to me if I—if I—"

"Hand over Harry?" Hermione finished for him [...].

"They will be here at any moment. I must save Luna. I cannot lose Luna. You must not leave." He spread his arms in front of the staircase, and Harry had a sudden vision of his mother doing the same thing in front of his crib. (DH, 419)

Xenophilius Lovegood has simply decided to prioritize his daughter's safety over that of Harry, Ron, and Hermione. We know that he knows that this is immoral, for his newspaper articles have expressed as much. He is simply deciding that Luna's physical safety is more important than his own moral integrity. It is not hard to empathize with Xenophilius Lovegood in this instance. Even Harry recognizes the similarity in his actions to that of his own mother in the face of Tom Riddle. Both parents stand up to protect the lives of their child. However, Lily

Potter is willing to sacrifice her own life to this end, not someone else's. Xenophilius Lovegood is willing to sacrifice other people's children in order to protect his own. His choice reveals his priority. Does Xenophilius Lovegood "care [. . .] too much," a trait Dumbledore saw as a flaw?

This theme is strongly echoed in a short story by Hermann Hesse writing under the pseudonym Joseph Knecht. The story was published alongside Hesse's final novel, *The Glass Bead Game*. The title of the story is "The Indian Life," and it has a character whose name, Pravati, suggests a connection to the Harry Potter series (Parvati Patil). The main character, Dasa, is in charge of a small territory. One day he gets word that there has been a raid on his borders.

> Dasa immediately made his preparations [...]. The moment before he rode off, he took his small son into his arms and kissed him; and love flared in his heart like a fiery pang [...]. What power, he wondered, was causing him to undertake such efforts? [...] What was the reason that the duty of vengeance was no trivial one [... He was afraid that] ultimately the enemy would stand directly before him and would strike him where he was prone to the bitterest pain: in the person of his son [...] So that was the reason he was riding off so zealously [...]. Out of intense, painful, irrational love for this child, and out of intense, irrational fear of the pain he would feel at the loss of this child [...]. He had realized how entirely ensnared he was [...]. Out of affection grew conflict, out of love war. (GBG, 543–5)

Dasa, in part spurred on by his wife, Pravati, escalates the war that brings about the death of his son. His efforts to provide for the safety of his son result in the boy's violent death. The desire for safety, particularly for that of a loved one, can inspire a willingness to perform violence. My prioritization of the physical safety of my loved one can rise in superiority to the point that any moral resistance I might have against violence can be overwhelmed. My love for the safety of my son or daughter can inspire me to kill yours.

When we are forced to choose between the safety of our dearest loved ones and the importance of our own ethical identity, many of us choose safety. Few of us however recognize that in making this decision, we have relegated our ethical principles to second-class status. When the desire for the power that provides safety rises to the level of my top priority, my ethical principles thereby become sacrificable. When I make power my priority, I will also make my moral principles bow in subservience. In other words, when the safety of my loved one is on the line, many of us become capable of previously inconceivable acts. Nowhere is this easier to see than in the figure of Xenophilius Lovegood.

So we are back once again to the definition of good. Am I a good father if I am willing to sacrifice my morals to protect my children? Am I a good father if I am willing to sacrifice your children to protect mine? Does a good parent prioritize moral principles or physical safety? Should I be willing to participate in nonviolent resistance in the name of civil rights even if it puts my children at risk of violent reprisal, or is it better to forego participation in such rebellion in the name of the safety of my kids (go along to get along)? Is justice more important than safety, or safety more important than justice? The one thing we know is one will have to win. Neither can be my priority while the other one is.

So which should it be? This returns us to the strange advice that Harry gives Tom Riddle during their final duel. "Be a man ... try ... Try for some remorse...." Harry does not gaze upon Tom Riddle with hatred in vengeance. He does not sling the word "bitch" at him like a dagger, the way that Molly Weasley does to Bellatrix Lestrange. Astoundingly, Harry never forgets the most important implication of Kant's categorical imperative, that no one is ever greater than any other one. Despite the immense magnitude of Tom Riddle's determination to cause pain and suffering in the name of his own domination, Harry will not stoop to this level. Harry stares across the gap between himself and his adversary and is still capable of recognizing the absolute and majestic significance of Tom Riddle's human free rational will. Harry is playing Jacob Marley to Riddle's Scrooge, calling him to remorse, calling him to the recognition that ethical principles matter more than power.

The otherworldly Dumbledore from the mystical King's Cross Station calls this "Voldemort's one last hope for himself" (DH, 710). However, how do we know that Harry and Dumbledore are right? Why should every human being be regarded with equal importance? Why should this intention rise in importance over my own desire for power and safety? The answer to this question is one of the main and most important themes of the entire Harry Potter series. In *Harry Potter and the Sorcerer's Stone*, the centaur Firenze reveals, "The blood of a unicorn will keep you alive, even if you are an inch from death, but at a terrible price. You have slain something pure and defenseless to save yourself, and you will have but a half-life, a cursed life [...]. Only one who has nothing to lose, and everything to gain, would commit such a crime" (SS, 258). In the same work, Dumbledore says, "To one as young as you, I'm sure it seems incredible, but to Nicolas and Perenelle, [death] really is like going to bed after a very, *very* long day. After all, to the well-organized mind, death is but the next great adventure" (SS, 297). In both quotes we can see the idea that it is a mistake to worry about death too much.

Sirius Black makes a similar point in *Harry Potter and the Prisoner of Azkaban*.

> Imagine that Voldemort's powerful now. You don't know who his supporters are, you don't know who's working for him and who isn't [...]. You're scared for yourself, and your family, and your friends. Every week, news comes of more deaths, more disappearances, more torturing ... Well, times like that bring out the best in some people and the worst in others. (GOF, 526–7)

It is clear here that Sirius believes that an overly great fear of death can bring out "the worst" in some people. We can see the template for the behavior of Xenophilius Lovegood in this passage.

However, as we've said, it is not merely Tom Riddle who fears death. In *Harry Potter and the Order of the Phoenix,* Ron says "[b]ut there can't be anything worse than the Avada Kedavra Curse, can there ... What's worse than death?" (OP, 100). This is remarkably similar to Tom Riddle's statement at the end of *Harry Potter and the Order of the Phoenix*. "'There is nothing worse than death, Dumbledore!' snarled Voldemort" (OP, 814). Clearly Molly Weasley's Boggart reveals that she agrees. Rowling has said in numerous interviews that her own experience with the death of her mother colored almost every page of the Harry Potter series. Her portrayal of Harry's emotions regarding the death of his parents, the death of Sirius Black, and the death of Albus Dumbledore show a keen and caring sensitivity for the overwhelming magnitude of mourning and grief. It is achingly painful to watch Harry in the moments just after Sirius's death.

> It was unbearable, he would not think about it, he could not stand it ... there was a terrible hollow inside him he did not want to feel or examine, a dark hole where Sirius had been, where Sirius had vanished; he did not want to have to be alone with that great, silent space, he could not stand it. (OP, 821)

It is also terrible to watch Harry hopelessly look for Sirius in the magic mirror or in the company of Nearly Headless Nick.

> He turned the mirror over. There on the reverse side was a scribbled note from Sirius.
>
> > This is a two-way mirror, I've got the other. If you need to speak to me, just say my name into it; you'll appear in my mirror and I'll be able to talk in yours. James and I used to use them when we were in separate detentions.
>
> And Harry's heart began to race. He remembered seeing his dead parents in the Mirror of Erised four years ago. He was going to be able to talk to Sirius again, right now, he knew it [...]
>
> "Sirius Black!"
>
> His breath misted the surface of the glass. He held the mirror even closer, excitement flooding through him, but the eyes blinking back at him through the fog were definitely his own.

Nothing happened [...] Harry remained quite still for a moment, then hurled the mirror back into the trunk where it shattered. He had been convinced, for a whole, shining minute that he was going to see Sirius, talk to him again [...] (OP, 857–8)

We might just as easily have considered the moment in *Harry Potter and the Deathly Hallows* in which Harry gazes upon his parents' gravestones for the first time. Considering his parents, Harry thought,

But they were not living [...]. His parents' moldering remains lay beneath snow and stone, indifferent, unknowing. And tears came before he could stop them [... Harry looked down at] the place where the last of Lily and James lay, bones now, surely, or dust not knowing or caring that their living son stood so near, his heart still beating, alive because of their sacrifice and close to wishing, at this moment, that he was sleeping under the snow with them. (DH, 328–9)

One thing that the incredible scale of the Harry Potter series affords Rowling is the space to do justice to the nature of anguish and mourning. Rowling does not offer her readers a watered-down image of death or grief. She presents it honestly echoing the words of "impostor Moody" who said, "[y]ou've got to appreciate what the worst is [...y]ou've got to know. It seems harsh, maybe, but you've got to know. No point pretending ..." (GOF, 217, 219). This is particularly true regarding the scene in *Harry Potter and the Deathly Hallows* in which the orphan Harry "beseeches" the dead Remus Lupin concerning Lupin's newly orphaned son.

No one can accuse Rowling of trying to diminish the immense impact that death and grief can have. As we have said, much of the Harry Potter series is dedicated to giving full-fledged expression of this impact. Only a fool would not be afraid of the death of his or her loved ones. Yet even in acknowledging the sheer weight and menace of death, we are nonetheless presented with a Dumbledore who contradicts Riddle's claim that there is nothing worse than death.

"You are quite wrong," said Dumbledore, still closing in upon Voldemort and speaking as lightly as though they were discussing the matter over drinks [...].

"Indeed, your failure to understand that there are things much worse than death has always been your greatest weakness." (OP, 814)

Dumbledore reiterates this idea at the end of *Harry Potter and the Deathly Hollows*. "The true master [of death] does not seek to run away from Death. He accepts that he must die, and understands that there are far, far worse things in the living world than dying" (DH, 720–1). Those who seek power so as to avoid death are on a fool's errand. Yes, death can result in "families [...] torn apart" and this can produce "maimed [...] souls," and so one should not be reckless, as Sirius sometimes was, in the face of death. Each precious human life must be treated with the utmost seriousness, "care and caution" (DH, 717, 722).

Nonetheless, since death is inevitable, the pursuit of survival alone can never provide meaning to a human life in the long run. This is what the master of death understands. The decision to prioritize safety as one's highest concern is the decision to dedicate one's whole life to a pointless pursuit. Such a pursuit is an ignorant squandering of potential and embarrassingly futile. In *Tales of Beedle the Bard*, Dumbledore writes, "Human efforts to evade or overcome death are always doomed to disappointment" (TBB, 94). To chase survival is to guarantee myself eventual failure as a forgone conclusion. Dumbledore calls death the "enemy who cannot lose" (TBB, 95). To identify myself with this hopeless pursuit, to ground and dedicate myself to it is to reduce myself to an obvious and pathetic joke. Only fear keeps us from seeing this more quickly and easily. As a friend once said to me, "last time I checked, all Christians die ... so, if you became a Christian so as to avoid death, you might want to rethink your plan."

This leads us back to the definition of good and the idea of remorse. If we, like the master of death, accept that we must inevitably die, then it will be impossible for us to make survival and its requisite power our highest priority. Nonetheless, this is precisely what Tom Riddle has done, and it is this that turns him into Voldemort. Dumbledore says,

> Tom Riddle was doing all he could to find out how to make himself immortal [...] so determined [was he] to evade death [...]. (HBP, 499–500)

Riddle himself says,

> I, who have gone further than anybody along the path that leads to immortality. You know my goal—to conquer death [...]. I took [steps], long ago to guard myself against mortal death. (GOF, 648, 653)

Tom Riddle is that simple fool who decided to prioritize power for the sake of safety and physical survival. Kant's categorical imperative, the internal awareness that all humans are equal in importance and significance, has simply never occurred to Tom Riddle. For Tom Riddle "there is only power and those too weak to seek it" (SS, 291).

For Tom Riddle there is one and only one possible definition and ground of good. More power is good, less power is bad, less power is weakness, and there is no other possible consideration. Tom Riddle does not experience a conflict between power and moral principle because, for him, subjective rational principles of morality that "press" on us from within, simply do not exist. Tom Riddle has detached himself from parts of what Dumbledore calls his "soul." Dumbledore believes that "these crucial parts of himself have been detached for so long, he does not feel as we do" (HBP, 507).

These ideas have never "pressed" on him, so he believes them a ruse. He believes that what others call ethics are nothing more than a weak person's pitiful strategy to eke out a modicum of power. He believes moral principles to be a fraud or a con job, and he fancies himself too sharp and clever to be taken in by such superstition. This is what Dumbledore is trying to express when he says,

his knowledge remained woefully incomplete, Harry! That which Voldemort does not value, he takes no trouble to comprehend. Of house-elves and children's tales, of love, loyalty, and innocence, Voldemort knows and understands nothing. *Nothing*. That they all have a power beyond his own, a power beyond the reach of any magic, is a truth he has never grasped. (DH, 709–10)

Rowling discusses this directly in an interview. Rowling founded a charity called Lumos that responds to the needs of institutionalized children. She says that one

> of the many disturbing things I found out from being involved closely with that charity is how much measurable brain damage is done when a child is taken from its mother and placed in an institution. And when I say measurable you can scan the brain and you will see that pathways haven't been made and you can never get that back—So in fact what I wrote about Harry being incredibly loved in his earliest days is measurably true, that it will literally give him protection that no one can undo. His brain will have developed in a way that Voldemort's brain didn't because Voldemort was from the moment of his birth institutionalized. ("The Women of Harry Potter." 2011)

This idea is strongly echoed in a conversation we discussed earlier between Professor Dumbledore and Harry held while they are considering the death of Merope Riddle, Tom Riddle's destitute mother.

> "She wouldn't even stay alive for her son?"
> Dumbledore raised his eyebrows. "Could you possibly be feeling sorry for Lord Voldemort?"
> "No," said Harry quickly, "but she had a choice [...]."
> "Yes, Merope Riddle chose death in spite of a son who needed her [...]. (HBP, 262)

The description of Tom Riddle's childhood orphanage, what with its obvious negligence and its alcoholic supervisor, lead us to believe that it was a place completely lacking in compassion, appropriate oversight, or sufficient care. From his earliest days Tom Riddle would have to have learned to fend for himself. In his reality, all favors come at a price. Riddle expresses as much to Professor Dumbledore in *Harry Potter and the Half-Blood Prince* where he says, "nothing I have seen in the world has supported your famous pronouncements that love is more powerful than my kind of magic, Dumbledore" (HBP, 444). Tom Riddle had never been "incredibly loved" as Harry had been. Tom's early experience presented a world that was violently competitive, relentlessly cruel, indifferent, Machiavellian, and merciless. From such a vantage point the ideas of ethical principles or of the voluntary care for others must have seemed like ridiculous jokes. It is not hard to see why the very young Riddle, undoubtedly the victim of constant bullying, would've learned to prioritize power at any cost and dismiss the possibility of compassion forever.

Tom Riddle does not consciously feel an internal rational draw of respect for universal human equality. He is not troubled by a conscience that would call him to decency. He knows only the evidence of the material world with its preference for power, the law of the jungle. This echoes a point made by C. S. Lewis in *Mere Christianity*. Lewis writes, "Anyone studying Man from the outside as we study electricity or cabbages [...] merely observing what we did, would never get the slightest evidence that we had this moral law" (MC, 33). Tom Riddle does not feel, therefore, a tension between an internal subjective call for mutual human respect and an external demand for sustaining material power. If I have an angel on one shoulder and a devil on the other, a conflict is sure to arise. However, if the devil is alone with no angel to contradict it, there will be no conflict. Uncontested, the devil's suggestions will rule. What will result is Machiavellian cruelty in a drive to dominance unhindered by even wisps of remorse. As we have said, without access to internal ethical principles, there is nothing to base remorse on.

For such a person there is no real problem figuring out what the word good means. Power is the only contender, so good is based on and defined by the acquisition of power. Further, people like Tom Riddle can't imagine any other way to be. Therefore, people like Tom Riddle believe that those who do not pursue power do so for lack of courage, skill, or effort. For people like Tom Riddle the acquisition of power is merely a product of determination and daring. That is why Riddle says of Dumbledore "he was weak! [...] Too weak to dare, too weak to take what might have been his, what will be mine!" (DH, 739). A person like Tom Riddle is simply incapable of imagining any other reason why Albus Dumbledore would not have pursued a path to power like his own.

This does not seem to have been the case, however, for Gillert Grindelwald. Grindelwald was the Dark wizard who had been bent on wizard domination of Muggles and was also the temporary possessor of the fabled Deathly Hallow, the Elder Wand. Imprisoned in Nurmengard for his overwhelming crimes, Grindelwald was eventually confronted by Tom Riddle there.

> *Kill me, then. Voldemort, I welcome death! But my death will not bring you what you seek.... There is so much you do not understand[...] . Kill me, then! ... You will not win, you cannot win!* (DH, 469, 472)

Perhaps Grindelwald recognizes his younger self in Tom Riddle. Perhaps the elderly Grindelwald, having been afforded long years for personal reflection, recognizes his own ignorant and futile pursuit of power in Voldemort. In welcoming death and in his certainty that Riddle "cannot win," it is clear that Grindelwald has left the world view that prizes power and survival over everything else, the world view currently occupied by his attacker.

Harry and Dumbledore discuss Grindelwald in the mystical version of King's Cross Station. Harry says,

> "Grindelwald tried to stop Voldemort going after the wand. He lied, you know, pretended he had never had it."

Dumbledore nodded, looking down at his lap, tears still glittering on the crooked nose.

"They say he showed remorse in later years, alone in his cell at Nurmengard. I hope that it is true. I would like to think he did feel the horror and shame of what he had done. Perhaps that lie to Voldemort was his attempt to make amends … " (DH, 719)

It is very important to pay special attention to Dumbledore's hope for Gindelwald, his boyhood companion. For Dumbledore, showing remorse is a matter of really feeling the "horror and shame" of immoral acts. Why would Dumbledore hope such a thing for a person he once cared for perhaps as much Hermione does Ron and as James did Lily? What could be worse than coming to recognize the "horror and shame" of one's own decisions and actions? And why would someone like Dumbledore "like to think" that Grindelwald had actually gone through such suffering? Why would that be good?

It is not as if Dumbledore doesn't know what the experience is like. We who have followed Harry's story encounter the character of Dumbledore as an old wise man and careful steward of Hogwarts School of Witchcraft and Wizardry. However, we must also acknowledge, that the young Albus Dumbledore was responsible for inspiring and assisting one of the Darkest wizards in history to a position of cruel and dominating power.

I wanted to shine. I wanted glory […]. And then, of course, he came … Grindelwald. You cannot imagine how his ideas caught me, Harry, inflamed me. Muggles forced into subservience. We wizards triumphant. Grindelwald and I, the glorious young leaders of the revolution […] I assuaged my conscience with empty words […] I had proven as a very young man, that power was my weakness and my temptation. (DH, 715–16, 18)

Dumbledore's youthful relationship with Grindelwald was hindered by his, Dumbledore's, responsibility to his troubled sister.

I did not want to hear that I could not set forth […] with a fragile and unstable sister in tow […]. The argument became a fight. Grindelwald lost control. That which I had always sensed in him, though I pretended not to, now sprang into terrible being. And Ariana … after all my mother's care and caution … lay dead upon the floor […]. I was left to bury my sister, and learn to live with my guilt and my terrible grief, the price of my shame. (DH, 717)

We are given a front row seat to Dumbledore's experience of grief and guilt in *Harry Potter and the Half-Blood Prince*. In pursuit of Horcruxes, Harry and Dumbledore enter a cave where Dumbledore must drink a dangerous emerald potion. The potion seems designed to force the drinker to relive his or her worst experience. For Albus Dumbledore, the potion forces him to relive the events surrounding the violent killing of his sister, Ariana, without emotional defense.

"No, no, no, no, I can't, I can't, don't make me, I don't want to […]. It's all my fault, all my fault," he sobbed. "Please make it stop, I know I did wrong, oh please make it stop and I'll never, never again […]."

Dumbledore began to cower as though invisible torturers surrounded him; his flailing hand almost knocked the refilled goblet from Harry's trembling hands as he moaned, "Don't hurt them, don't hurt them, please, please, it's my fault, hurt me instead" […] he kept his eyes tight shut and shook from head to foot. And now he fell forward, screaming again, hammering his fists upon the ground, while Harry filled the ninth goblet.

"Please, please, please, no … not that, not that, I'll do anything […]."

"No more, please, no more […]."

Dumbledore began to scream in more anguish than ever, "I want to die! I want to die! Make it stop, make it stop, I want to die!" […] Dumbledore drank, and no sooner had he finished than he yelled, "KILL ME!" (HBP, 573)

This is remorse. This is what Albus Dumbledore hopes happens for Gillert Grindelwald. This is also what Dumbledore means when he tells Harry "that there are far, far worse things in the living world than dying" (DH, 721). Childish Tom Riddle, simple and ignorant worshiper of survival and power, is completely unaware of the force of an internally enforced and rationally guaranteed experience of guilt. Riddle is simply unaware that guilt can be so overwhelmingly powerful, so bitingly penetrating that death itself can emerge as preferable. Harry expresses this to Aberfoth Dumbledore in *Harry Potter and the Deathly Hallows.*

> The night that your brother died, he drank a potion that drove him out of his mind. He started screaming, pleading with someone who wasn't there. 'Don't hurt them, please ... hurt me instead.' ... He thought he was back there with you and Grindelwald, I know he did," said Harry, remembering Dumbledore whispering, pleading. "He thought he was watching Grindelwald hurting you and Ariana ... It was torture to him, if you'd seen him then, you wouldn't say he was free." (DH, 567–8)

For people like Albus Dumbledore, guilt can be far more daunting than the threat of death.

We know that the Dumbledore of the mystical King's Cross Station is no longer alive and thus no longer concerned with the desire for survival. After he finishes telling Harry the story of Ariana's murder, King's Cross Dumbledore "gave a little gasp and began to cry in earnest" (DH, 717). The Dumbledore of King's Cross Station no longer needs to worry about fear of death or the power needed for staying alive or even safe. This is why he weeps so openly. There is nothing to get in the way of his awareness of moral responsibility. As we have said, power and decency are the only two contenders for our definition of good. When the desire for power is gone, only moral principles remain to direct our thinking and judgment. Just as Tom Riddle had selected power as the lone competitor for the definition of good, so the King's Cross Dumbledore has only one competitor for the definition of good. No longer being alive, the King's Cross Dumbledore has lost the ability

to prize or even to be concerned with physical world power. Being dead, he no longer has the ability to fear death. Where Tom Riddle defined good as power, the King's Cross Dumbledore has no choice but to define good by means of eternal ethical principles.

This may help us understand a curious little point Dumbledore makes to Harry in *Harry Potter and the Half-Blood Prince*, in reference to Harry's question about whether Tom Riddle can feel the different fragments of his mutilated soul. Dumbledore says, "[p]erhaps, at the point of death, he might be aware of his loss" (HBP, 507–8). Why would that be so key? As we have said, being alive, being in the world means being concerned with power. As Mundungus Fletcher says, "oh, well, gotta scrape a living" (HBP, 245). However, for those who have approached their "deathbed" as Dumbledore had by the time he had reached the Astronomy Tower, all concern for power is released for it can be of no more use (HBP, 593).

This helps us understand the "small, maimed creature ... under the chair" in the mystical King's Cross Station. The creature "had the form of a small, naked child, curled on the ground, its skin raw and rough, flayed-looking, and it lay shuddering under a seat where it had been left, unwanted, stuffed out of sight, struggling for breath" (DH, 706). What happens when a person defines him or herself by power only to find that in death power has no use or purpose. This is what Harry means during the final duel when he says, "I've seen what you'll be" (DH, 742). In a manic relentless drive for power, Tom Riddle severed himself from the part of his persona that would've pressed universal principles upon him from within. It is as if he abandoned that part of himself like a discarded infant at a train station (just as he, himself, had been abandoned at an orphanage), only to find, quite to his shock and amazement, that this is all there is left of him when, in death, power has become utterly superfluous.

As humans we will forever find ourselves torn between legitimate and understandable concerns for power and for moral principles. While we live, we are destined to paradoxically define good in both directions. This is one of the reasons why we get so easily confused about important things.

Consider Dumbledore's insightful comments in *The Tales of Beedle the Bard*.

> But which of us would have shown the wisdom of the third brother, if offered the pick of death's gifts? Wizards and Muggles alike are imbued with a lust for power; how many would resist the "Wand of Destiny"? Which human being, having lost someone they love then could withstand the temptation of the Resurrection Stone? Even I, Albus Dumbledore, would find it easier to refuse the Invisibility Cloak; which only goes to show that, clever as I am, I remain just as big a fool as anyone else. (TBB, 107)

However, each of us is also destined to establish our priorities. Each of us must decide whether power or decency is more important, the higher priority. So which should it be?

Dumbledore contends that power is a "lure for fools" (DH, 713). Power is only useful to the living, and none live forever. The inevitability of death makes fools of those who would seek the power to outrun it. Further, as death approaches we will lose the ability to concern ourselves with power. In other words, our ability to prioritize power will abandon us no matter how loyal we have been to it, as the approach of death reveals power's inevitable eventual irrelevance. This is a simple and obvious truth of human experience. Machiavelli can teach us how to acquire a royal crown, but he has nothing to say about what to do when death comes to take it. Lastly, when the ability to prioritize power abandons us, we will be left alone with an unfettered concern for our own ethical principles that press upon us from within. The approach of death will make all of us drinkers of Riddle's emerald potion.

For most of us it is the often unrecognized fear of death or pain that tempts us into prioritizing power over our own ethical principles. "The master of death" learns to accept the inevitability of death and thereby masters his or her fear of it. In doing so, this person allows for the ascendancy of universal moral principles to the position of top priority, or "ultimate concern" (ST 1967, 11). In other words, if I can get past my fear of death and suffering and with it my unflattering desire for power and safety, I can become a person who sees every other person as equally and transcendently important. For such a person the word good can finally be defined by universal moral principles. Only such a person could adopt "Dumbledore's insane determination to see good in everyone" as a ruling and defining personal principle (HBP, 569).

This is what Harry means when he asks Tom Riddle "to think about what you've done…. Think, and try for some remorse" (DH, 741). Power is not evil and there is nothing wrong with desiring it. None who are living can afford to disregard it, and it is a pity to remember those who are in desperate need of it. Power is not the problem. We make it a problem when we make the desire for personal power more important than decency. For most of us, the desire for power is little more than a desire to prioritize our own concerns over the equally important concerns of those around us. Such a desire is rationally inconsistent. Equally important concerns cannot be simultaneously unequal. Equally important people cannot somehow become unequal. However, Tom Riddle has always assumed and deeply believed that he "was different […] special" (HBP, 271). Dumbledore explains that Riddle had an "increased […] sense of self-importance" (HBP, 360).

Remorse is nothing more complicated than coming to the awareness and acceptance of having prioritized one's own concerns over the equally valid concerns of other people. Albus Dumbledore wants to die and weeps piteously when he acknowledges that he prioritized his own desire for "glory" over his responsibility to care for and love his sister, Ariana (DH, 715). One of the most powerful examples of inappropriate priority within the entire Harry Potter series involves Albus Dumbledore and Severus Snape.

> "If she meant so much to you," said Dumbledore, "surely Lord Voldemort will spare her? Could you not ask for mercy for the mother, in exchange for the son?"
>
> "I have—I have asked him –"
>
> "You disgust me," said Dumbledore, and Harry had never heard so much contempt

in his voice. Snape seemed to shrink a little. "You do not care, then, about the deaths of her husband and child? They can die, as long as you have what you want?" (DH, 677)

Dumbledore is disgusted by Severus precisely because he has so obviously prioritized his own desires over the lives of other people. After Tom Riddle has killed both of Harry's parents, Albus Dumbledore and Severus Snape speak again.

> "Her son lives. He has her eyes, precisely her eyes. You remember the shape and color of Lily Evans's eyes, I'm sure?"
>
> "DON'T!" bellowed Snape. "Gone … dead …"
>
> "Is this remorse, Severus?"
>
> "I wish … I wish *I* were dead…."
>
> "And what use would that be to anyone?" said Dumbledore coldly. "If you loved Lily Evans, if you truly loved her, then your way forward is clear […]. You know how and why she died. Make sure it was not in vain. Help me protect Lily's son." (DH, 678)

Remorse is not as simple as feeling bad about a past mistake in priority. For most of us it is simply not enough to "feel the horror and shame" of what we have done. It is simply not enough to wish we "were dead," for that would be of no "use … to anyone." Once we come to acknowledge past mistakes in priority, the first thing we must do is change our priorities. We must stop making power and our own sense of self-importance our top priority, opting instead for an acknowledgment of the universal equality and transcendent importance of human beings.

In other words, we must redefine the essence of good from power to decency. Once our base definition of good is shifted from a preference for power to a preference for integrity, our resultant actions will reflect this shift. Our behavior will reflect the fact that we prioritize the unconditional importance of all people over our own individual safety or interest in dominance. This is what Dumbledore means when he says, "I had to do what I could" (DH, 718). It is this that Dumbledore is asking of Severus. It is this that Harry is asking of Tom Riddle when Harry says during the final duel, "Be a man" (DH, 742). Remorse is a shift in priority that results in a shift in behavior. It is the shift from fear to courage. It is because of this that Ginny and Harry Potter name their son after two excessively flawed men, Severus Snape and Albus Dumbledore.

CHAPTER 11
Women and Violence

One of Rowling's most important early influences was the cultural critic and human rights advocate Jessica Mitford. Jo Rowling was given a copy of Mitford's *Hons and Rebels* by one of her aunts. Rowling reported, "I remember reading the book *Hons and Rebels* at the age of fourteen, and it changed my life" (Shapiro 2004, 39). *Hons and Rebels* is a delightful autobiography of Jessica "Decca" Mitford, privileged upper-class daughter of David Bertram Ogilvy Freeman-Mitford, 2nd Baron Redesdale, and Sydney Bowles. Much of the work functions as an insider's relentless and biting critique of the British noble class or "peers of the realm." The book follows Decca's emerging awareness of injustice both inside and outside of her family's estate. As Dumbledore says, "magic always leaves traces," and traces of *Hons and Rebels* can be found all over the Harry Potter series (HBP, 563).

First of all, *Hons and Rebels* is an honest and self-effacing presentation of the fact that ethical maturity takes a long, long time to develop. Mitford grants us access to her own ethical progress through her careful and efficient first-person recounting of her own childhood and youth. She does not present herself as an ethical hero who emerged fully formed to escape with Esmond Romily to fight the Spanish dictator Franco. Mitford uses careful, detailed, and personally embarrassing family stories to express just how messy and time-dependent the progress towards ethical maturity can be. Mitford writes,

> The Bible asserts glibly, "when I was a child a spake as a child [...] when I became a man, I put away childish things"— as though it were that easy, with never a word about the uneasy transition, the restless search for one's own personality, the longing, not only for independence, but for that particular kind of independence which one dimly feels will come with self-knowledge [...]. A 13-year-old is a kaleidoscope of different personalities, if not in most ways a mere figment of her own imagination. At that age what and who you are depends largely on what book you happen to be reading at the moment. (HR, 52–3)

There can be little doubt of the similarity this bears to certain elements of the Harry Potter series. Many of my students tell me they were attracted to the Harry Potter series by its honest and realistic reflection of their own experiences. Rowling shares this honest presentation of youth with Mitford.

There are many specific traces of Mitford's influence on he Harry Potter series. Within *Hons and Rebels* we find that the Mitford daughters spend a lot of time in a "cupboard ... our hiding place under the stairs" (HR, xxii, 17). The name of the Redesdale estate where Jessica grew up was called Swinbrook House which resembled a "boarding school ... [or] a fortress or citadel of medieval times" (HR, 2). This house was said to be "ridden with ghosts and legends" (HR, 1). The "swine" in Swinbrook mirrors the "hog" in Hogwarts. Mitford tells of an adversarial older brother whose name was Tom and who had friends who were called the Fat Friars. The younger Mitford sisters wore badges with the words "League against Tom" on them (HR, 7). The fact that Swinbrook House stood two "miles up the hill from Swinbrook village" calls to mind Rowling's village of Hogsmeade. Jessica's sister went to fancy balls wearing a tiara "resplendent with rubies, emeralds and pearls" and carrying a "pet rat" (HR, 66).

Jessica Mitford's father was a strong believer in hereditary privilege. He was once quoted as saying, "May I remind your lordships the denial of the hereditary principle is a direct blow at the crown? Such a denial is, indeed, a blow at the very foundation of the Christian faith." He later "explained that just as Jesus became God because he was the son of God, so the oldest son of our Lord should inherit his father's title and prerogatives" (HR, 16). Such ideas clearly echo the theme of purebloods and blood status in the Harry Potter series. Further, it seems that Rowling may have even based the Black family on Mitford's family with Sirius perhaps playing the role of Jessica. Mitford also mentions an uncle Tommy who "presided as magistrate at the local police court and [...] doled out his own ideas of justice" (HR, 24). It is in response to these ideas that Jessica will become a "rebel."

Much of what Jessica will discover through her adolescent development will lead to a building appreciation of the importance of legitimate social justice.

> It suddenly occurs to you that the hundreds of people you see in the course of the day [...] are as real as yourself each with his own individuality, with the past, even a childhood in his background [...]. You discover suffering [...]. You catch disturbing, vivid glimpses of the real meaning of poverty, hunger, cold, cruelty [...] ragged children ... gaunt young women in men's caps wheeling pallid babies ... What could be done about it all? (HR, 54–5)

As we have said, Joanne Rowling read *Hons and Rebels* at fourteen. Similarly, Jessica Mitford revealed that "when I was fourteen I read *Cry Havoc*, Beverly Nichol's indictment of war" (HR,

63). It seems that Nichol's formative impact on Mitford was prophetic of the formative impact Mitford was to have on Rowling. Interestingly Nichols claims to have been profoundly influenced by H. G. Wells and the optimistic utopianism recounted in his *The Work, Wealth and Happiness of Mankind*. In opposition to the classist idea of family lineage espoused by Mitford's parents, we seem to see here emerging a sort of intellectual and ethical lineage. Each of these works seems to have been grounded on the idea of universal human equality as a fervent conviction and each seems to have significantly influenced the next. Mitford called this fervent conviction "the instinctive respect for the fundamental dignity of every other human being—even his enemy" (HR, 280). We should bear in mind that many of Rowling's own readers were also fourteen. It is amazing to reflect on the idea that it is so often a single book that rides to a young person's rescue, reaching in through the haze of one's inherited, normalized, and accepted reality with an overturning and redeeming new world view.

Harry Potter himself may also owe something to Jessica Mitford. *Hons and Rebels* is in part a love story between Jessica and Esmond Romilly, family rebel and injustice fighter. In describing Esmond she says, "He seemed to have that magic combination of determination, intelligence, and courage which would take him wherever he intended to go" (HR, 133). This description of Esmond could just as easily have been a description of Harry. Harry also resembles Esmond in regard to their shared tendency to be hotheaded and significantly imperfect. Mitford writes,

> Esmond's encounter with fascism in Spain [...] had done much to solidify the direction his life had taken since the age of fifteen. He was no

longer a dilettante, playing around the edges of the struggle of his generation […]. He had become a committed partisan of the fight against fascism. […] Like most eighteen-year-olds, his personality was still a state of flux. To me he seemed part hero, part adventure, part bad boy—just as I had always imagined him, in fact. […] Living with Esmond was like going for a walk in a fairy story, I decided. You never knew whether some sinister troll disguised as a British consul or croupier might be lying in wait round the next corner, or when the thorny briar forest would magically part to admit you into the enchanted palace. (HR, 140, 144, 171)

Mitford's description of Esmond Romilly is a product of her intimate and long-term relationship with him. Her portrait of his character is subtle and detailed, with unexpected specifics that often take the reader by surprise. Her portrayal is not that of a caricature, hyperbole, or stereotype. Instead it rings with the truth of real-life experience. Rowling was able to capture some of this in her fictional Harry.

On another note, Mitford and Rowling are both women writers. We should not be surprised then by a certain sophistication in their presentation of women and women's issues. Both writers handle the topic with a delicate grace, seriousness, and care. During Jessica's childhood, her sister Diana married Bryan Guinness. Mitford writes about this from the point of view of a far younger sister,

Diana seemed different since her marriage. […] her portrait was painted by a dozen artists. Her face always seemed to come out looking the same—large, calm, gazing rather vacantly into space; and she seemed to be getting like that in real life, too. She had almost given up laughing or frowning, and developed a permanent expression for all occasions not unlike that of Mona Lisa. Her eyes […] remained in a wide stare, her mouth slightly open, relax but not set […]. This made me uncomfortable in her presence. Regretfully, I demoted her from Favorite Sister. (DH, 48–9)

For the elementary-school-aged Jessica, Diane's behavior is a mystery. For those familiar with the nature of domestic abuse, however, the traces are not hard to discover here. Mitford prefers to leave her presentation of violence perpetrated against women within the perspective of a child, leaving the details and implications to the imagination and insight of her adult readers.

There is a similar tendency in the Harry Potter series. In a television special about women in Harry Potter, Rowling said, "I am a female writer and what's interesting about the wizarding world is when you take physical strength out of the equation, a woman can fight just the same as a man can fight" (The Women of Harry Potter. 2011). In the Muggle world women are commonly in the presence of physically stronger men. This power difference is part of the context under which most first dates occur. A woman's decision to get into the car of a man she only recently met represents a tangible risk for her. Men often fail to consider the implications of this difference in physical power.

However, the entire plot of the Harry Potter series is set within a shifted male-female power context. Take Ginny Weasley for instance. George Weasley is considered a capable wizard. However, in *Harry Potter and the Order of the Phoenix* George says to Harry,

"Yeah, size is no guarantee of power," said George. "Look at Ginny."
"What d'you mean?" said Harry.
"You've never been on the receiving end of one of her Bat-Bogey Hexes, have you?" (OP, 100)

Professor Slughorn makes a similar comment saying, "You want to be careful, Blaise! I saw this young lady perform the most marvelous Bat-Bogey Hex as I was passing her carriage! I wouldn't cross her!" (HBP, 146). Witches on a first date are just not under the same male-female power difference that Muggle women are.

Nonetheless, careful and subtle presentations of violence perpetrated on women haunt the Harry Potter series. Take, for instance the fact that the spiral staircase in to the girls' dormitory of *Gryffindor* Hall collapses whenever a boy steps on it, even though girls can step on the boys' staircase. Hermione says, "Well, it's an old-fashioned rule […] but it says in *Hogwarts, A History* that the founders thought boys were less trustworthy than girls" (OP, 353).

Further, Katie Bell, under the Imperius Curse, was asked to carry a cursed opal necklace. Dumbledore says, "She appears to have brushed the necklace with the smallest possible amount of skin; there was a tiny hole in her glove" (HBP, 259). At the moment the opals touched her skin:

> At once, Katie rose into the air […] gracefully, her arms outstretched, as though she was about to fly. Yet there was something wrong, something eerie….Then, six feet above the ground, Katie let out a terrible scream. Her eyes flew open but whatever she could see, or whatever she was feeling, was clearly causing her terrible anguish. She screamed and screamed […] they lowered her to the ground where she thrashed and screamed, apparently unable to recognize any of them. (HBP, 248)

The character, Katie Bell, is not being sexually attacked in this scene. And yet, there is something very "eerie" about the details in this description. Just as with Mitford's description of her sister's marriage, the details presented imply something that is not directly mentioned on the surface. The opals touch her "skin" through a "tiny hole" leaving "her arms outstretched" and screaming terribly. Katie Bell is not being raped and yet the description of her curse seems to echo such a thing.

In the Harry Potter series, few characters are more despised by readers than Dolores Umbridge. She is sadistic and tyrannical. However, near the end of *Harry Potter and the Order of the Phoenix*, we see Professor Umbridge confronting centaurs in the Forbidden Forest. She insults them and they carry her off.

> "Nooooo!" he heard Umbridge shriek. "Nooooooo … I am Senior Undersecretary … you cannot — Unhand me, you animals … nooooo!"

Harry saw a flash of red light and knew she had attempted to Stun one of them; then she screamed very loudly. Lifting his head a few inches, Harry saw that Umbridge had been seized from behind by Bane and lifted high into the air, wriggling and yelling with fright. […] Harry saw Umbridge being borne away through the trees by Bane. Screaming non-stop, her voice grew fainter and fainter until they could no longer hear it over the trampling of hooves surrounding them. (OP, 755–6)

Later, Professor Dumbledore retrieved her from the centaurs. She was then brought to the hospital wing.

> Professor Umbridge was lying in a bed opposite them, gazing up at the ceiling […]. Since she had returned to the castle she had not, as far as any of them knew, uttered a single word. Nobody really knew what was wrong with her, either. Her usually neat mousy hair was very untidy and there were still bits of twigs and leaves in it, but otherwise she seemed to be quite unscathed.
> "Madam Pomfrey says she's just in shock," whispered Hermione.
> "Sulking, more like," said Ginny
> "Yeah, she shows signs of life if you do this," said Ron, and with his tongue he made soft clipclopping noises. Umbridge sat bolt upright, looking around wildly. (OP, 848–9)

We see Dolores Umbridge again during the funeral of Albus Dumbledore. "At the sight of the centaur Firenze, who was standing like a sentinel near the water's edge, [Dolores Umbridge] gave a start and scurried hastily into a seat a good distance away" (HBP, 642).

In Greek mythology, centaurs are generally seen as "wild, lawless, and inhospitable beings, the slaves of their animal passions" (*The New Encyclopaedia Britannica*). They're also associated with Dionysus and Eros. For many, Greek centaurs are associated with rape. Clearly Rowling's centaurs are her own creation and bear only a passing resemblance to their predecessors in Greek mythology. Nonetheless, the description of

Umbridge's encounter with the centaur herd bears an uncomfortable resemblance to a violent gang rape motivated by rage.

In the hospital wing, Umbridge seems in a near catatonic state with "twigs and leaves" in her hair. The fact that they can see no apparent damage invites the reader to consider the possibility of hidden damage. Umbridge's reaction to both Firenze and Ron suggests that she associates trauma with centaurs. Perhaps most importantly, three females—Hermione, Ginny, and Madam Pomfrey—all downplay and even ridicule Umbridge's experience. Many victims of rape report similarly callous and insensitive female responses from some in the real world.

However, there is another angle to Dolores Umbridge's encounter with the centaurs. If Rowling is indeed trying to call attention to sexual violence, then why choose a character as reviled as Umbridge to be a poster child? Perhaps the answer lies in something Remus Lupin said in *Harry Potter and the Prisoner of Azkaban.*

> "They call it the Dementors' Kiss," said Lupin, with a slightly twisted smile. "It's what Dementors do to those they wish to destroy utterly. I suppose there must be some kind of mouth under there, because they clamp their jaws upon the mouth of the victim and — and suck out his soul […] you exist without your soul, you know, as long as your brain and heart are still working. But you'll have no sense of self anymore […]. It's the fate that awaits Sirius Black. It was in the *Daily Prophet* this morning. The Ministry have given the Dementors permission to perform it if they find him."
>
> Harry sat stunned for a moment at the idea of someone having their soul sucked out through their mouth. But then he thought of Black.
>
> "He deserves it," he said suddenly. "You think so?" said Lupin lightly. "Do you really think anyone deserves that?" (PA, 247)

Rowling shares her readers' distaste for the character of Dolores Umbridge, and yet it is not hard to see her encounter with the centaurs as a stark metaphor. Perhaps she uses this sadistic and unrepentant character to make the point that sexual violence is an abomination that goes beyond these considerations. Perhaps she is taking the opportunity to make the point that rape, like the Dementors' kiss, is a violence and a violation too great for anyone, even the worst, to deserve. Sexual violence is a profound tragedy no matter what kind of person it happens to. The Grey Lady and the Bloody Baron are two of the resident ghosts of Hogwarts School of Witchcraft and Wizardry. Throughout the first six volumes of the Harry Potter series they comprise two elements of the detailed atmosphere of life at Hogwarts. They are part of the color of the place. However, we find out more in *Harry Potter and the Deathly Hallows.*

> "When I lived," she said stiffly, "I was Helena Ravenclaw […] my mother fell ill—fatally ill […] she was desperate to see me one more time. She sent a man who had long loved me, though I spurned his advances, to find me. She knew that he would not rest until he had done so."
>
> Harry waited. She drew a deep breath and threw back her head.
>
> "He tracked me to the forest where I was hiding. When I refused to return with him, he became violent. The Baron was always a hot-tempered man. Furious at my refusal, jealous of my freedom, he stabbed me."
>
> "The Baron? You mean—?"
>
> "The Bloody Baron, yes," said the Grey Lady, and she lifted aside the cloak she wore to reveal a single dark wound in her white chest. "When he saw what he had done, he was overcome with remorse. He took the weapon that had claimed my life, and used it to kill himself. All these centuries later, he wears his chains as an act of penitence … as he should," she added bitterly. (DH, 615–6)

Each of the seven books in the Harry Potter series follows the main characters as they go through their seven years at school. Each of the books becomes a more sophisticated reflection on the development of the characters within. As a result, each of the seven books demands and expects a little more of the reader. As the characters and themes get more complex so do the demands on even youthful readers. In other words, with each book, Rowling trusts her reader with a little more and pushes them a little harder.

With The Grey Lady, Rowling presents her reader the violent reality of a male intent on controlling a female. Rowling makes sure her reader knows that the murder was motivated by furious anger and possessive jealousy. Rowling reveals that the Bloody Baron was enraged by the idea that Helena Ravenclaw would not bend to his will. The Baron kills Helena Ravenclaw with a knife, not a wand, a fact that connects him with the mad violence of Bellatrix Lestrange. Finally, Rowling makes sure her reader sees the wound. This is a stark and powerful presentation of an all too common form of violence against women. In a footnote within The Tales of Beedle the Bard, Albus Dumbledore notes, "No witch has ever claimed to own the Elder Wand. Make of that what you will" (TBB, 106).

Both the Bloody Baron and the Grey Lady haunt the seven books of the Harry Potter series just as thoroughly as they do the halls of Hogwarts. The Bloody Baron has remained bloody and chained for "centuries." These seemingly perpetual marks of his guilt and penitence remind us once again of Dickens' Marley. They also succeed in fixing his fleeting and impulsive act of naked rage and maniacal dominance in eternal amber. His crime committed without witness remains on permanent display under the gaze of the generations that pass through the school. While it may seem fitting and even satisfying that a crime this unjust and violent is held to such an undying exposure, we must not forget that the Grey Lady remains just as fixed a testament to the act. Rowling is making a statement about the lasting, perhaps perpetual impact acts of sexual violence can have on both perpetrator and victim. While we are not surprised that remorse over such an act can leave the aggressor permanently altered, we must never forget the undying impact such acts have on the victims. The Baron's act has arrested both of them in what Nearly Headless Nick refers to as the "neither here nor there" of ghostly limbo (OP, 861).

The plot lines of Albus Dumbledore and Harry Potter are two of the most important in the series. At the inception of Dumbledore's plot line we find the disturbing story of his sister, Ariana Dumbledore. While there were many rumors surrounding the circumstances of Ariana and her eventual death, we get closest to the truth with the story as told by Albus's brother, Aberforth.

> "When my sister was six years old, she was attacked, by three Muggle boys. They'd seen her doing magic, spying through the back garden hedge: She was a kid, she couldn't control it, no witch or wizard can at that age. What they saw, scared them, I expect. They forced their way through the hedge, and when she couldn't show them the trick, they got a bit carried away trying to stop the little freak doing it."
>
> Hermione's eyes were huge in the firelight; Ron looked slightly sick [...].
>
> "It destroyed her, what they did: She was never right again. She wouldn't use magic, but she couldn't get rid of it; it turned inward and drove her mad, it exploded out of her when she couldn't control it, and at times she was strange and dangerous. But mostly she was sweet and scared and harmless." (DH, 564)

It is not clear whether the three Muggle boys raped, molested, or beat Ariana. However, we do know that what they did was severe enough to motivate Ariana's father, Perceval, to attack the three boys so severely that he was locked up in Azkaban for it. We might also consider the fact that Rowling uses the phrase "forced their way through" in the above passage. She is again using the suggestive language we saw in regards to both Dolores Umbridge and Katie Bell.

We also know that whatever the boys did, it left Ariana permanently altered and in need of constant care. Such an outcome is reminiscent of the permanent damage done to the Longbottoms by Bellatrix Lastrange. Ariana is said to have had magic that "turned inward and drove her mad,'z' magic that "exploded out of her" beyond her control. These images and ideas are so consistent with sexual abuse that it's hard to disregard the possibility. Further, we must remember that Rowling took the needs of her juvenile audience very seriously. It seems quite likely that Rowling is offering clear intimations of sexual abuse even while she crafts the language in such a way so as to allow younger readers to remain appropriately oblivious to this.

As we saw in the last chapter, much of what Albus Dumbledore said to Harry in the mystical King's Cross Station relates directly or indirectly to his sister, Ariana. Dumbledore's plot line is initiated largely by the atrocity perpetrated upon his sister in his parents' backyard. Just as Rowena Ravenclaw haunts Hogwarts Castle without calling much attention to herself, so Ariana haunts every detail of Albus Dumbledore's story and character. By initiating Albus Dumbledore's plot line with Ariana's attack, Rowling gives quiet and yet profound expression to the incredibly powerful and long-ranging implications of violent abuse. The impact of rape does not end with the initial victim. Rape affects everyone in its vicinity. Rape is a violence that "maim[s] … souls" and tears families (DH, 722).

This leaves us with Harry. Harry's plot line is at least partly initiated by Merope Riddle. The only time we catch a glimpse of Harry Potter not immediately connected to Tom Riddle is through a note written by Lily to Sirius, a note that describes one-year-old Harry as "so pleased with himself" on a toy broomstick (DH, 180). Shortly after this point in his life, Harry's plot line becomes irresolvably entangled with Tom Riddle's. Riddle's plot line begins with his mother, Merope. Her story begins in the house of Gaunt. In an earlier chapter we discuss the fact that young children will often accept the judgments of their parents about them as fact. There we saw how Neville simply accepted his family's negative comments about him as a simple statement of fact. Merope's indoctrinating parent was Marvolo Gaunt. Harry is afforded a glimpse into Merope's life through Professor Dumbledore's Pensieve. While in the Gaunt house,

Harry realized that there was somebody else in the room, a girl whose ragged grey dress was the exact color of the dirty stone wall behind her. She was standing beside a steaming pot on a grimy black stove, and was fiddling around with the shelf of squalid-looking pots and pans above it. Her hair was lank and dull and she had a plain, pale, rather heavy face. Her eyes, like her brother's, stared in opposite directions. She looked a little cleaner than the two men, but Harry thought he had never seen a more defeated-looking person. (HBP, 204–5)

Where the Bloody Baron would seek to control Helena Ravenclaw and fail, here we find a woman whose free will and agency has been almost completely crushed by her brutal and oppressive father.

"Pick it up!" Gaunt bellowed at her. "That's it, grub on the floor like some filthy Muggle, what's your wand for, you useless sack of muck?" […] Gaunt screamed, "Mend it, you pointless lump, mend it!" (HBP, 205)

Marvolo Gaunt controls his daughter by means of Machiavellian fear.

Merope picked up the pot and returned it, hands trembling, to its shelf. She stood quite still, her back against the wall between the filthy window and the stove, as though she wished for nothing more than to sink into the stone and vanish. (DH, 206)

What Marvolo Gaunt cares most about is his family ancestry founded on Salazar Slytherin. He is among the many wizards who pride themselves on what some call the purity of family lines. Marvolo Gaunt shares this passionate belief with Jessica Mitford's aristocratic father. Why would so many put such stock in the importance of bloodlines and heredity? The answer probably has something to the fact that no matter how many mistakes I make or how inept I am, I cannot screw up my own DNA. The nobility of my own family tree is an elitism that remains safely out of the reach of my own incompetence. Therefore, I can count on it. It is solid. The twentieth-century French philosopher Jean-Paul Sartre wrote in his *Anti-Semite and Jew*,

There are people who are attracted by the durability of a stone. They wish to be massive and impenetrable; they wish not to change [...]. They want [their ideas] to be innate [...]. By treating the Jew as inferior [...] I affirm at the same time that I belong to the elite [...] an aristocracy of birth. There is nothing I have to do to merit my superiority, and neither can I lose it. It is given once and for all. It is a thing. [...] If [...] all the Jews were exterminated as [the anti-semite] wishes, he would find himself nothing but a concierge or shopkeeper in a strongly hierarchical society [...] (Sartre, 1968)

Jean-Paul Sartre seems to be saying that bigots like the idea of being better than someone else. However, bigots often believe that this superiority cannot be based on anything they actually do or achieve because none of their actions ever merit acclaim. Therefore, their superiority has to be based on something out of the reach of their own mediocrity. It has to be based on something inborn and inalienable. It must be something that I cannot lose no matter how stupid I am. This is Marvolo Gaunt through and through.

With a howl of rage, Gaunt ran toward his daughter. For a split second, Harry thought he was going to throttle her as his hand flew to her throat; next moment, he was dragging her toward Ogden by a gold chain around her neck.

"See this?" he bellowed at Ogden, shaking a heavy gold locket at him, while Merope spluttered and gasped for breath.

"I see it, I see it!" said Ogden hastily.

"Slytherin's!" yelled Gaunt. "Salazar Slytherin's! We're his last living descendants, what do you say to that, eh?"

"Mr. Gaunt, your daughter!" said Ogden in alarm, but Gaunt had already released Merope; she staggered away from him, back to her corner, massaging her neck and gulping for air.

"So!" said Gaunt triumphantly, as though he had just proved a complicated point beyond all possible dispute. "Don't you go talking to

us as if we're dirt on your shoes! Generations of purebloods, wizards all — more than you can say, I don't doubt!" (HBP, 207–8)

There is nothing in Marvolo Gaunt's history or character worth bragging about. He has no individual claims to any form of superiority. He is therefore left to rely completely and utterly on whatever respect he can glean by means of his family lineage. Without his assertion of pureblood superiority, Marvolo Gaunt would be nothing but an alcoholic old man wasting to nothing "in squalor and poverty" (HBP, 212).

So, what does it matter that Marvolo Gaunt is a hopeless curmudgeon? Why does it concern us? It is because his belief in pureblood superiority directly impacts his daughter, Merope. If purity of blood is of primary concern, then it is of utmost importance that female sexuality be controlled. Wizards who brag about nothing other than their pureblood status must make sure that their daughters date and marry only purebloods. The problem for such people is that these daughters often have wills and desires of their own. For the wizard overly concerned with pureblood status, a daughter's will and desire must be crushed in deference to the will of the patriarch. She must be terrified into relinquishing her discretion to her family. This is what motivates the diminishing and destructive language Gaunt uses on his daughter. The desire to control and guarantee paternity grounds much of the world's violent sexism.

"Is it true?" said Gaunt in a deadly voice, advancing a step or two toward the terrified girl. *"My daughter—pureblood a descendent of Salazar Slytherin—hankering after a filthy, dirty veined Muggle?"*

Merope shook her head frantically, pressing herself into the wall, apparently unable to speak. (HBP, 210)

The destructive and controlling nature of Merope's upbringing left her all but incapable of forming real human relationships. We can see this in her desperate and hopeless attempt at a marriage by means of manipulative love potions. In response to this, Dumbledore says, when her husband abandoned her, Merope stopped using magic. I do not think that she wanted to be a witch any longer. Of course, it is also possible that her unrequited love and the attendant despair sapped her of her powers; that can happen. In any case, as you are about to see, Merope refused to raise her wand even to save her own life. (HBP, 262)

Merope's despair leads directly to the extremely regrettable institutionalization of the baby Tom Riddle. We might also consider the possibility that the Gaunt household may have held more than verbal abuse for Merope.

Merope's loss or abandonment of magic resembles Ariana's inability to control her magic. In both cases, the majesty of their true potential is squandered at the hands of males who would stop at nothing to control them. Nowhere is this more in evidence than in the murder of Helena Ravenclaw. Every major plot line in the Harry Potter series is initiated directly or indirectly by the long-ranging impacts of violence on women. In *Hons and Rebels*, Jessica Mitford expresses how important it is to have an "enormous curiosity about people . . . [and a] passion to find out things, to know about details and motivations, to trace big events to their small human beginnings" (HR, 257). Mitford also observes how essential this quality is to the writings of Jane Austen. We can also see how important this quality was to J. K. Rowling in her production of the Harry Potter series.

Fenrir Greyback, clearly one of the most disturbing characters in the entire series, also initiates a plot line with a violent act. It is Fenrir Greyback who bites and thus infects Remus Lupin when he was a boy. It's hard to imagine the "Marauders" coming to fruition without Remus's "furry little problem" (HBP, 335). Just as Tom Riddle comes to ever increasingly resemble a snake as the series progresses, so Fenrir comes to increasingly resemble a wolf. Where Lupin would render his greatest effort in the service of maintaining his humanity, Fenrir chooses instead to foster his primitive animal nature. By the time we reach the Astronomy Tower at the end of *Harry Potter and the Half-Blood Prince*, Fenrir's rapacious single-mindedness resembles nothing more than

the Basilisk from *Harry Potter and the Chamber of Secrets* who says, "Come … come to me…. Let me rip you…. Let me tear you …. Let me kill you …" (CS, 120) The werewolf, Fenrir Greyback,

> had […] a rasping bark of a voice. Harry could smell a powerful mixture of dirt, sweat and, unmistakably, of blood coming from him. His filthy hands had long yellowish nails […]. Blood trickled down his chin and he licked his lips slowly, obscenely.
>
> "But you know how much I like kids, Dumbledore."
>
> "[…] you have developed a taste for human flesh that cannot be satisfied once a month?"
>
> "That's right," said Greyback. "Shocks you, that, does it, Dumbledore? Frightens you?"
>
> "Well, I cannot pretend it does not disgust me a little," said Dumbledore […].
>
> "I wouldn't want to miss a trip to Hogwarts, Dumbledore," rasped Greyback. "Not when there are throats to be ripped out … delicious, delicious …" (HBP, 593–4)

Not only does Fenrir resemble Slytherin's Monster and even Naigini, but we might also notice that Dumbledore uses the word "disgust" in reference to him. This is the same word that Dumbledore uses when he discovers that Severus Snape would be willing to sacrifice the lives of James and Harry Potter so that he, Severus, could have Lily Evans for himself. What disgusts Albus Dumbledore, in both himself and in others, is our tendency to forget our "instinctive respect for the fundamental dignity of every other human being" (HR, 280). What disgusts Albus Dumbledore is our tendency to reduce the transcendent majesty of an individual human being to a mere object of our discretion, a trinket at our disposal—nothing in of itself. We can see something tamer yet similar in Professor Slughorn who "contemplated Harry for a moment as though he was a particularly large and succulent piece of pheasant" (HBP, 145) or Dolores Umbridge who says, "The Ministry places a rather higher value on my life than yours, I'm afraid" (OP, 752).

In Rowling's 2008 commencement address at Harvard, she discussed her experience working in the African research department at Amnesty International's headquarters in London. She said, "Every day, I saw more evidence about the evils humankind will inflict on their fellow humans, to gain or maintain power." She recalled a terrible scream "of pain and horror" coming from a young man in one of the Amnesty offices. She was to discover that "in retaliation for his own outspokenness against his country's regime, his mother had been seized and executed." Every day she saw "eye-witness accounts of summary trials and executions, of kidnappings and rapes."

It gave her nightmares.

However, she said she also saw,

> the power of human empathy [...]. Ordinary people [...] join[ing] together in huge numbers to save people they do not know, and will never meet [...]. Unlike any other creature on this planet, humans can learn and understand, without having experienced. They can think themselves into other people's places [...] we have the power to imagine better.

An unfettered desire for power and control can tempt us into the worst decisions. Our own ability to legitimate and prioritize a drive for power will abandon us in the moment we come to seriously recognize the inevitability of our own mortality. The call to "respect the fundamental dignity of every other human being—even [our] enemy" is not, at base, a product of culture, indoctrination, or prejudice. It is a rational certainty that emerges out of the pristine sovereignty of our own subjective reflection, our own truest self.

CHAPTER 12

Eternal Life in the Miraculous Transformation

I. Existential Courage

Some of the most profound and important ideas come across to us in the form of bumper sticker clichés, graduation speeches, or greeting card platitudes. We hear these ideas so often and at such an early age that they can begin to withdraw into the background noise of our lives. Sometimes the most profound and penetrating ideas can be presented so frequently that we begin to unconsciously disregard them. Like a crucifix that has hung over a kitchen door unmoved for seventeen years, these images and ideas can fade right into the woodwork and disappear from our conscious consideration or reflection. Over time, images like that crucifix, itself a blindingly brutal and overwhelmingly violent murder scene, can dissolve and fade from conscious recognition even when they are right in front of us. The crucifix, an image originally intended to shock and move us, can be reduced to something of an ignored good luck charm gathering dust in obscurity. Such objects lose their ability to seize, arrest, or even reach us.

It doesn't take much space to express the idea that all people are created equal or that there is good and evil in all of us. Kingsley Shacklebolt, first Minister of Magic of the post-Voldemort era, expresses as much in one line during the broadcast of *Potterwatch* in *Harry Potter and the Deathly Hallows* when he says, "I'd say that it's one short step from 'Wizards first' to 'Purebloods first,' and then to 'Death Eaters' [. . .] We're all human, aren't we? Every human life is worth the same, and worth saving" (DH, 440). If these really are the take-away messages of the Harry Potter series then why did Rowling need 4,224 pages to express them? It is because Rowling is saying more than this. What Jo Rowling is trying to

express cannot fit on a bumper sticker or a greeting card. Rowling is saying something new, something different, and yet what she is saying is based on some of the oldest writings in human history. If Jo Rowling had been doing nothing more than reheating literary and moral leftovers, her series would never have met with the reception it did. In the Harry Potter series, Jo Rowling has produced something powerful, important, and perhaps dangerous. The question is, what? She is expressing what it means for a real person to select ethical principles as his or her top priority even under the real threat of pain and death. It is one thing to merely say that human equality is a top priority and another thing entirely to behave that way in a dangerous real-life situation. She is trying to explain what it really means to put your money (and everything else) where your mouth is.

Let us begin with the difference between thought and action. In C. S. Lewis's *The Screwtape Letters*, we find the following passage:

> "It's all very well discussing that high dive as you sit here in an armchair, but wait till you get up there and see what it's *really* like": here "real" is being used in the … sense to mean … the emotional effect those facts will have on a human consciousness. (Lewis 2001, 168)

The character Screwtape and the writer Lewis both seem to be making the point that watching or thinking about something is just not the same as living through it yourself. The definition of a wedding doesn't change whether you are watching it on television or participating in it as the bride or the groom. However, the meaning does change depending on where you're sitting even if that basic definition doesn't. Harry gives an example of this difference in *Harry Potter and the Goblet*

of Fire. In bed one night Harry imagines becoming the Hogwarts champion for the Triwizard Tournament, safe in the security that he cannot actually be chosen.

> Harry rolled over in bed, a series of dazzling new pictures forming in his mind's eye … He had hoodwinked the impartial judge into believing he was seventeen … he had become Hogwarts champion … he was standing on the grounds, his arms raised in triumph in front of the whole school, all of whom were applauding and screaming … he had just won the Triwizard Tournament. Cho's face stood out particularly clearly in the blurred crowd, her face glowing with admiration … Harry grinned into his pillow. (GOF, 192)

It is easy to imagine the adventure and glory of being the Hogwarts champion from the safety of his bed and imagination. It is something altogether different when his wish turns into reality.

After Harry's name does come out of the Goblet, he has to face the reality of very dangerous tasks. Under these conditions, he no longer sits and imagines the cheering crowd. Faced with the reality, he wishes he could return to being just a spectator.

> What wouldn't he have given to be one of these people, sitting around laughing and talking, with nothing to worry about but homework? He imagined how it would have felt to be here if his name hadn't come out of the Goblet of Fire … Ron [and Hermione] would be sitting with him. The three of them would probably be happily imagining what deadly dangerous task the school champions would be facing on Tuesday. He'd have been really looking forward to it, watching them

> do whatever it was … cheering on Cedric with everyone else, safe in a seat at the back of the stands … (GOF, 320–1)

As the task approached Harry felt that "a barely controlled panic was with him everywhere he went" and on the day of the event

> he felt much more aware of his body than usual; very aware of the way his heart was pumping fast, and his fingers tingling with fear … yet at the same time, he seemed to be outside himself, seeing the walls of the tent, and hearing the crowd, as though from far away … He stood up, noticing dimly that his legs seemed to be made of marshmallow. He waited. And then he heard the whistle blow. He walked out through the entrance of the tent, the panic rising into a crescendo inside him. (GOF, 317, 352–3)

Any of us can recall moments like this one in which our fear and panic mount as we approach a challenge that may be too much for us. Many of us can also attest to the fact that the fear can overwhelm us and prevent us from even attempting a daunting challenge. Fear can stop us dead in our tracks.

The decision to approach and confront that which scares us is not a thought, it is an act. It is not something that can be understood, it can only be experienced. No amount of watching other people face their fears can help us learn to face our own. There is a fundamental and important difference between thought and action, between imagination and reality that we cannot afford to forget. Our discussion of aesthetic distance in the second chapter reaches its full fruition in this idea. There we talked about the difference between the reader safe in bed and the characters who are facing severe challenges. At base, we must not allow ourselves to cheer Harry on as he marshals his forces and accepts his challenges only to fail to do so ourselves.

The transitional movement from fear to courage is not a thought to be understood. If I am waiting for the day when I understand how to face fear before I act, I will never act. Even the person who has gone through such experiences may not be able to explain them well, even to themselves. Harry again gives us an example. Just above we watched Harry as his legs turned to marshmallow. He walks out into the crowd and summons his broom.

> He swung his leg over the broom and kicked off from the ground. And a second later, something miraculous happened …
>
> As he soared upward, as the wind rushed through his hair … He realized that he had left not only the ground behind, but also his fear. … He was back where he belonged….
>
> This was just another Quidditch match, that was all … Just another Quidditch match, and that Horntail was just another ugly opposing team…. "Okay," Harry told himself … "let's go." (GOF, 354)

Something miraculous does happen here. Harry moves from fear to determination. Even Rowling does not attempt to explain how such a thing happens. She contents herself with explaining *that* it happened. She leaves the question about how to the category of the "miraculous" and the unexplainable.

It is, however, interesting to note that Harry's experience playing a game, Quidditch, contributed significantly to his ability to find himself capable of confronting a real dragon. Even if I don't completely understand the process of learning how to face my fear, I can practice the act of facing my fears even in a game. This is one of the reasons why sports have so long been an important part of the development of young people while in school. Rowling did not include Quidditch in her series so as to merely add color. The facing of fear in real time events has to be practiced. Practicing may be more important than

understanding when it comes to facing fear and learning to act. Just as Quidditch functioned as training to help Harry face the Hungarian Horntail, so the Horntail eventually became training for the moment he would face Tom Riddle.

II. *Ariadne's Thread*

With every new year at Hogwarts we see the main characters facing ever more intimidating demands. Each year Harry, Ron, and Hermione face adventures that push them to the limits of their capacity. And yet each of these individual experiences becomes a stepping-stone for something even more demanding the following year. Each individual instance of courage and determination is not merely its own adventure, but also participates as a step to the next one that had heretofore been beyond their reach or comprehension. Rowling is saying something very important about the development of individual character. Real action requires courage in the face of that which scares us, and the facing of fear requires practice. However, we can only practice facing our fears if we confront what really scares us. Offering children sanitized, unthreatening challenges will not help them to develop courage. As Neville says in *Harry Potter and the Order of the Phoenix*, it is important to "do something real" (OP, 761).

We have considered the famous mythologist Joseph Campbell in an earlier chapter. His thoughts about the archetypal path of the epic hero seem to echo through the Harry Potter series. For example, Campbell tells a story about an Iroquois woman who has inadvertently married a great magician who happens to turn into a great snake from time to time.

> "Like many [magicians] of this kind, their hearts are not in their bodies. Go back into the lodge, and in a bag that is hidden under the bed of the one to whom you are married, you will find a collection of seven hearts." This is a standard worldwide shamanic motif. The heart is not in the body, so the magician can't be killed. You have to find and destroy the heart. (PM, 157)

This bears a striking resemblance to Tom Riddle's Horcruxes. Campbell also discusses the transition from childlike obedience to teenage independence. He says, "But the period of youth is the period of self-discovery and transformation into a lion. The rules [of childhood authorities] are now to be used at will … not submitted to as compelling" (PM, 154). This calls to mind certain Gryffindor Lions who demonstrate "a certain disregard for rules" (CS, 333).

Campbell also talks about Ariadne's thread. The story of Theseus and Ariadne is alluded to at least twice in the Harry Potter series. Ariadne is the Greek form of the name Ariana whom we recognize as the crucially important sister of Albus Dumbledore. Also the story of Theseus and Ariadne centers on a labyrinth that readers will recognize as playing a major role at the end of *Harry Potter and the Goblet of Fire*. In one of the versions of the original mythological story, Ariadne helps the hero Theseus escape the labyrinth by giving him a spool of thread. He simply unwinds it as he goes into the labyrinth and then follows the thread back out to escape. Campbell sees the thread as a metaphor for mentors or teachers. This recalls our earlier chapter on trusted guides. Campbell says,

> That's all you need—an Ariadne's thread […] That's not always easy to find. But it's nice to have someone who can give you a clue. That's the teacher's job, to help you find your Ariadne thread. […] Each of us is a completely unique creature and that, if we are ever to give any gift to the world, it will have to come out of our own experience and fulfillment of our own potentialities, not someone else's. […] We have to give our students guidance in developing their own picture of themselves. […] What each must seek in his life never was, on land or sea. It has to be something out of his own unique potentiality for experience, something that has never been and never could have been experienced by anyone else. (PM, 150–1)

This is not the message most children receive. Most children and teens are not given the repeated message that theirs is a fundamentally unique and crucially important potential. Most children are not raised to believe that they are destined for a heroic voyage that will require their utmost strength, courage, and skill. Most children are not told that they will discover who they really are only within the searing onslaught of this voyage and that there is no other path to self discovery. Most children are not told that they harbor a unique and critical gift for the world that will arise out of both their absolutely unique individuality and realized courage.

Instead most young people find that they are being asked directly or indirectly to stuff their unique but as yet unknown and mysterious potential into a prefabricated and predetermined box. College freshmen are inevitably asked to choose a major. They are asked whether or not they want to spend the rest of their lives immersed in the study of something like history or psychology. College professionals and parents alike will often ask these questions in the same offhanded and matter-of-fact tone they would use to ask about lunch menu choices. Many adults simply assume that young people should just know what they want to do as a matter of course. These adults often become frustrated if they meet with a moment's uncertainty or hesitation in the young person and often react with something of the dismissive tone of Slytherin former Headmaster Phineus Nigellus who said, "this is precisely why I loathed being a teacher! . . . my poor puffed-up popinjay. . . Like all young people, you are quite sure that you alone feel and think" (OP, 495–6). In short, most young people encounter adults who resemble Mr. and Mrs. Dursley who "were proud to say they were perfectly normal, thank you very much. They were the last people you'd expect to be involved in anything strange and mysterious, because they just didn't hold with such nonsense" (SS, 1). Anyone with a unique potential, anyone who might be destined for an heroic quest would be considered "as unDursleyish as it was possible to be" (SS, 2).

So how does this happen? How do infinitely unique people become Confunded and Imperiused into the Dursleys? Why would someone abandon Ariadne's thread only to be left lost inside the labyrinth? Well, in the last chapter Jean-Paul Sartre told us that many of us are happy to believe in irrational stereotypes so long as it makes us feel superior to someone else. However, the problem goes deeper and further than deliberate and convenient bigotry. The problem has to do with the definition of good. More specifically the problem centers on the battle within us between power and decency for supremacy. Will safety/dominance rule my definition of good, or will an internal certainty about the universal equality of humans so rule?

III. *Ultimate Concern*

We found in the chapter on priorities that only one of these two concerns can alone rise to the status of top priority, my own ultimate concern. However, we commonly allow ourselves to disgracefully linger in the illusion that we can have both without embarrassment, shame, or hypocrisy. This tendency is so common that our society in general has allowed the word good to vaguely wander between them. Few of us even notice that we indiscriminately refer to both power and ethics as good. However, if we linger too long in this delusion we threaten ourselves with the fate of Xenophilius Lovegood. For, as Plato suggested, if you don't know what matters most to you, you are at risk of selling that very thing in order to buy something that matters less. Imagine what it would feel like to sacrifice your highest concern only to acquire something that matters far less. You might ask Peter Pettigrew.

This brings us to Albus Dumbledore and Ariana's tombstone. In the last chapter we considered the idea that two of the major plot lines in the Harry Potter series begin with Ariana Dumbledore and Merope Riddle. In reference to Ariana's thread, we have heard from Aberforth Dumbledore that Ariana died during a skirmish between Aberforth, Albus, and Gillert Grindelwald. We've also considered Albus Dumbledore's immense remorse over Ariana's killing during both the scene with the emerald potion and the scene in the mystical King's Cross Station. It is this seventeen-year-old Albus who places the following line on Ariana's gravestone: "Where your treasure is, there will your heart be also" (DH p. 326). Harry, for one, admits that he does not know what this means. It is both a confession and a commitment. What Dumbledore is saying with this line is that your heart will be in whatever you care most about. You will be most deeply drawn to whatever you think your highest treasure is. Dumbledore says that before Ariana's death "I wanted to escape. I wanted to shine. I wanted glory" (DH, 715). After her death Albus Dumbledore desired "to see Ariana, and my mother, and my father, and to tell them how very, very sorry I was …" (DH, 720). What we see here is a change in what Albus Dumbledore would see in the Mirror of Erised. What we see is a change in the identification of what his treasure was. It is a change in his highest priority, his ultimate concern.

The name Ariana can be translated as "most holy." The twentieth-century American philosophical theologian Paul Tillich discussed the idea of highest priority in reference to holiness or religion. He said

> that everything which is a matter of uncon-ditional concern is made into a God. If the nation is someone's ultimate concern, the name of the nation becomes a sacred name and the nation receives divine qualities which far surpass the reality of the being and functioning of the nation. (DF, 44)

In other words, according to Paul Tillich, whatever we care most about we make into our God. This makes us all religious. There is no one who is without an ultimate concern. There are no atheists of individual meaning or purpose. All of us have one *thing* that we care most about. In that thing or concern we "live and move and have [our] being" (Acts 17:28). Consider the following examples. Tom Riddle has made physical survival and its requisite power his top priority. In reference to protecting her son Draco, Narcissa Black says,

"There is nothing I wouldn't do anymore!" (HBP, 21). Sirius Black said of Bartemius Crouch Sr., "Anything that threatened to tarnish his reputation had to go; he had dedicated his whole life to becoming Minister of Magic" (GOF p. 528). We all love our top priority, our "God with all [our] heart, and with all [our] soul and with all [our] mind, and with all [our] strength" (Mark 12:30). Our ultimate concern "is a matter of infinite passion and interest, making us its object whenever we try to make it our object" (ST, 12).

That last point is an important one. Whatever we care most about, owns us. Whoever would become the master of death is mastered by it. Whoever would become the master of power becomes the servant of the rules of power. Further, everything else in our lives takes a back seat to our highest priority. In other words, in reference to our ultimate concern, everything else can be sacrificed. If Albus had made Ariana his top priority, she would never have ended up "dead upon the floor." If Bartemius Crouch Sr. had made his family his top priority, his son would almost certainly not have ended up in Azkaban only to become a Death Eater (and his father's murderer) later.

After Ariana's death, Albus Dumbledore changes his ultimate concern. He says, "I had learned that I was not to be trusted with power" (DH, 717). He learned that under the influence of his desire for power, he became capable of sacrificing real people. Under the influence of power, he found that he was capable of violating the most basic form of his profound belief in the universal equality of all people. So, in the name of his faith in the universal equality of people, he sacrificed his desire for power and along with it, the post of Minister of Magic. He changed his "treasure" from power to decency. And with this change in treasure came a change in his "heart."

We can see something similar in Ron Weasley's use of the Deluminator. After having abandoned Harry and Hermione in *Harry Potter and the Deathly Hallows*, he allows his concern for his friends to literally enter his heart and direct him to where they were. His concern literally allows his heart to be where his treasured friends are. His commitment to them becomes his highest priority. Both Ron Weasley and Albus Dumbledore

go through a shift in ultimate concern. Further, Ron seemed to know that Dumbledore knew this about him (DH, 391).

We saw in the chapter on priorities that our desire for power will likely abandon us as our life comes to a close. Those who prioritize power will eventually lose the ability to do so as the utility of power dissolves with the approach of death. What significance can worldly power have for those who are leaving the world? All who are mortal have to face this. Why do so few of us actually get around to acknowledging this? The answer is that we are both physical and ideal. We care about both our bodily and our rational/ spiritual needs even though they are often in contradiction to each other. This is a very important point. We so often fear being hungry or at risk and yet we are also ashamed of the prospect of sacrificing our moral ideals. We therefore have a tendency to hide our prioritization of power from everyone, even ourselves. We do this at least in part in order to hide from ourselves the truth about that which we sacrifice to our desire for power. Many of us wish both to hide and hide from the truth about this, perhaps in the Room of Hidden Things.

IV. The Grand Inquisitor

In an effort to understand this better we will turn to the character of Dolores Umbridge once again. Of Umbridge, Rowling said, "One of the things I find most revolting in life is self-righteousness that covers self-interest—that was Umbridge from beginning to end. And she was actually quite as sadistic as Bellatrix but it was all justified because 'I work for the Minstry'" ("The Women of Harry Potter" 2011). Many clues in the Harry Potter series that suggest that Rowling deeply favors Christianity and religion in general. However, there is also much to suggest that she is deeply critical of religion. Take, for example, her use of the phrase "High Inquisitor" in *Harry Potter and the Order of the Phoenix* (OP, 306). First of all, this word calls to mind the history of the medieval Spanish Inquisition, one of the most violent atrocities ever committed in the name of God. However, the use of this specific phrase also calls to mind a very famous chapter from Fyodor Dostoyevsky's *The Brothers Karamazov,* a chapter called "The Grand Inquisitor." This chapter is a modern reflection on religion and human free will.

One of *The Brothers Karamazov*'s main characters produces a story about a brutal cardinal performing torture and executions during the Spanish Inquisition. On one particular day someone who genuinely appears to be the real risen Christ arrives and is confronted by the cardinal, the Grand Inquisitor. The Inquisitor addresses this figure as the real Christ. The Inquisitor explains that human nature is an "unsolved historical contradiction" (BK, 228). He is expressing the idea that humans are irresolvably torn between the demands of the body and the demands of the conscience. The Inquisitor agrees with Lewis and Kant that our reason gives us access to an eternal truth concerning human equality and significance. He also agrees that this grants us freedom in that we are thus empowered to choose between physical and rational definitions of the word good. We are free because we can understand the word good as grounded on either power or ethics. We are free precisely because this definition is at our discretion. Further, the actions and decision that result from this chosen definition are also at our discretion. We have freedom over much more than just our actions and decisions. We have freedom over the motives of our actions and decisions. We have freedom over our ultimate concern, the bedrock foundation of all our motives and conclusions.

The Inquisitor contends that this makes us miserable. We hate having to choose between our bodily and rational selves. Hunger puts us at risk of downplaying our conscience, and our conscience puts us at risk of accepting hunger for a cause. Our freedom over our own motives also proves that we must be responsible for these motives and choices. We hate being stuck between hunger and conscience and we also hate the guilt that can so often accompany our responsibility. The Inquisitor then suggests that our resistance to freedom and guilt can tempt us into relinquishing our own "knowledge of good and evil" in favor of accepting the dictates of an external authority. The Inquisitor says that by letting someone else

make up the rules, we feel excused from the responsibility of freedom and guilt. The Inquisitor says, "And they will be glad to believe our answer, for it will save them from the great anxiety and terrible agony they endure at present in making a free decision for themselves" (BK, 235).

The Inquisitor says that he will be able to draw people to a false Church, "and to teach them that it's not the free judgment of their hearts, not love that matters, but a mystery which they must follow blindly, even against their conscience" (BK, 232). He says,

> They will love us like children because we allow them to sin. We shall tell them that every sin will be expiated, if it is done with our permission, that we allow them to sin because we love them, and the punishment for these sins we take upon ourselves. And we shall take it upon ourselves, and they will adore us as their saviors who have taken on themselves their sins before God. [...] The most painful secrets of their conscience, all, all they will bring to us, and we shall have an answer for all. And they will be glad to believe our answer, for it will save them from the great anxiety and terrible agony they endure at present in making a free decision for themselves. (BK, 235)

He is admitting that his Church is a fraud that is grounded on the human desire for power and comfort without guilt. The cardinal acknowledges that no real church has the power, discretion, or authority to lift "all responsibility from [our] shoulders" (DH, 716). We own what we do and every single one of us knows that. When we violate the principle of universal human equality, the 1 = 1, our own criticism of this act "presses" on us from within. This happens even when no one else knows that we have done this thing. The dictates of our conscience (those not based on cultural prejudice or indoctrination) are, for most of us, undeniable feelings. These feelings of obvious and undeniable responsibility prove our freedom to us. We would not feel responsible if we did not fundamentally believe that we were free in the first place. The Grand Inquisitor admits the truth of all of this.

This Grand Inquisitor also addresses our fear of our own death and that of our loved ones. Not only will this false church allow us to believe that they have the power to relieve us of our inalienable responsibility, this church will also allow us to believe in an afterlife. The cardinal says, "Peacefully they will die, peacefully will they expire in thy name, and beyond the grave they will find nothing but death. But we shall keep the secret, and for their happiness we shall allure them with the reward of heaven and eternity" (BK, 235). The cardinal is saying that we fear death and that a story about eternal life would make us happy. The cardinal's false church is happy to provide such a story.

He does, however, admit that these followers of his false church will not be able to sustain the fraud forever. He says "their childish delight will end; it will cost them dear … man's nature cannot bear blasphemy, and in the end always avenges it on itself" (BK, 232). This is because there is an

> everlasting craving of humanity—to find something to worship. So long as man remains free he strives for nothing so incessantly and so painfully as to find something to worship. […] For the secret of man's being is not only to live but to have something to live for. Without a stable conception of the object of life, man would not consent to go on living, and would rather destroy himself than remain on earth, even if he had bread in abundance. (BK, 230)

Despite the fact that we are deeply drawn to the desire for power, dominance, and safety, we nonetheless have the potential to rebel against the proposed sovereignty of this desire. We can resist power's aspiration to an internal tyranny. People have the potential to disregard the demands of fear and selfishness and "at the great moments of their life, the moments of their deepest, most agonizing spiritual difficulties, cling only to the free verdict of the heart" (BK, 231). The free verdict of the heart is our rational awareness of the primacy of human equality.

In his conversion with what appears to be the risen Christ, the Grand Inquisitor admits that we all know that we are free to follow the dictates of our conscience and that it is our own fault if we don't. He admits that we should follow the "free verdict of the heart" without thought of reward in either this or the next life. The cardinal explains that his false eternal life is a bribe that undermines the idea that we should follow our conscience for its own sake. The cardinal admits that any reward-based image of heaven puts us at risk of being motivated by the pay-off. He admits that "free verdict of the heart" needs to be chosen without any other incentive than its own validity. The principles of conscience have to be followed for their own sake. Either we love our neighbor as our selves or we "love" them as a mere means of getting into heaven. There is a big difference between the two and that ought not be confused or conflated. Using people in order to achieve our self-centered afterlife desires cannot honestly be considered love of anyone but ourselves.

So, the Grand Inquisitor is saying that many of us desire an easy religion that allows us to relinquish our responsibility and side-step our fear of death. According to Dostoyevsky's violent cardinal, we want someone else to pay for our sins and to offer us eternal life in the company of deceased loved ones. All we have to do is blindly follow someone else's definition of good. We want what Rowling calls the Imperius Curse.

> It was the most wonderful feeling. Harry felt a floating sensation as every thought and worry in his head was wiped gently away, leaving nothing but a vague, untraceable happiness. He stood there feeling immensely relaxed, only dimly aware of everyone watching him.
>
> And then he heard Mad-Eye Moody's voice, echoing in some distant chamber of his empty brain: *Jump onto the desk …*
>
> Harry bent his knees obediently. (GOF, 231)

Even though the Imperius Curse is one of the Unforgiveable Curses, it is always described as pleasurable for the victim. This is not surprising. It is almost always easier to let someone else do the thinking. However, according to Rowling, this is the very thing, this very temptation and tendency that we need to grow out of. We need to grow out of our childlike reliance on the authority of others while we develop an ever weightier reliance on our own responsibility to define good independently.

The Grand Inquisitor admits that very few actually want to follow the example of Christ because the real thing is hard. Remember, the Inquisitor is directly addressing a person he believes to be the actual Christ.

> And behold, instead of giving a firm foundation for setting the conscience of man at rest for ever, Thou [,the Christ,] didst choose all that is exceptional, vague and enigmatic; […]. Thou didst desire man's free love, that he should follow Thee freely, enticed and taken captive by Thee. In place of the rigid ancient law, man must hereafter with free heart decide for himself what is good and what is evil, having only Thy image before him as his guide […] for they could not have been left in greater confusion and suffering than Thou hast caused, laying upon them so many cares and unanswerable problems. (BK, 230–1)

The Inquisitor is acknowledging that real moral independence is hard in part because our consciences are not always clear. Even if I am aware that I should treat all other people as equally and infinitely important, knowing just what to do next remains seldom obvious. This principle to treat everyone as equals is a general guide at best. It does not offer specific instruction. I will have to be the one who applies the general principle of the universal equality and unbounded importance of all people to the complexity and unpredictability of real life. That part of the process is left in my hands alone. While the Divinity/reason can produce the law, the application of the law is (and can only be) in human hands alone. Specific real-world application of this law requires the specific perspective and location of actual existence. It is only by means of a human being that the ideal can be applied to the specific. This is hard and requires "constant vigilance" (GOF p. 213). This, says the Inquisitor, will send most of us running back to

his easy fraud religion with its mindless Imperiused obedience to external authority and comforting images of a weakened death.

V. Daunting Self-Reliance

Applying the general principle of my conscience to real-life situations requires cleverness, creativity, fortitude, and resilience. It can be quite intimidating. This difficulty is given vivid and beautiful expression in *Harry Potter and the Deathly Hallows*. There we see Harry, Ron, and Hermione thrown out into wilderness with only the sparest of instructions from the deceased Dumbledore and nothing less than the safety of the world in their hands. All three of them feel completely insufficient to the task.

> Harry's hand brushed the old Snitch through the moleskin and for a moment he had to fight the temptation to pull it out and throw it away. Impenetrable, unhelpful, useless, like everything else Dumbledore had left behind— And his fury at Dumbledore broke over him now like lava, scorching him inside, wiping out every other feeling. Out of sheer desperation they had talked themselves into believing that Godric's Hollow held answers, convinced themselves that they were supposed to go back, that it was all part of some secret path laid out for them by Dumbledore; but there was no map, no plan. Dumbledore had left them to grope in the darkness, to wrestle with unknown and undreamed-of terrors, alone and unaided. Nothing was explained, nothing was given freely, they had no sword, and now, Harry had no wand. (DH, 351)

Moral maturity requires that we find ourselves left alone to solve immense problems on our own. We rise to the challenge in part because we have no one else to turn to, and thus no other choice. I embark on an epic voyage not because I fancy myself a hero, but because there is no one else there to do it. Eventually I must decide to say "Forget Dumbledore. This is my choice, nobody else's" (DH, 234). This is an essential part of Ariadne's thread.

Learning to forgo or release the advice of an elder in favor of self-reliance is something that is also easier to live through than understand. It is existential. It is more of an action than a thought. It is like Screwtape's high dive. More importantly, this transition changes who we are. By the time they reach Shell Cottage and have buried Dobby, Harry, Ron, and Hermione are no longer as desperate to know what Dumbledore would have them do. Harry in particular has given up the role of passenger and has deliberately taken the wheel, so to speak. In this particular scene, Harry must decide in the heat of the moment whether he will pursue Hallows or Horcruxes and needs to talk to both Griphook and Ollivander.

> "No," Harry said and Bill looked startled. "I need both of them here. I need to talk to them. It's important." He heard the authority of his own voice, the conviction, the voice of purpose that had come to him as he dug Dobby's grave. (DH, 482)

The Harry who had complained about being left to "grope in the darkness" without a plan from Dumbledore is a Harry who is still in the last stages of his childhood reliance on guidance. The later Harry, the one who speaks with his own voice, with the voice of purpose and conviction is no longer a child. We must remember that Harry dug Dobby's grave by hand.

> He had set to work, alone, digging the grave [...]. He dug with a kind of fury [...]. On Harry dug, deeper and deeper into the hard, cold earth, subsuming his grief in sweat [...] understanding blossomed in the darkness. [...] He felt as though he had been slapped awake [...]. Deeper and deeper Harry sank into the grave [...] Harry lost track of time [...] Harry placed the elf into the grave, arranged his tiny limbs so that he might have been resting, then climbed out. (DH, 478–80)

Dobby is not the only one who goes into this grave. Harry descends into the "hard, cold earth" as well. There is something of Harry that is buried along with the elf. Yet, even as one part of Harry dies, another part rises. Joseph Campbell discusses rituals

> through which a child is compelled to give up his childhood and become an adult—to die, you might say [...] and come back as a responsible adult. [...] The adventure is [...] necessarily dangerous, having both negative and positive possibilities, all of them beyond control. We are following our own way, not our daddy's or our mother's way. So we are beyond protection in a field of higher powers than we know. (PM, 124,158)

If you're going to break into Gringotts Wizarding Bank, steal Helga Hufflepuff's Cup, and escape on a nearly blind dragon, you cannot be waiting around for instructions from someone else. Someone like that will eventually have to decide to figure things out on his or her own. Real moral independence and maturity requires the application of an internally discovered principle onto the unpredictability, unprecedentedness, and complexity of real life. Applying the dictates of one's conscience to one's own lived experience is always a hero's quest. Those who would prefer the Grand Inquisitor's easy religion are not likely to embark on such a thing. They, like Vernon Dursley, are much more likely to "put [their] hopes in the establishment" (DH, 33).

This self-reliance also applies to the eudaiminia. As I begin my search for my own most appropriate long-term drive to excellence, I can lean into the advice and insight of those around me. I will pay attention to people like Mad-Eye Moody (Barty Crouch Jr.) when they convince me that I may have a future as an Auror, partly on the ground of their own excellence, experience, and expertise. I will also have to rely on coaches and the like to help me focus and direct my training toward my potential. However, I will have to learn to forgo the temptation for external advice when it comes to choosing the direction of my ambition. Deep within the authentic individuality of each person is a voice or a sense for that person's true calling. This is something that, like other parts of my personal morality, I will have to figure out largely on my own.

Most importantly, I will have to learn how to listen to this voice and give it credibility. This voice, this muse, is where artists, composers, and authors have gone for centuries for inspiration. We must come to see our own potential excellence as something new, something unprecedented and unplagiarized. Like all independent morality, this requires self-reliance. Like all independent morality, this requires practice. I must learn to practice judgment about my own appropriate life direction. Like all independent morality, this practice can be messy, leaving the floor strewn with unsuccessful attempts and fleeting whims. Nonetheless, we simply must learn to allow the question of our own most fitting potential to linger as an unanswered question while we give ourselves the time to listen for a answer that can only emerge from within ourselves. There is very little in our culture that offers us this advice.

VI. The Empty Consolations of Religion and the Master of Death

This brings us finally to the subject of death that haunts almost every page of the Harry Potter series. We have already received a warning from Dostoyevsky about comforting images of the afterlife. C. S. Lewis addresses the issue of mourning and grief in his profoundly beautiful *A Grief Observed*, which he wrote in the period immediately following the death of his wife. Lewis also warns against vacant platitudes regarding life after death.

It is hard to have patience with people who say, "There is not death" or "Death doesn't matter." There is death [… and it] has consequences. […] Already, less than a month after her death, I can feel the slow, insidious beginning of a process that will make the [wife] I think of into more of an imaginary woman […]. What pitiable cant to say, "she will live forever in my memory!" Live? That is exactly what she won't do […]. Will nothing persuade us that they are gone? […] It was [my wife] I loved. As if I wanted to fall in love with my memory of her, an image of my own mind! (GO, 15, 18, 20)

Lewis calls us to take death seriously and admit its serious implications. No human memory can capture the infinite complexity of another person. Only the actual person themselves in reality can manifest that person's magnificent complexity, unpredictability, and mind-blowing detail.

Like Dostoyevsky, Lewis also talks about convenient and comforting ideas about the afterlife.

don't come talking to me about the consolations of religion or I shall suspect that you don't understand.

Unless, of course, you can literally believe all that stuff about family reunions "on the further shore," pictured in entirely earthly terms. But that is all unscriptural, all out of bad hymns and lithographs. There is not a word of it in the Bible. It rings false. We know it couldn't be like that. Reality never repeats. The exact same thing is never taken away and given back. How well the spiritualists bait their hook! "Things on this side are not so different after all." There are cigars in heaven. For that is what we should like. The happy past restored.

And that, just that, is what I cry out for, with mad, midnight endearments and entreaties spoken into empty air. (GO, 25–6)

C. S. Lewis's *Mere Christianity* is a testament to his faith and commitment to his understanding Christianity. There can be little doubt that he thinks of himself as a firm believer in the Christian message. However, he does not seem to believe in a material heaven that closely resembles Earth. He does not seem to believe in "family reunions on that further shore" as one of the "consolations of religion." He admits that all we want is the "happy past restored" and that it is exactly this that we "cry out for, with mad midnight […] entreaties." However, Lewis reminds us that this desire is exactly what fraudulent spiritualists, such as Dostoyevsky's Inquisitor use to take advantage of us.

The Harry Potter series is loaded with fantastic and magical elements. Ghosts commonly frequent the Great Hall and corridors of Hogwarts. Long-dead former headmasters remain available for consultation in their portraits. And yet, Rowling does not give us anything like the image of heaven that Lewis recalls from "bad hymns and lithographs." Instead, she offers us something quite sophisticated and unpredicted. Rowling does not offer us any image of a "further shore" nor does she leave us any suggestion that "death does not matter." Instead we find images of Harry standing in front of the Mirror of Erised, a magical object that offers "neither knowledge or truth" (SS, 213). Dumbledore warns Harry in the very first book of the series that it "does not do to dwell" on a hopeless desire for the return of deceased loved ones, "the happy past restored." Dumbledore offers the orphan Harry none of the traditional "consolations of religion."

As Harry, Ron, and Hermione interact with Xenophilius Lovegood in *Harry Potter and the Deathly Hallows*, Hermione offers her own interpretation of Beedle's "The Tale of the Three Brothers." "'The Tale of the Three Brothers' is a story," said Hermione firmly. "A story about how humans are frightened of death" (DH, 427). People are frightened of death. This is what motivates Tom Riddle among very many others. Xenophilius Lovegood, for example, is perusing the Deathly Hallows because he is trying to become the "*Master . . . Conqueror ... Vanquisher*" of death (DH, 429). For Xenophilius Lovegood, being the master of death is synonymous with the words conqueror and vanquisher. He desires control over the threat of death both for himself and his loved ones. Xenophilius Lovegood has good reason to desire this having both a dead wife and a kidnapped daughter.

Toward the end of *Harry Potter and the Deathly Hallows* we find that Albus Dumbledore desired something very similar.

"The Hallows, the Hallows," murmured Dumbledore. "A desperate man's dream [...]. A lure for fools [...]. Master of death, Harry, master of death! Was I better, ultimately, than Voldemort? [...] I too sought a way to conquer death, Harry [...] the legend said that the man who united all three objects would then be truly master of death, which we took to mean 'invincible.'" (DH, 713, 716–7)

Both Xenophilius Lovegood and Albus Dumbledore mirrored Tom Riddle's "goal—to conquer death" in their desire to control death through possession of the Deathly Hallows (GOF, 653). Harry's own fear of death at the hands of Tom Riddle and the prophesy tempts him into a desire for the Hallows himself.

Three objects, or Hallows, which, if united, will make the possessor master of Death ... Master ... Conqueror ... Vanquisher ... The last enemy that shall be destroyed is death....

And he saw himself, possessor of the Hallows, facing Voldemort, whose Horcruxes were no match ... *Neither can live while the other survives....* Was this the answer? Hallows versus Horcruxes? Was there a way, after all, to ensure that he was the one who triumphed? If he were the master of the Deathly Hallows, would he be safe? [...] Harry was [...f]eeling as though great new vistas of truth were opening all around him ...

He felt armed in certainty, in his belief in the Hallows, as if the mere idea of possessing them was giving him protection, and he felt joyous. (DH, 429–30)

As we discuss the issue of death we must bear in mind that there is absolutely nothing wrong with the human desire for survival. In *Harry Potter and the Prisoner of Azkaban*, Lupin refers to our desire for survival as one of the happy feelings that can help us produce The Patronus Charm. He says, "The Patronus is a kind of positive force, a projection of [. . .] hope, happiness, the desire to survive" (PA, 237). Rowling fills the Harry Potter series tip to tail with beautiful and delightful images of the joy of being alive. From the feasts of the Great Hall, the delirious selection of candy at Honeydukes, the feel of a four-poster bed with a warming pan in it, the Yule Ball and mistletoe to Harry's reception of Ginny's face, ("Ginny gave Harry a radiant smile: He had forgotten, he had never fully appreciated, how beautiful she was") and Remus Lupin's announcement of the birth of his son, Rowling never misses a chance to remind us how much glorious fun it is to be alive (DH, 582).

"Yes—yes—a boy," said Lupin again, who seemed dazed by his own happiness […]. Harry felt overwhelmed, astonished, delighted […]. Tidings of new life were exhilarating. (DH, 514–5)

Even mourning and grief are ways of expressing the magnificent importance of life. Our own yearning and appreciation for life is one of our greatest qualities. This desire only becomes a problem when we lift it to the exalted status of ultimate concern, highest priority. It is under this condition that we become no "better, ultimately, than Voldemort" (DH, 713). It is not the desire for life that makes us like Tom Riddle, it is the desire for life at all costs. When we make survival our highest priority, we become prepared to sacrifice all other concerns to it. When we make survival our highest priority, it owns us. When survival and power own us, nothing else can.

Hermione's pronouncement "about how humans are frightened of death" does not merely refer to our fear of our own death. Many of us are perhaps even more frightened of the deaths of those we care most about. In his commentary on Beedle, Albus Dumbledore asks, "Which human being, having lost someone they loved, could withstand the temptation of the Resurrection Stone?" (TBB, 107). It is hard not to be moved by the image of eleven-year-old Harry standing in front of the Mirror of Erised or thirteen-year-old Harry trying to contact Sirius Black through a hand mirror. This idea is given more vivid expression in *Harry Potter and the Deathly Hallows*. There Hermione is questioning the value of the Hallows. She says,

"what about the Resurrection Stone? […] No magic can raise the dead, and that's that!"

"When my wand connected with You-Know-Who's, it made my mum and dad appear .,. and Cedric … " [said Harry.]

"But they weren't really back from the dead, were they?" said Hermione. "Those kind of—of pale imitations aren't the same as truly bringing someone back to life."

"But she, the girl in the tale, didn't really come back, did she? The story says that once

people are dead, they belong with the dead. But the second brother still got to see her and talk to her, didn't he? He even lived with her for a while …"

He saw concern and something less easily definable in Hermione's expression. Then, as she glanced at Ron, Harry realized that it was fear: He had scared her with his talk of living with dead people. (DH, 427)

Hermione's response to this hopeless desire seems to reflect Albus Dumbledore's when he says," It does not do to dwell on dreams and forget to live, remember that" (SS, 214). Rowling seems to echo Lewis's warning against the hopeless attempt to hold on too tightly to those who have passed.

However, if Rowling thinks it is dangerous and unwise to hold out hope for "family reunions on the further shore" and "the happy past restored" in some kind of heaven, then why does she give us so many images of returned dead people? Hermione interprets the gravestone of Harry's parents in Godric's Hollow saying, "It means . . . you know . . . living beyond death. Living after death" (DH, 328). She herself does not seem to hold with this idea. Harry instantly dismisses these as "empty words." If Rowling agrees with their skepticism of living beyond death in some literal way, then why does she provide us with the apparently literal return of Harry's parents at the end of both *Harry Potter and the Goblet of Fire* and *Harry Potter and the Deathly Hallows*? The answer has to do with the way in which we address and encounter death.

Joseph Campbell says,

The riddle of the Sphinx is the image of life itself through time—childhood, maturity, age, and death. When without fear you have faced and accepted the riddle of the Sphinx, death has no further hold on you, and the curse of the Sphinx disappears. The conquest of the fear of death is the recovery of life's joy. One can experience an unconditional affirmation of life only when one has accepted death, not as contrary to life but as an aspect of life. Life in its becoming is always shedding death, and on the point of death. The conquest of fear yields the courage of life that is the cardinal initiation of every heroic adventure. (PM, 151–2)

Dumbledore is suggesting something very similar when he says to Harry, "You are the true master of death, because the true master does not seek to run away from death. He accepts that he must die" (DH, 720–1). However, we have just seen that Harry desired the Deathly Hallows precisely because he did "seek to run away from death." Is Dumbledore wrong about Harry?

No. The Harry that became intoxicated with the idea of a reprieve from his death sentence, the Harry that became obsessed with the Deathly Hallows, is the Harry that descended into the grave with Dobby and did not climb out. Something happens to Harry as he digs Dobby's grave by hand. The process makes him feel as if he has been "slapped awake" (DH, 479). For a brief amount of time Harry had become possessed by the idea of sharing Tom Riddle's pursuit of the Hallows. He even says, "'The last enemy shall be destroyed is death,'" to which Hermione has to respond "I thought it was You-Know-Who we were supposed to be fighting?" (DH, 436). At this particular point Harry has shifted his priority to his own survival, a priority that unites him at some level with Tom Riddle.

However, "Grief, it seemed, drove Voldemort out [. . .] though Dumbledore, of course, would have said that it was love" (DH, 478). Through his grief for Dobby, Harry is able to remind himself that he cares more for people than he does for survival. As he descends into Dobby's grave, he is able to lift his concern for other people to the status of highest priority and ultimate concern. In doing so Harry is able to demote survival to the status of a secondary concern.

Courage is little more than the decision and ability to prioritize a worthy cause over one's own survival. Courage is not a matter of being unafraid of death. It is simply a matter of realizing that there are things more important than death. It is the importance of these things, their deep relevance that grants us the ability to confront our own fear. It is our own recognition of the transcendent importance of the cause that grants us the strength

to stand up to our own fear. It is my acceptance of the priority of the cause, not the strength of my own fortitude that allows me to be brave. It is this that initiates me for the hero's quest.

> But he understood at last what Dumbledore had been trying to tell him. It was, he thought, the difference between being dragged into the arena to face a battle to the death and walking into the arena with your head held high. Some people, perhaps, would say that there was little to choose between the two ways, but Dumbledore knew—*and so do I*, thought Harry, with a rush of fierce pride, *and so did my parents*—that there was all the difference in the world. (HBP, 512)

As mortals we will all face death, that is not going to change. Further, we have to weigh our concern for pain and death against the other competitors for our esteem and respect. We will have to decide whether esteem for justice and decency rises above our interest in survival and power. The choice as to which of these to prioritize will make a difference, "all the difference in the world."

VII. Gethsemane

This brings us at long last to Harry's voluntary walk into the Forbidden Forest to submit to Tom Riddle. Upon seeing Severus Snape's memories in the Pensieve, Harry finally comes to realize that he himself is a Horcrux and thus harbors a piece of Tom Riddle's soul and immortality within himself.

> Finally, the truth. [. . .] Harry understood at last that he was not supposed to survive. His job was to walk calmly into Death's welcoming arms. [. . .] Slowly, very slowly, he sat up, and as he did he felt more alive and more aware of his own living body than ever before. Why had he never appreciated what a miracle he was, brain and nerve and pounding heart? [. . .] He stood up. His heart was leaping against his ribs like a frantic bird. Perhaps it knew it had little time left, perhaps it was

determined to fulfill a lifetime's beats before the end […]. He could no longer control his own trembling. It was not, after all, so easy to die. Every second he breathed, the smell of the grass, the cool of the air and space, was so precious: to think that people had years and years, time to waste, so much time it dragged, and he was clinging to each second. (DH, 691, 692, 694, 697–8)

With incredible care and detail, Rowling juxtaposes Harry's determination to fulfill his mission against his passionate desire to live. Rowling refuses to allow us the illusion that the voluntary submission to death is somehow easier for heroes. In this scene Rowling's prose stretches out, offering us far more vivid descriptions of Harry's feelings and reflections than at any other point in the entire series. Rowling invites us to relate to Harry. She encourages us to understand what he is going through. She is calling us to empathize with him and thus to imagine seriously the incredible possibility that we could do it too.

This is Harry's Gethsemane scene. This element of the Harry Potter series calls to mind some similar elements in *Steppenwolf*, a novel by Hermann Hesse. The two main characters in *Steppenwolf* are Harry and Hermione. It is not likely that the recurrence of these names in Rowling's work is coincidental. Hesse once wrote,

Whenever […] I hear or see the word "Jesus," what leaps into my mind first is not Jesus on the cross, or Jesus in the wilderness, or Jesus the miracle worker, or Jesus risen from the dead, but Jesus in the garden of Gethsemane, tasting the last cup of loneliness, his soul torn by woes of impending death and a higher rebirth. And as he looks about him for his disciples, in a last touching, childlike need for comfort seeking a little warmth and human closeness, a fleeting comforting illusion in the midst of his hopeless loneliness. (MB, 86–7)

Much of what is said here coincides with Harry's experience during his walk in the Forest. Hesse was trying to emphasize that aspect of Christ that we all can relate to. So many of us

have been presented with a superhero image of Christ that bears an only fleeting resemblance to our own human experience. Hesse would seem to agree with Dostoyevsky regarding the dubiousness of such an image. The Grand Inquisitor's fraud religion would probably need a superhero Christ who could release us from our unreleasable responsibility. For Hesse, Christ is to be seen as a model, not a surrogate. I am to follow Him, not be excused by Him. If I am to be able to emulate Christ, I have to be able to imagine such a thing as possible. I will have to be able to relate to Christ, to empathize. I will have to be able to realistically imagine myself in His place. I will have to be able to actually believe that my heroic quest could be like His.

In *Steppenwolf*, the main character, Harry, receives a pamphlet written by some mysterious unnamed writer. According to this mysterious author,

As for […] the way to immortality, [Harry] has, it is true, an inkling of it […]. He knows too well that [the way to immortality] leads to still greater sufferings, to proscription, to the last renunciation, perhaps the scaffold and even though the enticements of immortality lies at the journey's end, he is still unwilling to suffer all those sufferings and to die all these deaths […]. He is resolved to forget that the desperate clinging to the self and the desperate clinging to life are the surest way to eternal death, while the power to die, to strip one's self naked, and the eternal surrender of the self bring immortality with them. [… He must bear the] loneliness of the Garden of Gethsemane. (S, 62–3)

The Harry of *Steppenwolf* is not able to do what Harry Potter is able to do. Harry Potter is able to relinquish the "desperate clinging to life." The Harry of *Steppenwolf* has not yet become what Dumbledore would've called "the true master of death" who accepts that he must die.

So how does Harry do it? This is the big question. The facing of death is existential. It is much more something we experience than it is something we understand. It is a product of existence, not thought. Like Screwtape's high dive or the determination to rely on oneself, if we are waiting to understand it before we act, the act will never occur. This returns us to the questions concerning Rowling's use of the Resurrection Stone during Harry's Gethsemane scene.

> He closed his eyes and turned the stone over in his hand three times. [...] He knew it had happened [...]. They were neither ghost nor truly flesh, he could see that. They resembled most closely the Riddle that had escaped from the diary [...]. Less substantial than living bodies, but much more than ghosts, they moved toward him, and on each face, there was the same loving smile [...].
>
> Lily's smile was widest of all [...].
>
> "You've been so brave." [...].
>
> "You are nearly there," said James. "Very close. We are [...] so proud of you." [...]
>
> "You'll stay with me?"
>
> "Until the very end," said James.
>
> "They won't be able to see you?" asked Harry.
>
> "We are part of you," said Sirius. [...]
>
> And he set off. The Dementors' chill did not overcome him; he passed through it with his companions, and they acted like Patronuses to him [...]. Beside him, making scarcely a sound, walked James, Sirius, Lupin, and Lily, and their presence was his courage, and the reason he was able to keep putting one foot in front of the other. (DH, 699–700)

The entire seven-volume Harry Potter series drives toward this point. What we know is that Harry is confronting something so terrifying that few would be able to pull it off. We also know that he would not be able to continue toward the goal without the presence of his "companions." As we've said, the decision to face death is an existential leap that is beyond conception or comprehension even for the person who does it.

VIII. Empowering Symbols

In reference to this, Paul Tillich talks about empowering symbols. According to Tillich, a symbol is something that helps me grasp that which I would not be able to grasp on my own. The unthinkable and transcendent is normally beyond my conception. However, according to Tillich, I can catch a glimpse of the unthinkable and transcendent as it breaks through into my experience through a symbol. These momentary glimpses into the infinite have the capacity to help me orient my concerns in relation to the eternal. In other words, I only have to glimpse the eternal for a moment to come to the realization that some of my biggest worries are really not that big a deal.

These momentary and yet orienting symbols have the capacity to help me reprioritize. Harry's experience digging Dobby's grave is just such a glimpse. They can be a slap in the face, and an awakening. More importantly, these glimpses into the eternal through a symbol can empower me, encourage me to risk the existential leap required to face the threat and fear of death. Harry would not have been able to continue walking had it not been for his companions. The King's Cross Dumbledore explains that Harry is "the worthy possessor of the Hallows" because Harry used the stone "to enable [his] self-sacrifice" (DH, 720). Consider philosophical theologian David Klemm's discussion of this:

> The theological depth of understanding appears [...] when the figure of authenticity becomes an enabling symbol [...]. I am empowered to become myself through the appearing symbol [...]. Ordinarily, I may be able to recognize what I should do or become in the situation of life, but I may be unable to actualize it on my own. For instance, I may face a situation in which I'm called on to act with courage. Let's say that some political refugees are being moved through my city and I am asked to put them up, at great risk to myself as well as to them, until further arrangements can be made. Let's say

as well that I think it to be morally imperative that I consent. If so, I may understand that courage is demanded here; but I may be capable only of fear. A theological depth overturns my understanding if, in view of a certain symbol, I am encouraged to do the thing, so that I am able freely to take the risk and to become authentic. (Klemm 1986, 48)

In other words, the symbol is part of the mystery by which I move in real life from fear to courage.

So, what does the symbol allow me to see? Well, a glimpse of the eternal allows a person to see what he or she already knew, that morality is more important than power and that decency is more important than survival. The glimpse merely allows me to believe this enough to base my actions upon it in real life. The glimpse allows me the opportunity to finally see that even the fear of death is not as big a deal as the principled purpose of my life. Under the influence of such a glimpse, I can prioritize my purpose over my fear. Under such an influence, I can manifest courage in the real world. Not even God could do this without first becoming human.

All of human experience, the entire human experiment, centers on the exercise of free will. Everything else is less important. It is our choices that really matter. As animals we cannot help but tend to prioritize our desire for power. As rational or spiritual beings we cannot help but tend to prioritize our glimpse of eternal truths, a glimpse that confirms universal human dignity. Only one of these may rise as our ultimate priority and fundamental motive of our actions and behavior. Will it be Hallows or Horcruxes?

Our desire for power is so basic and persuasive that for many of us it may seem impossible to stand against it. However, despite our awareness of the force of instinctual demands, we, nonetheless, also feel called to an unconditional respect for the fundamental importance of every human being. However, this call to treat all people as equally and infinitely important always seems to take a back seat to our personal safety and desire for dominance. Changing this can seem impossible.

A symbol, however, could do the trick. But what symbol? I need a symbol that can help me believe that I am actually capable of confronting my fear of death in the name of a cause or principle that matters more. I need a symbol that makes it possible for me to believe that such courage really can exist. There is only one symbol that can perform such a task. It is the firm and irrefutable belief that another human, just like me, has already been able to do it. It just so happens that Remus, Sirius, James, and Lily, Harry's Resurrection Stone companions, all faced the fear of death in the name of a more important cause. Harry and Remus Lupin discuss this in reference to Lupin's newborn son, Teddy. Remus says, "he will know why I died and I hope he will understand. I was trying to make a world in which he could live a happier life" (DH, 700). I cannot tell myself that such a thing is impossible if someone else I know has already done it.

We might also notice that this Resurrection Stone Lupin admits that he will never know his son. Rowling offers us no comforting images of protective, benevolent overseeing loved ones. Lupin will not be "watching over" Teddy. What the dead *can* do is leave us their example, and their example can empower us. For most of us, it is nearly impossible to allow our concern for ethics to champion our desperation for power. If it is to happen, it will require our greatest effort and most profound courage. It would probably be impossible were it not for the help of effective empowering symbols. It would probably be impossible without believing oneself to be intimately connected to another who has gone before and pulled it off. However, my respect for these people who have gone before must run so deep that I would rather die than disappoint them. It is this very respect that will, in part, permit me to rise to my courageous potential.

The battle between power and ethics for our loyalty wages within each one of us. When power wins, violence and injustice always follow. This is why Grundelwald's and Dumbledore's slogan "For the Greater Good" rings with such dissonance and hypocrisy. When ethics has been sacrificed for power, justice can only ever receive lip service from then on. The battle for the primacy of justice can only occur within one human being at a time and within the context of their own absolutely free will. Everything that occurs outside of us, from movements, to elections, to wars, is less important. This kind of change does not and cannot happen as a group activity. This change does not happen to whole generations or organizations. Each of us individually must come to realize that we have a destiny that resembles Harry's. We must never confuse *what* we are, a living embodied human, with *who* we are, a hero destined to uniquely ennoble the world in the name of universal human equality.

Sir Cadogan is a figure in a Hogwarts painting who is presented as ridiculous in his overzealous interest in courage and chivalry. In his day he was probably an important member of King Arthur's roundtable. However, he has long since died and remains nothing more than an image in an oil painting. The relevancy of his bravery and sacrifice has faded into the distant past. His long-gone decisions leave almost no trace on the lives of those living and deciding in the present. The center of human experience is the exercise of free will. The exercise of free will is in the hands of those with the ability to move things in the real world. Only living people have this ability. The dead only matter with regard to the free will of the living. Once we are gone, our exploits won't matter that much. Failure to recognize this would make us as comical as Sir Cadogan. Nearly Headless Nick says as much.

However, we do have the capacity to live on as the empowering symbol for the next generation. Note that both the dead Dumbledore and the dead Sirius insinuate that their existence is within Harry himself, perhaps a product of Harry's own spirit and desperate imagination. If I find a way to prioritize ethics over power, I thereby leave my children that model or example. If I rise to my true potential and respond to my authentic calling, if I embark on the legitimate quest for my own true individual dignity, my sacrifices and priorities may leave an empowering trace on those who come after me. And if, as by some miracle, my own daughter rises to her own challenge in part because of my example, then truly I can say I live there in her, for her achievement would have been impossible without my example as an empowering symbol. As Lupin says, "[Teddy] will know why I died and I hope he will understand. I was trying to make a world in which he could live a happier life" (DH, 700). This is in part why, in an earlier scene, Harry so desperately sends Remus back to his son ("Parents," said Harry, "shouldn't leave their kids unless—unless they've got to" (DH, 215), and why Neville keeps every wrapper he receives from his nearly delirious mother in St. Mungo's (OP, 515).

My ability to live on in the acquired and perhaps miraculous courage of those I inspire is why Jo Rowling included the following quote from William Penn in the epigraph of *Harry Potter and the Deathly Hallows.*

> Death is but crossing the world, as friends do the seas; they live in one another still. For they must needs be present, that love and live in that which is omnipresent. In this divine glass, they see face-to-face; and their converse is free, as well as pure. This is the comfort of friends, that though they may be said to die, yet their friendship and society are, in the best sense, ever present, because immortal. (DH, xi)

My individual life is not as important in and of itself as is my participation in a humanity that with every new generation learns to prioritize universal human equality and dignity to an ever-higher degree. We are individuals connected by a thread of our mutual and shared infinite importance, like a "fine golden chain" connecting friends on Luna's ceiling (DH, 417).

As Dumbledore says, "death is coming for me as surely as the Chudley Cannons will finish bottom of this year's league" (DH, 683). So it is for us all. This is one of the very few certainties we are afforded. So many people foolishly believe that heroic self-sacrifice is about dying. It is not, for even the most pathetic coward dies. It is not death that distinguishes the epic hero. The hero's quest and sacrifice is about coming to the simple realization that your life will have been emptied into something, for everyone's inevitably is. Vernon Dursley has emptied his life into mindless conformity and Grunnings Drills just as completely as Martin Luther King Jr. emptied his into the call for universal human equality. It is not a question of whether we will sacrifice our lives. We will, every one of us. We empty our entire human life into whatever we prioritize. So it all boils down to this. What is worth the sacrifice of an entire precious and transcendently important human life, your life?

We must all "bow to death" (GOF, 660). This is a forgone conclusion. Attempts to deny it make us into fools and worse, much worse. This is true of even religious attempts as the Grand Inquisitor reveals. Just as Harry says as he begins to walk toward the Forest, we are "not supposed to survive" (DH, 691). When I was about eleven-years-old, I asked my mother why Jesus wanted me to care about poor people. She said, "Perhaps it's because Jesus knows you and knows that you'd never be happy if you didn't. Perhaps He knows that deep down you've always been the kind of person who can't help caring about people who are struggling. Perhaps He is asking not because He wants you to but because you do."

The call to the heroic quest is not a call to recklessness or suicide. It is a call to our own most authentic and uniquely individual self. Each one us has the capacity and destiny to manifest an absolutely unprecedented response to our own internal awareness of the austere majesty of other people. It is a call to lean away from my understanding of myself as an isolated center of power and toward a realization that I reside within the connection I share with those I love and could love. If I can do this, my path usually becomes clear. Under these conditions, I can empty myself into a cause or a quest, and I can do so, not with a feeling of resisted or lamented duty, but with the spirit of deepest gratitude and appreciation of my good fortune. If I can do this, I may rise immortally as a symbol, the only symbol powerful enough to inspire those who will follow me.

IX. The Miracle of Shifted Priority

There are a number of strange references sprinkled throughout the Harry Potter series having to do with an unnamable force. Fawkes is a phoenix whose death and rebirth occurs numerous times. Phoenixes have long been associated with eternal life. Harry's wand is made of holly and phoenix feather. Holly is associated with Christmas because it, like evergreens, survives the winter with its leaves intact while so many other trees seem to die. As such holly became a symbol for eternal life. Harry's wand carries both references. In *Harry Potter and the Order of the Phoenix* Dumbledore tells Harry,

> "There is a room in the Department of Mysteries […] that is kept locked at all times. It contains a force that is at once more wonderful and more terrible than death, than human intelligence, than the forces of nature. It is also, perhaps, the most mysterious of the many subjects for study that reside there." (OP, 843)

Rowling protects the delicacy of this force by refusing to name it. She mentions it also near the end of *Harry Potter and the Goblet of Fire*.

> And then an unearthly and beautiful sound filled the air … It was coming from every thread of the light-spun web vibrating around Harry and Voldemort. It was a sound Harry recognized, though he had heard it only once before in his life: phoenix song.
>
> It was the sound of hope to Harry … the most beautiful and welcome thing he had ever heard in his life … He felt as though the song were inside him instead of just around him … It was the sound he connected with Dumbledore, and it was almost as though a friend were speaking in his ear … (GOF, 664)

Something similar seems to appear in *Harry Potter and the Half-Blood Prince* as Horace Slughorn seems to be discussing antidotes.

our primary aim is […] to find that added component which will … transform these disparate elements. (HBP, 375)

These all refer to the miracle of shifted priority. When I shift my priority from power to decency, I begin to identify with the principles I stand for. I lean away from identifying myself with my material situation in the real world and lean toward understanding the voice of my conscience as having been my own real voice all along. This voice that Lewis called conscience, Kant called reason, and Plato called eternal rises again like a phoenix with each new person who hears it and then manifests it in their courageous decisions within the real world. That which Albus Dumbledore and Lily Potter stood for dies with them but their living example allows for it to rise immediately in Harry. Harry, Hermione, and Remus Lupin carry the hope that it will rise again in Teddy Lupin and Albus Severus Potter and you. "They live in one another still. For they must needs be present, that love and love in that which is omnipresent […]. This is the comfort of friends, that though they may be said to die, yet their friendship and society are, in the best sense, ever present, because immortal" (DH, xi). We must make of our lives an extraordinary testament to our own highest principles for such is the only conduit through which the eternal and transcendent can burst forth into the temporal world. We must, like Luna, look past the *what* of a person in order to see so deeply into their *who,* that we would recognize their detailed, thorough, and unprecedented individuality even when disguised under polyjuice potion.

X. The Welcomed Obligation and Cherished Debt

J. K. Rowling understands that Galileo and the scientific tradition permanently damaged our society's ability to stomach superstition as a legitimate ingredient in faith and free will. She also understood that religious corruption has had a similarly devastating effect. Rowling understands that many of us have inherited a Christian tradition filled to the brim with dubious elements of magic and shameful examples of institutional depravity. Rowling understands that traditional Christianity's reliance on magic and external unquestionable authority has left many of us feeling permanently exiled from religion in general. However, she also understands that our exile from religion has left us at a loss.

In his book *Religion for Atheists*, Alain de Botton said,

> In rejecting superstition, we should take care that we aren't tempted to ignore […] longings which religions have been so successful in identifying and dignified in resolving […]. No existing mainstream secular institution has a declared interest in teaching us the art of living […]. [Religion] never leaves us in any doubt about what art is for: it is a medium to remind us about what matters. It exists to guide us to what we should worship and revile if we wish to be sane, good people in possession of well-ordered souls. It is a mechanism whereby our memories are forcibly jogged about what we have to love and to be grateful for […]. We know intellectually that we should be kind and forgiving and empathetic, but such adjectives have a tendency to lose all their meaning until we meet with the work of art that grabs us through our senses and won't let us go until we have properly remembered why these qualities matter and how badly society needs them for its balance and its sanity. (RA, 160, 176, 215, 217)

Botton acknowledges that ever-fewer modern-day people have the ability to make it past religion's reliance on magical or supernatural elements. Botton is also saying that there is far more to religion than a reliance on the supernatural. The secular world, claims Botton, has very little interest in helping us understand or develop "the art of living" or in reminding "us about what matters" and yet many of us desire guidance in regard to these very matters. Rowling, Botton, and Dostoyevsky's Grand Inquisitor all seem to be suggesting that it was never the supernatural elements of religion that really mattered. They all seem to be suggesting that what we really need is to be reminded "about what we have to love and to be grateful for." We need to be reminded about "what matters" and we need to be guided in the "art of living" and in the creation of a "well-ordered soul."

So J. K. Rowling has given us a presentation of immortality and transcendence that does not rely on anything supernatural whatsoever. Isn't it interesting that in her series about a school of magic she has presented us with an image of religion freed of its reliance on magic and external authority? At its most essential core, religion is about the independent individual establishment of priorities within the context of radical freedom and responsibility. It is about maturing into awareness that my choices are my own and that no one, *no one* can protect me from that. Religion is about understanding that the meaning of my life cannot be inherited or gleaned from another. I must come to grasp that the course of my life is astoundingly important to the appropriate progress of the world and that my contribution must emerge out of the perfect uniqueness of my own true individuality.

This is why her books have been so universally beloved. People treasure her books because she has given us what so few of us thought we wanted: an honest and daunting call to a heroic quest for our own integrity and authentic fulfillment. In an age in which all morality has so often been disgracefully reduced to the randomness of cultural bias, Jo Rowling has written a series for children and young adults assuring them that principles of friendship, honesty, character, justice, courage, and empathy not only exist, but matter more than anything else. So many of us cherish Rowling's books precisely because they invite and inspire us to what we always knew was true, that we are destined to launch ourselves onto a voyage of unfathomable importance in the face of devastating fears and dedicated to unquestionable principles. We have always known that we desire at the deepest levels to live a life so breathtaking and profound that it could move someone like Harry Potter to name his child after us if ever anyone were to hear the whole story.

What if what we owe, what if that which is required of us is also simultaneously what we most deeply desire to give and be? What if sacrifice is not about giving things up, but about recognizing the truth about what we actually want? What if what we have always wanted was a cause and a life worthy of everything we have to give and could become? In a world of Vernon Dursleys who want nothing more than the biggest paycheck for the smallest amount of work, the Harry Potter series reminds us of a truth we try hard to forget: that we desire a magnum opus, mission, and a purpose that merits the practiced acquisition of our own highest individual excellence and is worthy of our boundless commitment and the free sacrifice/dedication of our own individual and unrepeatable human life. This is the welcomed obligation, the yearned for responsibility, the self-actualization of subjectively appropriate potential.

Rowling is not offering a new religion, just a reminder about an old one and a fresh way of looking at it. Mainstream Christianity's significant reliance on elements of the supernatural and vicarious salvation have proven an impediment for so many who might have looked to it as a legitimate and trusted guide for the formation of their individual character. Harry's free and incredibly difficult decision to dedicate himself to integrity and compassion against all odds reminds us that there is a lot more to the world's great religions than dubious superstition and personal subjugation. His story reminds us that we may indeed desire a venerable voice like that of Professor Dumbledore that would call us to recognize that we, each one of us, have always been destined to our own individual and appropriate heroism grounded on universal human empathy.

XI. Mrs. Cole

Let us take one last parting look into the Harry Potter series. In *Harry Potter and the Half-Blood Prince*, we are privy to Merope Riddle's last day and Tom Riddle's first. This scene of a destitute and hopeless mother alone in the cold recalls a similar image witnessed by Marley and Scrooge in a scene mentioned earlier from Dickens' *A Christmas Carol*. The infant Tom Riddle is left in the hands of Mrs. Cole, the intelligent yet dismissive, negligent, and alcoholic caretaker at Tom's orphanage. She is a woman who receives the sufferings of children as mere frustrations, nuisances, and irritations. Imagine how differently Harry's story would have turned out had Mrs. Cole taken her job as to caretaker of children more seriously. Rowling includes the fact that Mrs. Cole started at the orphanage around the same time that Merope Riddle showed up on its steps. Like anyone in a new job, Mrs. Cole was in a position of assessing her new priorities. Where would her loyalties lie? It soon becomes clear that Mrs. Cole did not come to recognize the profound formative impact she was to have on the children under her care. She did not come to recognize she and she alone represented the only chance at childhood compassion and care these children would ever have. Mrs. Cole's callous disregard and deplorable self-centeredness became perfectly reflected in every decision ever perpetrated by Tom Riddle.

Mrs. Cole's decisions and priorities stand in marked contrast to those of the school-aged Sirius Black, James Potter, and Peter Pettigrew. Upon discovering Remus Lupin's closeted condition as a werewolf, these three individuals took upon themselves to help. Not only did they decide to accompany Remus during his monthly transformations, a decision of great risk, they also decided to take on the arduous task of becoming Animagi in an effort to better protect their friend during these times. These three Marauders put about as much effort into becoming Animagi as Tom Riddle did into opening the Chamber of Secrets. Where Riddle would seek private power, the Marauders would dedicate themselves to friendship and compassion.

Remus Lupin eventually becomes an individual capable of being a cherished husband and father. However, Lupin nearly abandons both of these possibilities. He has to be persuaded into accepting his role as husband to Nymphadora Tonks and then shamed into returning to his role as father to Teddy Lupin. How much of a role did the early and continued loyalty and compassion of his friends contribute to Lupin's eventual ability to rise to his potential in both of these roles? How close had he come to abdicating these opportunities? How much of the early compassion shown Lupin do we see reflected in the important compassion that Lupin in turn shows Harry? Left to abandonment and exile, what would Remus Lupin have become? We see a similar rising to potential in the epilogue where the adult Harry and Ginny have the orphan Teddy over "for dinner about four times a week" and yearn to invite him permanently into their family (DH, 757).

James Potter's parents adopt a Sirius Black in need. Sirius Black adopts a Remus Lupin in need. Remus Lupin adopts a Harry Potter who is in need. Harry Potter adopts a Teddy Lupin in need. No one adopts the Tom Riddle in need. Mrs. Cole does not rise to the heroic potential latent in her position as a caretaker of an orphanage. She does not shower those under her care with love. The clever Mrs. Cole opts to prioritize self-interest over empathy and the world nearly cracks under the weight of her all but anonymous decision. Heroes of empathy do not usually have to save the world in the majestic duel at sunrise, they just have to save the world. This can only happen one person at a time.

Love is a word that suffers from a vagueness of definition similar to that of the word good. The reason is because love is not as much of a concept as it is a decision, a commitment, a dedication, a determination, a prioritization of and to individualized empathy. Love doesn't mean something in general. It derives its definition out of specific relationships between specific individuals. Love is redefined, born anew like a phoenix each time people prioritize each other over their individual material concerns. The word love risks losing all meaning outside of a specific relationship in which each person knows the other in intimate and empathetic detail. These relationships absolutely require time, trust, respect, and voluntary reciprocity. I must know not only who you are but also who you have the potential to be. Knowing a person on this level takes all of our focused attention, skill, and cleverness. This can only happen one person at a time.

Mrs. Cole was probably disrespected and seriously underpaid. Her working conditions were probably deplorable. If she had risen like a phoenix to her potential in the face of Tom Riddle's need it would have been an overwhelming miracle, and yet none but the baby would likely have paid any attention. There are never parades for someone like this, someone whose care helped prevent and protect Tom Riddle from ever becoming Lord Voldemort. We must come to recognize that the arena of the potential empathetic hero is almost always free of fanfare. In order for there to be a Martin Luther King Jr., there has to be a million nearly unremembered partners whose individual courageous dedication gave his leadership whatever meaning it ever had. The quality of empathy and justice is never a matter of scale. Some of us will reach millions, most of us will reach a few, and some will reach only one person. However, given the infinite significance of each person, there is no difference in the end.

XII. Deathbed Insight: How to Open at the Close

The only way to avoid deathbed regrets is to creatively imagine the life you would most want to recall from the perspective of that deathbed. We must remember that there is an owl-borne letter destined for each of us inviting us to a magical life of meaning and relevance. So many fall into a muddled and gullible life (Muggle) wandering through barely understood traditions and priorities when a letter accepting us to an existence of unimagined aptitude and immeasurable impact has been trying to make it down our chimney all along. The world's great religions have, like Dumbledore, been calling individual people to a life of authentic individual consequence even as religious institutions, like the Grand Inquisitor, have so often been corrupting these authentic religions into their pure opposite. It is a mistake to dismiss the profound wisdom of generations of the wise when trusted guidance can be so illusive, rare, and necessary. These amazing people, the founders of the world's great religions and epics, dedicated their lives to

encapsulating their discoveries and deep insights in books like messages in bottles. Science has never occupied itself with an investigation into the meaning and purpose of human life for it cannot, and we should not let the inadvertent presumptions of a scientific age inure us against the great treasure that is old books. The life of character and integrity grounded on the irrefutable importance of all people, a life that is espoused by an honest reading of these works of epic literature and religion, is simply not diminished by suspicions about the supernatural or the devestating corruptions of religious institutions.

What life would be the best life to look back on from the vantage point of your last day? It is very likely that the desire for power and safety will no longer interest you whatsoever on that day. We must not let the threat of death cower us into inaction even as we never fail to bow to the overwhelming beauty and central importance of life. These works of epic literature and religion have always called us to the unbounded dedication of our lives to an appropriate and unquestionable cause, and it is this unconditional commitment to a life of worthy rigor and determination that we have each glimpsed in distant dreams all along. It is in this way that our lives resonate with Harry Potter's. Rowling's Harry Potter series is a "work of art that grabs us through our senses and won't let us go until we have properly remembered why these qualities matter." Yours is a unique and crucial potential that has exactly one chance at existence in a real world that needs it. How important is it that you make the decisions that will make it come true? What if what we owe, what if what is asked and required of us, what if what we are responsible for is also what we most deeply desire to do? What if what we should be is as such because that is also what we most genuinely want to be?

XIII. Last Words

This book began with a discussion of Aristotle's concept of eudaimonia. We saw that eudaimonia is an ancient Greek word that refers to our inherent desire for complete individual human flourishing or fulfillment or our own individually defined excellence. When we discuss racism, sexism, classism, and other terrible corruptions, we too often focus on an understanding of freedom as merely freedom from oppression. The twentieth century inspired many of us to envision an understanding of freedom as a freedom from ruthless dictators, technological warfare, insidious economics, and systematic prejudices. There is nothing in this to criticize or second-guess. However, if we are to strive for peace in the name of freedom, we must look beyond the idea of freedom as merely freedom *from* ... We must begin to envision freedom in the form of freedom *for* ...

Many are the works of art that stand as witness and testimony to the physical violence and suffering wrought by injustice and the prioritization of power for its own sake. It is easy to show a battered and bleeding body on a movie screen and reveal it to be the consequence of unchecked power. It is much harder to show the violence of lost individual potential. How do we display the grief associated with a life that never had the chance to occur or even be imagined? How do we learn to mourn the loss of an excellent life that was never manifested? Racism, sexism, classism, and the other forms of systematic oppression do more than limit me in the here and now. These oppressions do perhaps their greatest violence in their ability to sever me from my own true potential and calling. What does it mean when, as Virginia Woolf considers, a woman with the poetic potential to be a Shakespeare is squandered as a scullery maid?

The world and world view of the Dursleys who desire nothing more than anonymizing conformity is contrasted in Rowling's work with the wizarding world in which the "wand chooses the wizard" uniquely. If we can escape the gravitational pull of herd conformity, we may just find that there is a eudaimonia with our name on it waiting for us as Ollivander's. J. K. Rowling's wizarding world calls or reminds us to see people as more than a mere collection of general human rights. We must come to recognize that individual excellence can be discovered only on an individual basis. Further, eudaimonia is a mystery that emerges out of the profound individuality of each person. However,

the connection between a person and their most appropriate individual potential can so easily be severed. What does it mean to lose contact with this? If what we truly are is our own most eudaimonia, then what does it mean to lose it, forget it, smother it, or have it smothered?

In this book I have tried to show that the Harry Potter series follows the development and establishment of authentic individual responsibility over time. Far from being a mere recitation of external moral rules, we have seen how responsibility must emerge spontaneously and organically out of each individual person. It is not enough to learn that I should treat my neighbor as myself. I must come to recognize this idea as a product of my own persona and opinion. I must awaken to the legitimacy of universal human equality not merely as a good idea but also as my own idea. Maturity of character requires that I relinquish the easy assumption that moral rules are given, imposed, plagiarized, or inherited. As a maturing moral agent I must discover that I am responsible for not just my choices but also for the reasons for my choices. I am responsible for explaining my own definition of good.

However, we also saw that the idea of universal human equality is a rule that is too general to produce clear decisions in the real world. It is the responsibility of each person to determine how to apply this principle to specific situations. This is where eudaimonia comes in. Just as the principle of universal human importance must emerge out of my deepest subjective well-spring, so also must my plan to apply it. Eudaimonia in the name of the unbounded importance of each person *is* the epic voyage of Rowling's hero. Once I come to recognize the priority of the categorical imperative, the incalculable relevance of each person, I will then have to ask how I will bring that about through my particular story and subjective excellence. Every single one of the major characters in the Harry Potter series represents a different and detailed experiment with this question.

Eudaimonia is about the development of character and skill over a significant period of time. If we want to understand a character, it is not enough to look at that person's individual decisions. We must look at the full arc of a person's development and maturation. One of the most important characteristics of the Harry Potter series is Rowling's insistence of revealing characters as they progress and change over seven volumes. Eudaimonia is about the intentional development of practiced skill in name of an envisioned virtuosity and purpose. In other words, it is not enough to be a good person in the here and now. We must ask what we are doing to strive toward that potential excellence that emerges out of our authentic individuality and our willingness to train. It is not just about who we are but who we are endeavoring to become as well. This is what is being emphasized by Dumbledore's Army as they train in the Room for Requirement, developing not only practiced skill but also individual Patronuses.

This leads us to a last look at Tom Riddle and Harry Potter. Rowling went to great pains to emphasize both the similarity and difference between Harry and Tom. Nowhere is this made more apparent than in the culminating duel at sunrise. There they stood, two of the "abandoned boys of Hogwarts," each championing one of the two archetypal priorities, power and compassion. It is not hard to understand Tom's commitment to power, for such a commitment requires only the internalization of fear and its companion desire for dominance. The abandoned Tom Riddle simply abandons any concern other than power. As we have seen, for Tom there is only power. This is no mystery. The mystery is Harry. How does this "abandoned boy" rise into what Tom cannot even consider?

Well, what if you gave yourself over four thousand pages to craft and express an answer to that question? As we have said, Harry's walk into the Forest took everything he had and then a little more. Few would deny that the challenge was all but too much for this "wonderful boy. [This] brave, brave man." The task required every iota of his fortitude and developed strength. But it took more than that as well. The dedicated reader of the Harry Potter series will be able to recall every one of the various individuals who rose to Harry's need in exactly the way that Mrs. Cole did not rise to Tom's. From Lupin and Hagrid to McGonagall and the Weasleys, from Dumbledore and Snape to Sirius, James, Lily, Luna, Ron, and

Hermione, the devoted reader will be able to appreciate just how pivotal each and every one of these and other figures were to Harry's eventual rise. If just one of them had disregarded or disrespected their potential role in Harry's development, the Harry who had been asked to walk willingly into the Forest might not have been able to do it. In this we may see that we are called not only to be the Harry who develops into the kind of person who can stand resolute in the face of corruption and violence. In this we can see that we are also called to be among the contributing voices that help a person arrive at Harry's posture and potential in the first place. It is never a lone hero who stands before Voldemort. The Harry who stands before Tom Riddle stands both as an individual and as a testament to the courage, cleverness, and care of those living and dead who had risen for him. In the person of Harry Potter, a community and collaboration stands to confront Tom Riddle.

It is this that I believe is studied in the unnamed "room in the Department of Mysteries […] that is kept locked at all times." Harry rises as the chosen one to respond to the need of all those under the threat of Tom Riddle's mania, but he can only do this as a result of every single one of those who had already risen for him. What would you name that which Harry freely gives to those who surround him? What would you name that which he gives yet only as a result of their having already freely given it to him? We cannot allow ourselves to cheer the hero who rises to free us *from* Voldemort only to be at a loss as to what we were freed *for*. There is a place and a need for every eudaimonia. We are called to a life of gravity and relevant impact.

There is something miraculous that rises in Harry. It is this that lifts and accompanies him as he walks first into the Forest and then out of the mystical King's Cross Station and back into the realm of threat and pain. It acts as a Patronus, a shield against the threat of fear and the desire for power. It is expressed in the form of his Resurrection Stone companions, Remus, Sirius, James, and Lily but it is not limited to them. It is expressed in Harry's desire and ability to aspire to these, his forerunners and their proven prioritization of compassion and justice. It rises also in the combined and cumulative efforts of all those who helped carefully craft Harry's development. The existential ability and decision to stand on C. S. Lewis's high dive and sacrifice real-world safety in the name of justice and human dignity is one of the rarest and most delicate of human phenomena. The slightest thing can undermine it, and there are many who are utterly incapable of even imagining its possibility. And yet it can rise.

In the face of concrete and tangible power the priority of a miraculous ideal can rise. The self-evident majesty of this ideal can lift a courage in me such as to overwhelm the most instinctual resistance. The transcendence and eternality of this ideal even has the capacity to raise within me the patience and care needed to dismiss the taunts of daily frustrations and the toxic suspicions of personal obscurity so as to respond to the needs of the forgotten, disregarded, and powerless. When it rises in Dobby's grave it is called grief. When it rises in Grindelwald and Dumbledore, it is called remorse. Like a bird of fire rising impossibly out of inert ash, it can rise.

When it rises as the sword of Gryffindor in the hands of Neville Longbotton, it is called righteous courage. When it rises in Hermione Granger in her willingness to relentlessly embark with Harry on a hopeless mission, it is called loyalty. When it rises in the Weasleys so as to recover Percy, it is called forgiveness. When it rises in Remus Lupin so as to allow him to accept his role as husband and father, it is called gratitude. When it rises in Dumbledore from the depths of his guilt and shame so as to enable his rise to excellence as Hogwarts headmaster, it is called redemption. When it rises in Luna Lovegood in her response to Harry's needs after the death of Tom Riddle, it is called mercy. That which transcends human understanding is probably best left unnamed and so I, like J. K. Rowling, will do just that. However, "Dumbledore, of course, would have said that it was love."

Works Cited and
Abbrevations Used

Aristotle. *Nicomachean Ethics*. Translated by and introduction by Terence Irwin. Indianapolis, IN: Hackett Pub., 1999.

Beverley, Nichols. *Cry Havoc!* New York: Doubleday, Doran & Co., 1933.

Botton, Alain de. *Religion for Atheists: A Non-believer's Guide to the Uses of Religion.* New York: Pantheon, 2012.

Campbell, Joseph and Bill D. Moyers (collaborator). *The Power of Myth*. New York: Doubleday, 1988.

Campbell, Joseph. *The Hero with a Thousand Faces*. Novato, CA: New World Library, 2008.

Cates, Diana F. *Choosing to Feel: Virtue, Friendship, and Compassion for Friends.* Notre Dame, IN: University of Notre Dame Press, 1997.

Chesterton, G. K. (Gilbert Keith), *Tremendous Trifles*. Kindle Edition, May 17, 2012. First published 1920 by Methuen & Co. LTD.

A Christmas Story. Directed by Bob Clark. Turner Entertainment. 1983. Film.

"Seven Seconds," *Criminal Minds,* episode 50, CBS, Hollywood, CA, Oct. 24, 2007. Television.

Dickens, Charles. *Christmas Stories*. Racine, Wisconsin: Whitman Publishing Company, 1940.

Dostoyevsky, Fyodor. *The Brothers Karamazov*. Translated by Constance Garnett. Mineola, NY: Dover Publications, 2005.

Dostoyevsky, Fyodor. *Crime and Punishment*. Translated by Jessie Senior Coulson. Edited by Richard Arthur Peace. Oxford: Oxford University Press, 1998.

The Godfather. Directed by Francis Ford Coppola. Paramount Pictures. 1972. Film.

GoodFellas. Directed by Martin Scorsese. Warner Bros., 1990. Film.

"*Harry Potter and Me.*" Interview with J. K. Rowling. BBC Radio, 2001. Accessed on YouTube.

Hesse, Hermann. *My Belief; Essays on Life and Art*. Edited and translated by Theodore Ziolkowski. New York: Farrar, Straus and Giroux, 1974.

Hesse, Hermann. *The Glass Bead Game (Magister Ludi)*. New York: H. Holt, 1990.

Hesse, Hermann. *Steppenwolf*. New York: H. Holt, 1990.

Hobbes, Thomas. *Leviathan: With Selected Variants from the Latin Edition of 1668*. Editd by E. M. Curley. Indianapolis: Hackett Pub., 1994.

J. K. Rowling website, accessed Aug 19, 2014, including www.jkrowling.com/en_GB/#/timeline/early-influences.

"J. K. Rowling," *Who Do You Think You Are?* Series 8, episode 2, Aug. 17, 2011, Wall to Wall Television. Acorn Media, 2011. DVD.

Kant, Immanuel. *Grounding for the Metaphysics of Morals; With, On a Supposed Right to Lie Because of Philanthropic Concerns*. Translated by James W. Ellington. Indianapolis: Hackett Publishing Co., 1993.

Klemm, David E. *Hermeneutical Inquiry: Volume I: The Interpretation of Texts*. Atlanta, GA: Scholars Press, 1986.

Lewis, C. S. *The Screwtape Letters: With Screwtape Proposes a Toast*. San Francisco: Harper San Francisco, 2001.

Lewis, C. S. *A Grief Observed*. San Francisco: Harper San Francisco, 2001.

Lewis, C. S. *Mere Christianity: Comprising The Case for Christianity, Christian Behavior, and Beyond Personality*. New York: Touchstone, 1996.

Lewis, Sinclair. *Babbitt*. Introduction by Hugh Walpole. London: Jonathan Cape, 1922.

Machiavelli, Niccolò. "Discourse upon the First Ten Books of Livy," edited by George Klosko, *History of Political Theory: An Introduction*. Belmont, CA: Wadsworth/Thomson Learning, 1995.

Machiavelli, Niccolo. *The Prince: A Revised Translation, Backgrounds, Interpretations, Marginalia*. Edited and translated by Robert M. Adams. New York: Norton, 1992.

May, Herbert G., and Bruce M. Metzger. *The New Oxford Annotated Bible with the Apocrypha: Revised Standard Version, Containing the Second Edition of the New Testament and an Expanded Edition of the Apocrypha*. New York: Oxford University Press, 1977.

Mitford, Jessica. *Hons and Rebels*. New York: New York Review, 2004.

Moyers, Bill, and Joseph Campbell. *The Power of Myth: Program 1*. New York: Mystic Fire Video, 1988.

The New Encyclopaedia Britannica. Chicago: Encyclopaedia Britannica, 1976.

Nietzsche, Friedrich. *Thus Spake Zarathustra A Book for All and None*. Dover Publications, Kindle edition, 2012.

Ordinary People. Directed by Robert Redford. Paramount Pictures, 1980. Film.

Pirsig, Robert. *Zen and the Art of Motorcycle Maintenance: An Inquiry into Values*. New York: Morrow, 1974.

Plato. *The Republic*. Translated with an Introduction by Desmond Lee. 2nd Ed. Harmondsworth: Penguin, 1974.

Plato, *The Last Days of Socrates*. Translated by Hugh Tredennick. Edited by Harold Tarrant. London, England: Penguin, 1993.

Pottermore: A Unique Online Harry Potter Experience from J.K. Rowling." Accessed Aug. 19, 2014, http://www.pottermore.com/en-us/daily-prophet/qwc2014/2014-07-08/dumbledores-army-reunites.

Roth, Philip. *The Plot Against America*. London: Vintage, 2005.

Rousseau, Jean-Jacques. *The Essential Rousseau*. Translated by Lowell Bair. New York, NY: Penguin, 1983.

Rowling, J. K. *Harry Potter and the Goblet of Fire*. Illustrated by Mary GrandPré. New York, NY: Scholastic, 2002.

Rowling, J. K. *Harry Potter and the Chamber of Secrets*. Illustrated by Mary GrandPré. New York: Arthur A. Levine, 1999.

Rowling, J. K. *Harry Potter and the Deathly Hallows*. Illustrated by Mary GrandPré. New York, NY: Arthur A. Levine, 2007.

Rowling, J. K. *Harry Potter and the Half-blood Prince*. Illustrated by Mary GrandPré. New York, NY: Arthur A. Levine, an Imprint of Scholastic, 2005.

Rowling, J. K. *Harry Potter and the Order of the Phoenix*. Illustrated by Mary GrandPré. New York, NY: Arthur A. Levine, 2003.

Rowling, J. K. *Harry Potter and the Prisoner of Azkaban*. Illustrated by Mary GrandPré. New York, NY: Arthur A. Levine, 1999.

Rowling, J.K. *Harry Potter and the Sorcerer's Stone*. New York, NY: Arthur A. Levine, 1999.

Rowling, J. K. *The Tales of Beedle the Bard.* New York: Children's High Level Group in Association with Arthur A. Levine, 2008.

Rowling, J.K. "Very Good Lives: The Fringe Benefits of Failure and the Importance of the Imagination," Harvard University commencement address, NBCUniversal Media, 2008. Accessed on YouTube. Also published by Little, Brown and Company, 2015.

Sartre, Jean-Paul. "Anti-Semite and Jew," *Thirteen Questions in Ethics and Social Philosophy.* Edited by Meredith W. Michaels, Kathleen Marie. Higgins, Robert J. Fogelin, and G. Lee. Bowie. Fort Worth, TX: Harcourt Brace College, 1998.

Shakespeare, William. *The Tragedy of Hamlet, Prince of Denmark.* Edited by Barbara A. Mowat and Paul Werstine. New York: Washington Square, 2002.

Shapiro, Marc. *J.K. Rowling: The Wizard Behind Harry Potter.* New York: St. Martin's Press, 2004.

Tillich, Paul. *Dynamics of Faith.* New York: Harper, 1958.

Tillich, Paul. *Systematic Theology: Three Volumes in One.* Chicago: University of Chicago, 1967.

Twain, Mark. *The Annotated Huckleberry Finn.* Edited by Michael Patrick Hearn. New York: W. W. Norton & Company, 2001.

Unforgiven. Directed by Clint Eastwood. Warner Bros., 1992. Film.

Wall Street. Directed by Oliver Stone. Twentieth Century Fox Film Corporation, 1987. Film.

Wells, H. G. *The Work, Wealth, and Happiness of Mankind.* London: William Heinemann, 1934.

Who Do You Think You Are? magazine, October 2011, 26.

"The Women of Harry Potter." J. K. Rowling filmed interview, 2011, Warner Bros. Entertainment Inc. Accessed on YouTube, June 15, 2014.

Abbreviations Used

B   Lewis, Sinclair, *Babbitt ... with an Introduction by Hugh Walpole.*

BK   Dostoyevsky, Fyodor, and Constance Garnett (translator). *The Brothers Karamazov.*

CS   Rowling, J. K. *Harry Potter and the Chamber of Secrets.*

DF   Tillich, Paul. *Dynamics of Faith.*

DH   Rowling, J. K., *Harry Potter and the Deathly Hallows.*

GBG   Hesse, Hermann. *The Glass Bead Game.*

GO   Lewis, C. S. *A Grief Observed.*

GOF   Rowling, J. K., *Harry Potter and the Goblet of Fire.*

HBP   Rowling, J. K., *Harry Potter and the Half-blood Prince*

OP   Rowling, J. K., *Harry Potter and the Order of the Phoenix.*

HR   Mitford, Jessica. *Hons and Rebels.*

MB   Hesse, Hermann, *My Belief; Essays on Life and Art.*

MC   Lewis, C. S. *Mere Christianity: Comprising The Case for Christianity, Christian Behaviour, and Beyond Personality.*

PA   Rowling, J. K., *Harry Potter and the Prisoner of Azkaban.*

PM   Campbell, Joseph, and Bill D. Moyers. *The Power of Myth.*

RA   Botton, Alain de. *Religion for Atheists: A Non-believer's Guide to the Uses of Religion.*

SS   Rowling, J.K. *Harry Potter and the Sorcerer's Stone.*

S   Hesse, Hermann. *Steppenwolf.*

ST   Tillich, Paul. *Systematic Theology*

TBB   Rowling, J. K. *The Tales of Beedle the Bard. .*

ZMM   Pirsig, Robert. *Zen and the Art of Motorcycle Maintenance: An Inquiry into Values.*